T0135662

New Advances in Multimedia Security, Biometrics, Watermarking and Cultural Aspects

Prof. Dr.-Ing. Jana Dittmann
Dr.-Ing. Claus Vielhauer
Ass. jur. Jan Hansen
Editors

Logos Verlag Berlin

Bibliographic information published by the Deutsche Nationalbibliothek

The Deutsche Nationalbibliothek lists this publication in the Deutsche Nationalbibliografie; detailed bibliographic data are available in the Internet at http://dnb.d-nb.de .

This publication has been produced partly with the assistance of the European Union (project CultureTech, see http://amsl-smb.cs.uni-magdeburg.de/culturetech/). The content of this publication is the sole responsibility of the authors and can in no way be taken to reflect the views of the European Union.

ISBN 3-8325-1386-8

Logos Verlag Berlin
Comeniushof, Gubener Str. 47,
10243 Berlin
Tel.: +49 030 42 85 10 90
Fax: +49 030 42 85 10 92
INTERNET: http://www.logos-verlag.de

Preface

Sandra Gebbensleben, Jana Dittmann

This publication was produced by the project partners within a three-year project of the EU-India Economic Cross Cultural Program (ECCP) framework and based on the global scope of the ECCP research activities. The project is named Cultural Dimensions in Digital Multimedia and Security Technology (CultureTech) and focuses on integration of partner's research results and education concepts in the following domains:

- Digital Rights Management.

- Authentication of Media Data.

- Biometric User Authentication.

The project clearly addresses the dimension of University & Studies with a cross-sectional link to Media and Communication of the EU-India Cross-Cultural Programme. High relevance can be seen, as it strengthened the links between all partners from five different regions in three different countries. The co-operation resulted in a pooling of joint research activities and required a close co-operation between the partners in order to produce new research results, educational content and implement e-Learning facility, leading to a closer relationship between universities and research centres in all countries as well as spreading entrepreneurial research/know-how from academic media departments to business.

The main goal of the book is to spread a selection of the achieved results with regard to multimedia technologies, to their legal implications, and to the related intercultural issues.

With this aim the 3 European and 2 Indian partners involved the respective research communities (thought Research integration activities), the students (through the Education activities) and the wider international audience (through the dissemination activities). The Research integration concentrated on the technologies for cultural heritage, for biometrics user authentication, for media protection and authentication, for multimedia database management and on the related legal and cultural implications.

Organisation

Project Leader:

Prof. Jana Dittmann, Otto-von-Guericke University, Magdeburg, Germany

Project Coordinator:

Dipl.-Ing. Sandra Gebbensleben, Otto-von-Guericke University, Magdeburg, Germany

Project Partners - Main Contact:

Prof. Pranab Kr. Dutta, Indian Institute of Technology Kharagpur, India

Prof. Chandra Sekhar, Indian Institute of Technology Madras (Chennai), India

Prof. B. Yegnanarayana, International Institute of Information Technology Gachibowli (former: Indian Institute of Technology Madras (Chennai)), India

Jan Hansen, Hessisches Telemedia Technologie Kompetenz Center (httc e.V.), Darmstadt, Germany

Prof. Vito Cappellini, Media Integration and Communication Center - Università Italy di Firenze (MICC-UNIFI), Italy

Contents

Introduction

Sandra Gebbensleben, Jana Dittmann

Cultural Dimensions in Digital Multimedia and Security Technology is a project realised in the framework of the EU-India Cross Cultural Programme (ECCP). The three-year duration reached its end and this book represents a selection of achieved research results and main recommendations of all project partners.

The fundamental goal of the project was the promotion of links, the fusion of knowledge and the establishment of a durable open network between university media departments and non-profit associated partners from different cultural origin in Europe and India in respect to an interdisciplinary scientific area, bordered by technical, legal and cultural domains.

The grand challenge here was to bring together outstanding partners with specialisation in different scientific disciplines and to concentrate their expertise in respect to Multimedia into a knowledge base. Based on the global scope of the research activities of the participants, the partners focused on integration of their research results in the following domains:

- Digital Rights Management.
- Authentication of Media Data.
- Biometric User Authentication and technical impacts in different cultures.
- Legal aspects (in the field of data protection, copyright law, legally effective documents).
- Cultural aspects of Restoration and Authentication in the digital domain

The articles in this book describe and illustrate the work and results of the different research focuses in the project.

The authors A. Del Mastio, A. De Rosa, A. Piva, and V. Cappellini present "Image Registration in the Cultural Heritage field". This article proposes the use of a registration technique in the field of Cultural Heritage. The technique is based on the computation of the mutual information and it is able to determine the correct displacement to align points from one image with corresponding points coming from another one of the same object or scene.

"Issues in the Development of an Audio-Video based Person Authentication System" are discussed from B. Yegnanarayana, C. Chandra Sekhar, S. Palanivel, V. Suresh, Anil Kumar Sao and Dhananjaya N. The focus of this article is on face and video issues associated with the development of a person authentication system using audio and visual information. Motion information is used to localize and track a face in a video. The facial features are extracted relative to the locations of the eyes, and visual speech features are extracted relative to the locations of the eyes and mouth. Acoustic features represented by weighted linear prediction cepstral coefficients are derived from the speech signal.

In "Digital Speech Watermarking and its Impact to Biometric Speech Authentication" the authors Andrea Oermann, Andreas Lang and Claus Vielhauer present an approach for connecting biometric speech authentication and for digital watermarking illustrating the integration of metadata into the authentication process without significant quality and performance losses. Metadata in this case consists of ancillary information about the social, cultural or biological context of the owner of the biometric data as well as technical details of the sensor. The overall goal is to perform an evaluation of the recognition precision for selected algorithm in the context of the gender belongings of the persons.

The article "Verification and Watermarking Schemes of Biometric Signatures" from Biswajit Kar, Devesh Katiyar, P.K. Dutta and T.K. Basu focuses on signature verification and presents a new application of watermarking to secure electronic biometric signatures using digital watermarking techniques.

The authors A. Hemant Patil, P.K. Dutta and T.K. Basu present "Person Authentication Using Voice Biometrics: Final Report of CultureTech Project (2004-2006)". It illustrates the research work done in the area of person authentication using voice biometrics. Voice biometrics or Automatic Speaker Recognition (ASR) deals with person authentication based on his/her voice with the help of Machines, e.g. for banking transactions, forensic science, access control and information retrieval. The article summarizes contributions made in the area of speaker identification (for monolingual, crosslingual and multilingual mode), speaker classification (for open set and closed mode) and mimic recognition task.

Andrea Oermann demonstrates in the article "Cross-Cultural Analysis of Digital Media: From Fundamentals over Feature Extraction to Inter-Feature Fusion" that making semantic information available to digital applications has to be seen as the key in order to develop future trustworthy systems, which are trusted and accepted by different cultures at the same time. Further, the article provides a framework to evaluate digital applications such as biometric user authentication systems in a crosscultural context.

The article "Legal Chances and Restrictions in International Research Projects" from Jan Hansen and Katharina Selmeczi provides basic information about copyright, data protection and probative force of electronic documents.

In "Summary of Research in order to Evaluate Biometrics in Metadata Context" the impact of the cultural background of users of multimedial (different types media) and multimodal (different channels) applications such as biometrics is elaborate by the authors Andrea Oermann, Tobias Scheidat and Claus Vielhauer. The produced evaluations are facing in two directions: the impact of metadata on the performance of biometric authentication systems and deriving metadata from the available biometric data is focussed. Furthermore multimedial as well as multimodal applications in a cross-cultural context are benchmarked considering three dimensions, which have to be seen as criteria for the characterization of technologies in respect to their applicability in inter-cultural domains.

The authors G. Antini, S. Berretti, A. Del Bimbo and P. Pala present a method relying on curvature correlograms to perform description and retrieval by content of 3D objects in the article "Retrieval of 3D Objects by Structural Similarity". 3D models have raised a certain interest for, e.g. including advancements in 3D hardware and software technologies, their ever decreasing prices and increasing availability, affordable 3D authoring tools, and the establishment of open standards for 3D data interchange. This resulted in the demands for tools supporting their effective and efficient management, including archival and retrieval.

In "E-Learning in University Teaching" dissemination strategy and the dissemination activities of the project are presented from Irina Reuter and Jan Hansen. The strategies and activities can be seen in line with the worldwide progression of e-learning as a column of a university's teaching strategy.

"Overview to workpackages EI (1) to EI (5)" produced by all project partners presents an overview and background information to courses implemented by the project partners. The material for these courses was created or enriched by using project results of the different work packages.

Additionally two papers from partly non-project members are presented in the book:

"Digital Repatriation of Heritage and Visualization Technologies – The Contribution of the EPOCH Project" from Franco Niccolucci

"On the mono-lingual and cross-lingual speaker identification for Indian and European languages" from Hemant A. Patil, P. K. Dutta and T. K. Basu

Conclusion

Sandra Gebbensleben and Jana Dittmann

The impact of cultural background to Multimedia Technology can be clearly seen in the fact that Multimedia has become one of the most interesting technologies over the past years. Besides the technical dimension of Multimedia, aspects of legal and cultural nature with a number of inter-dependencies also need to be considered. A major goal of the book was to integrate knowledge from these three inter-related perspectives and develop and spread this knowledge into education. The work presented in the articles show, that we have been able to fulfil these goals.

In particular, legal aspects of multimedia technology have an impact due to its characteristic of allowing the reproduction of digital goods, which has triggered a lot of legal activity in the area of copyrights. While for the countries of the European Union, legal foundations relevant in multimedia have taken a very converging development and a harmonised legal basis is actually in a process of consolidation, differences in legal aspects in multimedia technology between India and the EU needed to be elaborated. The impact of multimedia technology especially to education is resulting from its applicability being used together with the well-developed communication networks. This cooperation allows the implementation of e-Learning in common education. This technology mainly aims to either convenience by relaying the consumption of a lecture from class room to home. Also, e-Learning is provided as a means of repetition of teaching content in academia. The need of simultaneous activities on both sides can be overcome to mutual benefit. The project's aim was to give the opportunity to fill this gap by use of existing technology for the purpose of spreading learning content over the wide geographical area spanned by the joining partners.

Finally, the impact of technologies on culture as well as the cultural influences on technologies has been an important focus of the project and also of the book. It is quite plausible that the perception of new multimedia technology varies a lot in different cultures and another aspect regards the cultural heritage field where the possibility of having multimedia tools able to (approximately) recover the original aspect of an artwork can increase the interest of people toward the art sector; this however can have different effects according to the cultural environment.

Acknowledgements

This publication has been produced with the assistance of the European Union within the framework of EU-India Economic Cross Cultural Programme (ECCP). The content of this publication is the sole responsibility of the project partners of the project Cultural Dimensions in Digital Multimedia and Security Technology (CultureTech) and can in no way be taken to reflect the views of the European Union.

Image Registration in the Cultural Heritage field

A. Del Mastio, A. De Rosa, A. Piva, V. Cappellini

Contents

Abstract

Over the past few years, the availability of new and more powerful technologies and algorithms have attracted the attention of researchers and managers of academies, museums and government bodies, working in the sector of Cultural Heritage.

We propose the use of a registration technique in the field of Cultural Heritage. It is based on the computation of the mutual information, which is a similarity measure coming from the information theory; it is able to determine the correct displacement (that is a geometrical transformation including sub-pixel translation, rotation and scaling) to align points from one image with corresponding points coming from another one of the same object or scene. Roughly speaking, mutual information is a measure of the amount of information one image contains about the other one. It is a highly performing similarity measure, when compared to previously proposed ones, such as cross-correlation, which can often fail when dealing with multi-source images (i.e. images coming from different sensors or regarding different frequency bands), for the inherently difference of the image structures and tone dynamics.

1   Introduction

The application of signal and image processing to the analysis of artworks is still a very uncommon practise, both among conservators and ICT specialists. Lately, however, many efforts have been made to acquire and process artwork image data, which proved the impact that digital image processing may have on all major issues, related to the conservation field, such as material analysis (and therefore dating and provenance determination), discovery and interpretation of ancient technologies, artists' environment and mutual relationships, better knowledge of materials and processes, and art dissemination and fruition.

Similarly to what happens in the medical fields, also for art diagnostics it is often needed to compare and integrate different sets of information, coming from different sources, and stored in different images. In order to successfully integrate these data, images corresponding to the same areas need to be registered. Registration is the determination of a geometrical transformation that aligns points in one picture with corresponding points in another picture. Similarly to what happens in the medical field, where this image processing tool has been initially developed, image registration can be an useful procedure in all the cases in which the analysis of the painting is performed by integrating information coming from different images taken at different time (e.g. historical pictures versus current pictures), or from different points of view or by means of different sensors acquiring the images in different spectral bands (e.g. IR-reflectograms, X-radiographies). In these cases, the acquired images will capture different and often complementary contents, allowing an integrated visualization of the images.

In the Cultural Heritage field, the registration is often performed manually by an user iteratively setting the parameters of the geometrical transformation. However, this approach is time consuming and can give subjective results. In the present work, the application of an automatic registration technique based on the computation of the mutual information for the analysis of artworks is proposed. We have applied the proposed method for the automatic registration of multispectral images, 7 relative to UV induced visible fluorescence images and 7 to white light acquisition. The multispectral images, acquired with a monochrome CCD camera equipped with a filter wheel, could result to be translated or scaled with respect to each other, due to a different optical path, a possible relative misaligned position of the corresponding filters in the filter wheel or a slightly different distance of the acquisition system from the painting in the various measuring sessions. The procedure was successful even on a small portion of the image, which made the processing much faster.

Image registration is also useful for a wide number of applications. They can be divided in four main groups [BJ03]:

- **Different viewpoints:** images represent the same scene or object observed from different points of view;

- **Different times:** the same scene is acquired in different times; this is a characteristic case when dealing with medical imaging used to outline the changes of some objects (monitor of tumor progression, for example);

- **Different sensors:** the same scene is observed by means of different sensors, thus acquiring the images in different spectral bands, being able to outline different characteristic of the same scene or object;

- **Scene to model registration:** what it is registered is an image of a scene and a corresponding model, for example for a more precise representation of the scene by a 3-D model.

As it can be seen, it is impossible to define a unique registration methodology, because of the different applications involving registration: every specific task has its own properties and its own difficulties, and registration procedures have to be fitted over the tasks themselves.

2 Classification of registration techniques

As said, it is impossible to design a universal registration method, due to the different deformations between the to-be-registered images, the different characteristics of the image data themselves, the accuracy which is required for the registration process.

When dealing with registration items, in general it is possible to define some subsequent steps to accomplish the task [BJ03]; note that we are generally talking about two different 2-D images which have to be registered each other, i.e. the *reference* (or *target*) one and the *sensed* (or *template*) one:

- *Feature detection:* by means of this step it is possible to extract some characteristic points (both manually or automatically) which are then used to find the transformation occurred between the two images; these points are often called *Control Points*;

- *Feature matching:* in this step the correspondence from the points previously extracted, over both the two images, is established, by means of various similarity measures;

- *Transform model estimation:* with this step it is possible to estimate the parameters of the transformation which is able to align the reference and the sensed images;

- *Image resampling and transformation:* the sensed image is transformed by means of the transformation parameters which have been estimated in the previous step, so as to perfectly match the reference image.

Although registration methods follow the same basic steps, they can be classified in a certain number of different ways. In the following, some of them have been reviewed; for a more detailed classification and explanation, and for a survey over the followed approaches, please refer to [Mas06].

2.1   Extrinsic vs. Intrinsic registration methods

A first kind of classification can be made distinguishing *extrinsic* and *intrinsic* methods [FHJ00].

The *extrinsic* registration approaches include all the methods which are based on the placement of some specific landmarks over the object whose image is acquired. In this way, the registration is accomplished estimating the transformation which these points have suffered. These points are often referred to as *fiducial points, fiducials* or *markers*. This kind of registration methods are most suitable for multi-sensor alignment of images taken in the same session after the object has been settled. Obviously, this procedure is feasible when (and only when) the object is correctly settled by means of markers; consequently, it is not useful for the alignment of previously acquired images without the aid of fiducial points.

On the contrary, the *intrinsic* registration approaches are not based on the need of accurately positioned markers. In this case, some specific features or specific measurements are extracted from the images themselves, in a completely automatic or a semi-automatic way; thus, it is also possible to accomplish registration over images which have been previously acquired and which are at disposal in archives or databases.

2.2   Classification according to the geometrical transformation

Since the proposed definition of registration is strictly related to the transformation of one image with respect to another, registration methods can also be classified according to the geometrical transformation involved, even if such a kind of classification highlights geometrical changing instead of the registration approach [FHJ00].

According to this, it is possible to point out some different transformations:

- *Rigid transformations:* defined as a transformation which preserves all the distances on the image. The general equation representing the rigid transformation is:

$$\vec{x}' = \mathbf{R}\vec{x} + \vec{t} \tag{1}$$

where R is the rotational displacement, and the translational displacement $\vec{t}$ is:

$$\vec{t} = (\ t_x, \quad t_y, \quad t_z\ ) \tag{2}$$

- *Nonrigid transformations*: are useful when dealing with non-rigid objects; they can be divided in a certain number of categories, among which the more general one is the *affine transformation*, defined by:

$$\vec{x}' = \mathbf{A}\vec{x} + \vec{t} \tag{3}$$

where there are no restrictions over the coefficients $a_{i,j}$ of the matrix $\mathbf{A}$ (a 3 by 3 matrix). The affine transformation preserves the straightness of the lines and the planarity of surfaces, preserves parallelism but allows non-zero angles to change. Sometimes, the affine transformation is represented by means of a single matrix $\mathbf{M}$ and the augmented vectors $\vec{u}$ and $\vec{u}'$:

$$\vec{u}' = \begin{pmatrix} u'_1 \\ u'_2 \\ u'_3 \\ u'_4 \end{pmatrix} = \mathbf{M}\vec{u} = \begin{pmatrix} a_{11} & a_{12} & a_{13} & t_1 \\ a_{21} & a_{22} & a_{23} & t_2 \\ a_{31} & a_{32} & a_{33} & t_3 \\ 0 & 0 & 0 & 1 \end{pmatrix} \cdot \begin{pmatrix} u_1 \\ u_2 \\ u_3 \\ u_4 \end{pmatrix} \tag{4}$$

where $u_i = x_i$, $u'_i = x'_i$ for $i = 1, 2, 3$ and $u_4 = u'_4 = 1$.

- *Rectification*: sometimes, images are distorted during the acquisition process. More precisely, let's suppose that the acquisition process acts such as a known transformation; thus, we assume that an image has been distorted during the acquisition step if the transformation from the actual object up to the image fails from the ideal behavior assumed for the acquisition. So, the *rectification* is the transformation, applied to the acquired image and leading to a different one, called the *rectified* image, for which it is possible to say that the transformation from the physical object to the rectified image follows the general model assumed for the acquisition process. For more detailed information, refer to [SVM92, CF92, SGBA93].

2.3   Classification according to the registration basis

This kind of classification of registration methods is based on the basis over which the classification is performed. With *basis* we intend the set of points or features that are involved in the registration task [FHJ00].

According to this, registration methods can be classified in three different categories: the *point-based methods*, the *surface-based methods* and the *intensity-based methods*.

The *point-based methods* are the ones in which it is essential to identify a priori a certain number of points over both the to-be-registered images; these points can be manually selected or externally superimposed to the images. As well as the extrinsic methods, these points are called *fiducials* and the process which is able to determine them is called *fiducial localization*.

The *surface-based methods* involve the determination of corresponding surfaces (instead of points) in both the two different images and try to find the transformation that best aligns these surfaces. Note that the item of determining some featuring surfaces in both the to-be-registered images is a further difficulty, which has to be solved by means of some preprocessing operations, increasing the computational complexity of the whole registration process.

The *intensity-based methods* are based on a completely different approach with respect to point-based and surface-based methods. They calculate the transformation by simply using the pixel (or voxel in the case of 3-D registration) values alone, with no reference to distinctive points or surfaces. In its basic implementation, it estimates the transformation by iteratively optimizing a *similarity measure* calculated starting by the pixel (voxel) values. In order to speed up the registration process, sometimes not all the pixels in the images are involved, but only a subset of them. Generally, they don't require any previous step, even if some pre-processing filtering can improve their performance.

2.4 Area-based vs. feature-based methods

Another kind of classification can be performed according to which step the emphasis is posed on, in the registration process. More clearly, and referring to the basic steps the registration is composed by (par. 1), this classification is based on the more or less importance of the feature matching with respect to the feature detection.

In this way, it is possible to talk about *Area-based methods* and *Feature-based methods*.

The *Area-based methods* pose more emphasis over the feature matching rather than their detection; often, the detection step is omitted and the registration is performed over the entire images or over smaller windows which have been shifted over the whole images.

The *Feature-based methods*, on the contrary, pose great care over the feature detection step. In this kind of approach, some salient structures are extracted from the images; the deformation estimation is then performed over these extracted features, which represent higher level information.

Apart from the greater computational complexity, these methods suffer from the great care needed to extract salient features. They have to be *remarkable*, even if this characteristic is intrinsic in the definition of "salient features"; they have to be *distinct* and spread all over the image; they have to be *clearly detectable* both in the sensed and in the reference images; for registration of images taken in different times, they have to be *stable in time* during the whole experiment; furthermore, they have to be *sufficiently numerous* to lead to good results.

Both the area-based and the feature-based methods have their advantages and suffer from some disadvantages; the most suitable approach has to be chosen with respect to the particular task we are dealing with.

3 Proposed method

As it can be seen in the previous section, Image Registration can be accomplished following some different approaches; regrettably, not all of them can lead us to useful results in all the field they could be used; particularly, in the Cultural Heritage field most of them often fail to get the correct registration parameters.

In fact, the acquisition of the good in different spectral bands is often obtained by means of a number of filters: a white light source floodlights the good through different filters; the emitted back light rays expose a suitable film, in order to get the whole image corresponding to the wavelength the filter let go by. The presence of the filters leads to a different length of the light path, and sometimes to some deformations of the path itself; in the final, this lead to some misalignment of the same painting points in the different images. So, if the purpose is to compare the different images in order to get a better knowledge of the good itself, the different images have to be correctly aligned, and it appears how the registration process is fundamental.

Furthermore, the diagnosis using a greater wavelength lead to a deeper inquiry, even under the painted layer and up to the preparatory drawing of the painting: it is possible in this way to appreciate how it was the art work in the very first thinking of the author, and, moreover, it is possible to discover the so called ***pentimenti*** of the author. Such a case is the most suitable to understand the difficulty of the registration process: because of the pentimenti of the painter, different images of the same good, taken in different spectral bands, could show some very different features, in particular showing details in one image which are not present or different in another image. So, it can be seen that registration techniques based on common features, such as points (point-based methods) or regions (area-based methods) can be applied with difficulty, because of the presence of non-common painting elements.

The approach we think the most suitable one is the one based on the **Mutual Information** and on the **Maximization of Mutual Information** (**MMI**) criterion. Mutual Information is a measure coming from information theory; roughly speaking, concerning a couple of images, Mutual Information is a measure of how much information the first image contains about the second one. In order to usefully use this measure, the MMI criterion states that *two images are correctly aligned when the Mutual Information reaches its maximum value*. So, the correct alignment of the two images can be found looking for the maximal value, over some different geometrical transformations applied to one of the images (called the *template image*) with respect to the other one (called *target image*), of the Mutual Information value. The geometrical transformation which satisfies the MMI criterion is the one we are looking for [VC05b, VC05a].

3.1 Mutual Information

Information theory is the discipline which studies signals and their transmission through some different communication channels. Each signal is joined to its quantity of information, and it arises the need of a parameter which is able to quantify this information. Each signal is also joined to a set of values it can assume: this set is often called the *alphabet* of the signal itself; each element of the alphabet is assumed more or less frequently from the signal. The probabilities of assuming an element of the alphabet by the signal are commonly a range, since some values are rare and some are common; in predicting what value a signal will have we can form an estimate of the *uncertainty* of our guess for that value, given the observed distribution of probabilities. Two extreme cases arise:

- **the signal can get only one value**: the uncertainty in guessing the value of the signal would be zero (*thus, each value of the signal is carrying a low amount of information*);

- **the signal can get all the values with the same probability**: all the probabilities are equal, thus uncertainty in guessing what value the signal might have is the largest (*thus, each value of the signal is carrying a large amount of information*).

It is often useful to look for the average amount of information provided by the set itself; in order to define a possible information measure behavior, a number of axioms and requirements for the measure itself have been given (see [Rez94]). Some possible attempts to define such a measure have been made ([Fis25]); the most commonly used one is the Shannon-Wiener entropy measure, such as presented in [Rez94].

Let's take a set of symbols S_i (an alphabet) of n elements, whose probabilities are given by $\{p_1, p_2, ..., p_n\}$; the average information supplied by this alphabet can be expressed as:

$$H(p_1, p_2, ..., p_n) = - \sum_{i=1}^{n} p_i \cdot \log(p_i) \tag{5}$$

This measure H is called *entropy* of the signal, and equation (5) gives a first order estimate of it.

Concerning the Image Processing field and images, the same previously exposed considerations hold; in particular, it is possible to think about images as two-dimensional generic signals, thus it is possible to get a measure of the entropy of the images. An important note has only to be posed on the index i, which has to be replaced by a two-dimensional index, varying in the interior of the image space. Thus, given a generic image A, and a generic pixel $a \in A$, the previous equation (5) can be rewritten as:

$$H(A) = - \sum_{a \in A} p_A(a) \cdot \log p_A(a) \tag{6}$$

Going ahead about eq. (6), it is possible to extend the concept to a couple of images and to the information they share. Thus, it assumes a great interest the probability of how often pairs of values occur together, a measure which is called *joint probability distribution*: in other words, if the *probability distribution* is a measure of the occurrence of a value referred to a single image, the *joint probability distribution* is a measure of the occurrence of a couple of values referred to a couple of images, a value for each image. Starting from this, it is also possible to define a measure of the quantity of information the two images are sharing from each other: this is called the *joint entropy* of the two images. Given A and B the two images (or the two views of the same good), and $a \in A$ and $b \in B$ a couple of pixel values belonging to the image A and B respectively, their joint entropy can be expressed as follows:

$$H(A, B) = - \sum_{a \in A} \sum_{b \in B} p_{A,B}(a, b) \cdot \log p_{A,B}(a, b) \tag{7}$$

The joint entropy is a very interesting measure of the information the two different images A and B are sharing; moreover, starting from eq. (7) it is possible to estimate the value of the Mutual Information for the two images involved. As said, Mutual Information is the amount of information one image contains about the other one; mathematically, it can be expressed such as in the following:

$$MI(A, B) = H(A) + H(B) - H(A, B) \tag{8}$$

where $H(A)$ is the entropy of the first image A, $H(B)$ is the entropy of the second image B, which can be written, similarly to eq. (6), such as:

$$H(B) = - \sum_{b \in B} p_B(b) \cdot \log p_B(b) \tag{9}$$

and $H(A, B)$ is the joint entropy value for the two images.

Marginal probabilities $p_A(a)$ and $p_B(b)$ can then be expressed as function of $p_{A,B}(a, b)$, such as in the following:

$$p_A(a) = \sum_{b \in B} p_{A,B}(a, b)$$
$$p_B(b) = \sum_{a \in A} p_{A,B}(a, b) \tag{10}$$

Combining the previous equations, Mutual Information can be expressed as:

$$MI(A, B) = \sum_{a \in A} \sum_{b \in B} p_{A,B}(a, b) \cdot \left[\log \frac{p_{A,B}(a, b)}{p_A(a) \cdot p_B(b)} \right] \tag{11}$$

Let's focus over some considerations. Marginal probabilities $p_A(a)$ and $p_B(b)$ can be approximated as the number of occurrence of the pixel with value equal to a in the image A; analogously for the number of occurrence of the pixel b of B and its probability $p_B(b)$. The number of occurrences of a value in an image can be extracted by the *histogram* of the image, which reports the value of all the grey levels with the number of pixel assuming it.

When dealing with a couple of images, the histogram of each one is often insufficient to get joint information. Thus, it is possible to go by the single histogram of each image, up to the so called *joint histogram*. The joint histogram is the natural extension of the single image histogram to a couple of it; it shows the grey levels of the first image on the x-axis, and the grey levels of the second image on the y-axis. Each entry of the joint histogram is the number of couples of pixels from the two images which get the corresponding values.

A very interesting property (even if it's obvious) of the joint histogram is its changing appearance corresponding to a misalignment of the two images. In the subsequent figure 1, two different couples of images with their corresponding joint histogram are shown; in particular, the right image of the second couple shows a significant misalignment. As it can be seen, the first joint histogram shows a very thin and sharp white line; the second one, instead, shows a cloud of white points, roughly following the course of the previous line. So, it is possible to see that the joint histogram is itself a first indicator of the correct alignment between two images.

The Mutual Information (MI) measure is not the only one used; a similar measure is the **Normalized Mutual Information** (**NMI**). Normalized Mutual Information is a measure

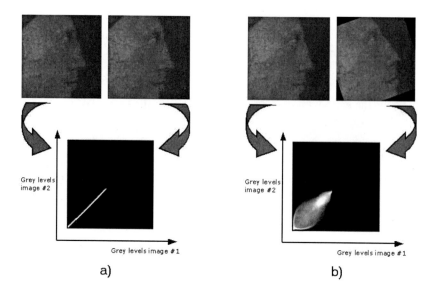

Fig. 1: Two couple of images and the corresponding joint histograms. The right image of the second pair shows a significant misalignment

which doesn't come from Information Theory (like Mutual Information actually does); it is simply a normalization of the Mutual Information measure. It has been developed in the field of Medical Imaging, and appears to produce more reliable results ([FHJ00]); mathematically, it can be expressed such as in the following:

$$NMI(A,B) = \frac{H(A) + H(B)}{H(A,B)} \qquad (12)$$

In equation (12), the entropies $H(A)$, $H(B)$ and $H(A,B)$ are computed exactly as in the previous equations (6), (9) and (7), and, with similar considerations, it is possible to infer the subsequent:

$$NMI(A,B) = \frac{\sum_{a \in A} \sum_{b \in B} p_{A,B}(a,b) \cdot \log\left[p_A(a) \cdot p_B(b)\right]}{\sum_{a \in A} \sum_{b \in B} p_{A,B}(a,b) \cdot \frac{1}{\log p_{A,B}(a,b)}} \qquad (13)$$

Actually, the most used measure is the NMI, because of its better behavior in this field.

3.2   Application of MMI criterion

As said, the MMI criterion states that when a couple of images are perfectly aligned, the Mutual Information value (or the Normalized Mutual Information value) reaches its maximum, with respect to all the other possible configurations of reciprocal position. Thus, it is possible to infer that the correct alignment of two different images can be retrieved by looking for the geometrical transformation which produces the maximum value of MI or of NMI, over a set of possible transformations; the following steps have to be performed:

Choice of the reference image: when dealing with two different featured images, first of all we have to choose which one of them is the "correct" one. Usually, this image is referred to as the *target* one; the other one is referred to as the *template* one. The target image is the "fixed" one, or reference one; image registration aims to find the correct geometrical transformation which is able to transform the template image towards the target one. Actually, it is not so important which one of the couple of images is the target one;

Choice of the geometrical transformation to be inquired: a geometrical transformation is chosen as likely to be the correct one;

Application of the geometrical transformation: the transformation is applied to the template image, leading to a new image (the *transformed* one);

Computation of the mutual information measure: the MI or NMI is computed over the transformed and target image; the result is a value for the measure of MI (or NMI) which is a function of the template image, the target image and the transformation applied;

Finding of the maximum value for the chosen measure: the previous steps from the second to the fourth are iterated until the maximum value for MI or NMI is found;

Reconstruction of the transformed template image: once the correct geometrical transformation has been found, it is possible to apply this transformation to the template image, in order to get a transformed template image which is aligned with the target one.

3.2.1 Application of the transformation to the template image

An important note has to be posed on the way the transformation has been applied to the template image.

First of all, we have to define the transformation model to be used; in the present work we selected the simpler *non-rigid transformation*, which can be obtained by a rigid transformation with a scaling, as in the following equation:

$$\vec{p'} = S \cdot R \cdot \vec{p} + \vec{t} \tag{14}$$

where the coordinate vector of a single point $\vec{p}$ (a 1 by 2 vector in the $2D$ case) is transformed in another point $\vec{p'}$ by the transformation. $\vec{t}$ is the translational displacement:

$$\vec{t} = [t_i, t_j] \tag{15}$$

R is the rotation matrix (a 2 by 2 matrix):

$$R = \begin{bmatrix} \cos\Theta & \sin\Theta \\ -\sin\Theta & \cos\Theta \end{bmatrix} \tag{16}$$

where Θ is the rotation angle; and S is a diagonal matrix:

$$S = \begin{bmatrix} s_i & 0 \\ 0 & s_j \end{bmatrix} \tag{17}$$

whose elements s_i and s_j represent the scaling factors along the two axes. In the simpler condition of isotropic scaling, as we assume, $s_i = s_j = s$; thus, the previous equation (14) can be simplified in the following:

$$\vec{p'} = s \cdot R \cdot \vec{p} + \vec{t} \tag{18}$$

where s is a scalar value. Thus, in our implementation the geometric parameters to be found are $\alpha = [tx, ty, \Theta, s]$.

Essentially, we considered two different ways this transformation has been applied. In the first case, the transformation has been applied to the whole image itself, by means of standard toolkits; in the second case, the transformation has been applied to the image pixel by pixel, in order not to generate a transformed image, but only to get the joint histogram. In the following, these two ways will be discussed.

Applying the transformation globally to the template image, we used a standard tool put at disposal in the MATLAB environment, the *imtransform* function. This function allows the user to apply one among a certain number of standard transformations, or to generate a completely user defined one. Moreover, it allows to set all the parameters featuring the particular transformation chosen. Nevertheless, some problems arise. Since this is a standard tool implemented for a general purpose use, no further refinements to the transformation parameters are allowed. Moreover, in order to generate a global transformed image, the tool interpolates some pixels which are lost in the transformation process. The joint histogram is then generated by comparing the two whole images.

The second way the transformation is applied is the one which deals with any singular point of the image. In this case, the joint histogram is not produced by the comparison of the target and the transformed image, but it is generated point by point. First of all, all the pixels of the template image are processed; please keep in mind that each pixel of the image is uniquely identified by its pair of coordinates. According to the transformation applied in the present step of the maximization procedure, the pixel is transformed up to the final position it would assume if the transformation would be actually applied; this means that the starting coordinates of the pixel we are dealing with are re-calculated in order to find the final coordinates of the pixel. If T is the transformation applied, and (i, j) and (k, l) are the starting and final coordinates of the pixel, the following equation shows this process:

$$(k, l) = T(i, j) \tag{19}$$

Then, the histogram entry which has to be updated is the one with coordinates:

$$(Template(i, j); Target(k, l)) \tag{20}$$

As it can be seen, we don't actually apply a transformation, but we only have a simulation of the transformation itself. This can help avoiding some approximation (thus some truncation errors); a comparison between these two different ways to generate the transformation is described in the following results section 4.1.

3.2.2 Interpolation items

Both of the previously explained methods to infer the joint histogram of the two images hurt with interpolation items, i.e. with the need of inferring the value of a number of pixels in some positions.

Strictly speaking, when applying the transformation globally to the image by means of specific functions, the interpolation problem is a marginal one, because the interpolation methods are built inside the function itself, and the user isn't able to perform any setting or improvements.

Some more degrees of freedom are available when applying the transformation locally pixel by pixel. Even in this case, some problems arise when pixels belonging to the new image (the transformed one) cannot be deduced by the starting image; nevertheless, in this case it is possible to use some ad-hoc solutions, since each pixel is shifted singularly.

There exists some different solutions to this problem, allowing the system to generate the joint histogram keeping into account the interpolation items.

In order to briefly review some interpolation algorithms, it is possible to remember the most used of them; mathematically, the interpolation aims to estimate the value of a general function in a point which doesn't belong to a grid, starting and basing on the grid point for which the function value is defined. In the following, only some few notes will be given on the most commonly used methods; for further details, please refer to [WHP92]:

Nearest Neighbor Interpolation Nearest Neighbor Interpolation is the simplest method and basically makes the pixels bigger. The color of a pixel in the new image is the color of the nearest pixel of the original image. Most image viewing and editing softwares use this type of interpolation to enlarge a digital image for the purpose of closer examination because it does not change the color information of the image and does not introduce any anti-aliasing.

Bilinear Interpolation Bilinear Interpolation determines the value of a new pixel estimating a linear function along both the two direction of coordinates, function which assumes the known points and by means of which it is possible to infer values in the required points. Practically, it is based on a weighted average of the 4 pixels in the nearest 2×2 neighborhood of the pixel in the original image.

Bicubic Interpolation Bicubic Interpolation is more sophisticated than the previously
   mentioned one; it is based on the estimation of a cubic function along both the directions; furthermore, it needs not only the value of the function, but also the gradient
   and the cross-derivatives of it, for each known grid points. Bicubic Interpolation produces smoother edges than Bilinear Interpolation.

Bicubic Spline Interpolation This is equivalent to a special case of Bicubic Interpolation. The interpolation function is of the same form of the function used in the case
   of the Bicubic Interpolation; nevertheless, the derivatives in the grid points are computed by means of one-dimensional *spline functions*. This is the numerically most
   accurate existing interpolation algorithm.

In order to compare some different solutions, we have tested two different procedures to
overpass the problem of the interpolation. Among the previously reported methods, we
chose the *Bilinear interpolation*; this because we think that this kind of method is the one
leading to the best results by means of the minimum computational effort. We compared it
with a different kind of method, the so called *Partial Volume interpolation*. Strictly speaking, this last one is not an exact interpolation method: as it will be seen, it is a some kind of
"trick", useful to overpass the problem of the interpolation itself.

Concerning the Partial Volume (PV) interpolation, as proposed in [CMD$^+$95], let's consider
the joint histogram of the target and the deformed images h_α: this joint histogram is strictly
related to the transformation T_α which has been applied to the target image in order to get the
deformed one. Following this approach, the joint histogram h_α's entries are incremented
accordingly to suitable weights w_k, for all the corresponding four nearest neighbors n_k
($k = 1, \cdots, 4$) of the pixel $T_\alpha(p)$; the weighting factors w_k are computed as inversely
proportional to the distance from n_k and $T_\alpha(p)$:

$$\sum_i w_k \left(T_\alpha(p)\right) = 1$$
$$\forall k : h_\alpha \left(X(p), Y(p)\right) = +w_k \tag{21}$$

see the following figure 2 for references.

More precisely, the values of weighting factors are computed in accord to their distance
between the position of the transformed pixel and the position of each one of the four neighboring grid pixels, thus accordingly to the areas of the four rectangles in the figure. Let's
pose that $T_\alpha(p) = p' = (i', j')$ is the transformed pixel and $n_{k,i}$ and $n_{k,j}$ the i and j coordinates of each neighboring pixel n_k of p'; thus, the weighting factors w_k are computed
as:

$$\begin{aligned}
w_1 &= (n_{3,i} - i') \cdot (n_{3,j} - j') \\
w_2 &= (n_{4,i} - i') \cdot (j' - n_{4,j}) \\
w_3 &= (i' - n_{1,i}) \cdot (j' - n_{1,j}) \\
w_4 &= (i' - n_{2,i}) \cdot (n_{2,j} - j')
\end{aligned} \tag{22}$$

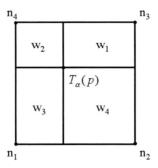

Fig. 2: Scheme of the weighting parameters for the proposed interpolation.

Since the distance between n_k and n_{k+1} is 1, being $(n_{3,i} - i') = a$ and $(n_{3,j} - j') = b$, it is possible to rewrite the previous equation (22) such as:

$$
\begin{aligned}
w_1 &= a \cdot b \\
w_2 &= (1 - a) \cdot b \\
w_3 &= (1 - a) \cdot (1 - b) \\
w_4 &= a \cdot (1 - b)
\end{aligned}
\tag{23}
$$

Note that the first expressions in equation (21) is satisfied; in fact:

$$
\begin{aligned}
w_1 + w_2 + w_3 + w_4 &= \\
= \ a \cdot b + (1 - a) \cdot b + (1 - a) \cdot (1 - b) + a \cdot (1 - b) &= \\
= \ a \cdot b + b - a \cdot b + 1 - a - b + a \cdot b + a - a \cdot b &= \\
= \ 1
\end{aligned}
\tag{24}
$$

Thus, referring to the equation (21), there are four entries in the joint histogram h_α, related to the transformation T_α, which are updated: the entries related to the four neighboring pixels of the transformed one; each one of them are incremented by a factor depending from the distance between the transformed pixel and the neighboring ones.

Experiments showed that PV interpolation introduces some artifacts in the MMI procedure; in particular, PV interpolation yields local maxima of MI for transformations imposing integer translations (more details on this effect can be found in [CMD+95]).

After that, we implemented the bilinear (BI) interpolation algorithm [CMD+95], which computes the intensity value of the lacking pixels as a weighted sum of the intensity values of the four nearest neighbors n_k ($k = 1, \cdots, 4$). Following this approach, the transformation is used to find the new position of the transformed pixel, whose values is then computed by means of its neighbors; thus, the joint histogram h_α is incremented according to this value, as described in the following equation:

$$\sum_i w_k \left(T_\alpha(p) \right) = 1$$
$$Y \left(T_\alpha(p) \right) = \sum_k \cdot Y(n_k) \qquad (25)$$
$$h_\alpha \left(X(p), Y(T_\alpha(p)) \right) = +1$$

The BI algorithm exhibits a better performance, with respect to the Partial Volume interpolation algorithm; it will be detailed more precisely in the following chapter 4.

3.3   Maximization procedure

As said, the MMI (Maximization of the Mutual Information) criterion states that the correct alignment between two images, representing the same good, is obtained for the transformation which is able to yield the maximum value of the computed Mutual Information. Thus, this directly imply maximization problems.

The maximization procedure is accomplished by changing and testing some different transformations, applied to the template image. The transformation which lets the maximum value of MI to be reached is the one performing the right alignment between the two images, target and template one.

In order to accomplish this task, several methods can be found, both in literature and as tools in many general purpose softwares (for example, MATLAB); for details, please also refer to [WHP92].

Regrettably, all of those methods are powerful when dealing with continuous or regular functions or, at least, with functions showing certain continuity and a known (or inferrable) course. As said, the Mutual Information related to a pair of images (the function we have to maximize) is strictly related to their joint histogram (see figure 1); since the joint histogram represents the occurrences of pairs of grey levels in the image, it is impossible to think about a regular function which is able to model the histogram's course; thus, it is possible to assert that histograms of the images are completely unpredictable.

As a consequence, usual methods, designed for regular functions, are assigned to fail.

In the present work, we dealt with two different approaches in order to apply the MMI criterion: performing the maximization by means of a standard MATLAB function, i.e. the *fminsearch* function, and performing the maximization by a simple and time consuming *exhaustive search*.

The MATLAB *fminsearch* function finds a minimum of a scalar function of several variables, starting at an initial estimate; this is generally referred to as *unconstrained nonlinear optimization*. This function is based on the simplex search method, which is a direct search method that does not use numerical or analytic gradients, as said above; for details, please refer to [JCL98]. We go back to a minimization problem for the MMI criterion simply by inverting the mark of the MI measure, i.e. multiplying it by a -1 factor. For the task we are dealing with, the *fminsearch* function is quite fast.

Nevertheless, it only give local solutions: this is a non-secondary problem, since we are trying to get the overall minimum of the measure, and a local minimum (if different from the global one) can lead to great misalignment of the two images. Furthermore, when dealing with a transformation involving a scaling factor, this function often fails in the minimum finding.

On the basis of such considerations, the *exhaustive search* has been implemented and used. By following this approach, all the transformations, belonging to a chosen set of all the possible ones, are applied once a time to the template image; the related MI value is stored in a sort of stack menu, paying attention to let the maximum value be the upper one; after having tested all the possible configurations of the transformations, the first element of the list is chosen, and consequently the related transformation parameters.

Based on the number of transformations we have to test, on the size of the under examination images and on the range the transformation parameters are allowed to vary, the exhaustive search method could be very time consuming, even involving several hours; nevertheless, this searching strategy is the only one able to guarantee a global maximum finding for the task we are dealing with.

4 Experimental results

In this section we show some of the experimental results obtained by applying the implemented MMI-based registration algorithm to a real case of art-works analysis. Please note that, due to copyright items, regrettably the whole images of the goods we used to test the registration technique can't be shown.

A set of different multispectral images (i.e. the UV induced visible fluorescence images and the white light acquisition images) have been used both to test the validity of the registration algorithm and demonstrate the usefulness of such a technology. The multispectral images, acquired with a monochrome CCD camera equipped with a filter wheel, could be translated or scaled with respect to each other, due to a different optical path, a possible relative misaligned position of the corresponding filters in the filter wheel or a slightly different distance of the acquisition system from the painting in the various measuring sessions. The final goal is the possibility to combine the registered UV and white light images in order to match correctly the information provided by the multispectral images.

Hence, the registration algorithm was applied firstly to register all the UV images, then to register all the white light images and finally to register the UV with the white light images. In particular the procedure was applied on a small portion of the images, to make the processing much faster, and then the estimated transformation $T_\alpha*$ was extended to the whole images.

As mentioned in the previous section, two interpolation techniques (partial volume PV and bilinear BI interpolation) have been implemented and compared.

4.1 Results of the work

Some preliminary tests have been accomplished over synthetic images, created ad-hoc for the tests: a synthetic image, showing some geometrical objects, has been drawn; subsequently, some deformations have been applied to it, in order to get some different template images. After that, small parts of the target and the template images have been extracted, in order to speed up the process, posing great care in order to avoid the introduction of further unpredictable misalignments: the registration algorithm has been performed on these sub-images.

In order to validate the process itself, the differences between the target and the template images and between the target and the registered template images (the "registered difference" for brevity) have been computed. As it can be seen in the following figure 3, the registered difference image shows a lower number of bright pixels, thus leading to a darker global image with respect to the difference image obtained by the target and the non-deformed template ones: this is a rough proof of the improvement the registration process implies to the correct alignment between the two images.

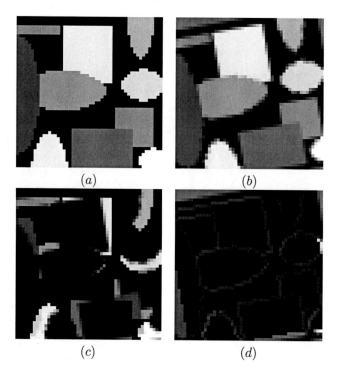

Fig. 3: Two parts of the synthetic images used for the preliminary tests: the target image (a) and the template one (b). In the second row, the differences between the target and the template images (c) and the target and the registered template images (d).

After that, since the main item is to deal with Cultural Heritage images, that kind of images have been used. We worked with images of a big painting, coming from the acquisition of it in several sub-bands of the visible spectrum; in order to avoid that the registration process would take too much time, we extracted by the whole image some smaller sub-parts; great care has been posed on the extraction of the smaller parts, in order to avoid further misalignment which could invalidate the whole registration procedure.

An example of the sub-parts which have been extracted can be found in the following figure 4, which shows a part of the visible band image taken at $\lambda = 700nm$ on the left and a similar part of the UV image taken at $\lambda = 450nm$ on the right. Once the correct transformation has

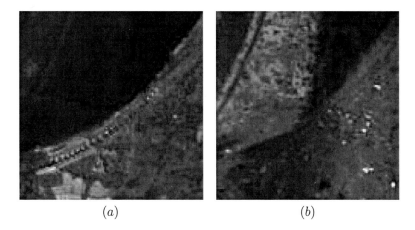

(a) (b)

Fig. 4: Images over which registration has been performed: visible band image at $\lambda = 700$ nm on the left and UV image at $\lambda = 450$ nm on the right.

been retrieved by means of the sub-parts, it has been applied to the related global image, in order to correctly align all the images taken in the different bands.

Referring to figure 5, the registration process has been tested on such images. In the figure, a couple of sub-images over which the registration process has been accomplished, the target and the template one, are shown. In the second row the differences between the target and the template images and between the target and the registered template images are shown. The registered difference image shows a lower number of bright pixels, i.e. it is a darker global image with respect of the other difference one: even in this case, this is a rough proof of the improvement the registration process implies to the correct alignment between the two images. The presence of bright pixels in the registered difference image is due to the interpolation step in the registration process and to the different details the two images show. These details are the ones we are interested to highlight, and are of great interest for restorers and curators.

Furthermore, a comparison between the different interpolation methods has been accomplished. Since we are interested to a sub-pixel precision for the geometrical transformation existing between target and template image, we found that the BI algorithm provides more reliable results, given that PV interpolation yields local maxima of MI at integer pixel positions, thus favoring integer values. Such a behavior is evident in figure 6 (a), where the MI is represented as a function of translation $[t_x, t_y]$ for a subpart of two UV images, using the PV interpolation method. In figure 6 (b) the corresponding result by using the BI interpo-

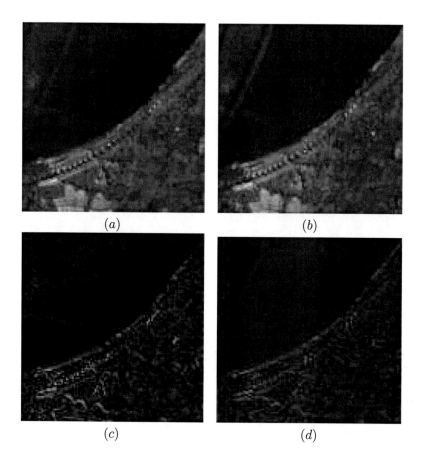

Fig. 5: Two sub-images which have been registered: the target image (a) and the template one (b). In the second row, the differences between the target and the template images (c) and the target and the registered template images (d).

lation is shown, and the two maxima (the one related to PV and the other related to BI) are pointed out, thus highlighting that, by means of PV, the real maximum is lost.

In the following tables, some comparative results are shown, regarding the different behavior of the process based on the PV and BI interpolation scheme; in particular, in table 1, the MI values for BI and PV are shown for the estimated $T_\alpha *$; this table refers just to the actual translation that occurred when the acquiring process was performed, and no further processing (such as rotation or scaling) have been applied. Similarly, in table 2 and in table 3 the MI values for BI and PV are compared, respectively when having applied a rotation angle and a scaling factor to the template images.

It is possible to note that BI interpolation often performs better than the PV interpolation; such a behavior can be proved both by the higher accuracy of the estimated parameters

	BI					PV				
UV Images	**R**	t_x	t_y	**S**	**MI**	**R**	t_x	t_y	**S**	**MI**
400uv - 450uv	0	-3,2	-0,2	1	0,94	0	-3,0	0,0	1	0,92
500uv - 450uv	0	-2,6	-0,2	1	2,67	0	-3,0	0,0	1	2,47
550uv - 450uv	0	-0,2	-2,2	1	1,77	0	0,0	-2,0	1	1,73
600uv - 450uv	0	-3,0	-0,8	1	1,63	0	-3,0	-1,0	1	1,60
650uv - 450uv	0	-2,6	-1,0	1	1,67	0	-3,0	-1,0	1	1,65
700uv - 450uv	0	-3,8	0,4	1	1,57	0	-4,0	0,0	1	1,52
W Images	**R**	t_x	t_y	**S**	**MI**	**R**	t_x	t_y	**S**	**MI**
400w - 700w	0	0,4	-1,2	1	1,33	0	1,0	-1,0	1	1,27
450w - 700w	0	3,8	-0,8	1	1,62	0	4,0	-1,0	1	1,59
500w - 700w	0	1,2	-1,0	1	1,87	0	1,0	-1,0	1	1,84
550w - 700w	0	3,4	-3,2	1	2,30	0	3,0	-3,0	1	2,16
600w - 700w	0	1,0	-1,8	1	2,78	0	1,0	-2,0	1	2,68
650w - 700w	0	1,2	-1,6	1	2,73	0	1,0	-2,0	1	2,42

Tab. 1: Comparison of BI and PV interpolation: in the first column the under process images are indicated (first the template, following the target image), where the number represent the λ used for the acquisition and the following letters stand for UV induced visible fluorescence (uv) and for white light acquisition (w).

		BI					PV				
UV Images	**Appl. Rot.**	**R**	t_x	t_y	**S**	**MI**	**R**	t_x	t_y	**S**	**MI**
400uv - 450uv	2	2	-3,2	-0,4	1	0,93	0	-3,6	-0,4	1	0,73
650uv - 450uv	-1	-1	-2,8	-1,0	1	1,60	0	-2,4	-1,4	1	1,35
W Images	**Appl. Rot.**	**R**	t_x	t_y	**S**	**MI**	**R**	t_x	t_y	**S**	**MI**
400w - 700w	1	1	0,4	-1,2	1	1,30	0	0,0	-0,6	1	1,04
600w - 700w	-2	-2	1,0	-1,8	1	2,50	-2	1,0	-2,0	1	2,10

Tab. 2: Comparison of BI and PV interpolation with images presenting a known angle of rotation: in the first column are indicated the template and the target images, pointing out the λ used for the acquisition and uv for UV induced visible fluorescence and w for white light acquisition; in the second column the applied angle of rotation.

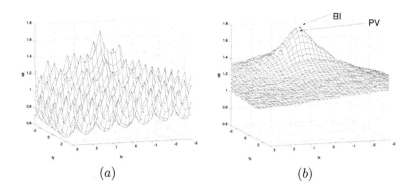

Fig. 6: Mutual Information as a function of translation $[t_x, t_y]$, by using the PV (a) and BI (b) inter-polation methods.

		BI					**PV**				
UV Images	**Appl. Scal.**	**R**	**t_x**	**t_y**	**S**	**MI**	**R**	**t_x**	**t_y**	**S**	**MI**
500uv - 450uv	1,1	0	-2,6	-0,2	1,1	2,28	0	-2,6	-0,2	1,1	1,91
700uv - 450uv	0,8	0	-4,0	0,4	0,8	2,18	0	-3,6	0,4	0,8	1,34
W Images	**Appl. Scal.**	**R**	**t_x**	**t_y**	**S**	**MI**	**R**	**t_x**	**t_y**	**S**	**MI**
550w - 700w	0,9	0	3,2	-3,2	0,9	2,19	0	3,4	-3,0	0,9	1,83
650w - 700w	1,2	0	1,2	-1,6	1,2	2,43	0	1,2	-1,6	1,2	2,07

Tab. 3: Comparison of BI and PV interpolation with images presenting a known scaling factor: in the first column are indicated the template and the target images, pointing out the λ used for the acquisition and uv for UV induced visible fluorescence and w for white light acquisition; in the second column the applied scaling factor.

(using the BI interpolation the sub-pixel accuracy is often reached even when the PV inter-polation restricts to the pixel accuracy) and by the higher value of the estimated MI value. The MMI-based registration algorithm with BI interpolation was applied to all the UV im-ages (with respect to a chosen UV target image) and, similarly, to all the white light images. A similar procedure has been applied for registering an UV with a white light image: even if in this case the structure of the two images is quite different from each other, the MMI algorithm leads to reliable results, as demonstrated by MI values for the estimated trans-formation, that is comparable with the MI value in the case of two UV or two white light images (e.g. MI = 1,29 for $[t_x = 0.2, t_y = -1.4]$). As last result, the multispectral reg-istered UV images have been used to obtain the RGB image, where all the information provided separately by the single images have been merged.

The maximization procedure we used to get such results is the exhaustive search procedure; the transformation applied is such as in equation (18), thus using the set of parameters such as $\alpha = [tx, ty, \Theta, s]$; i.e. there are four parameters which have to be found. In order to accomplish the exhaustive search procedure, a range is chosen for each one of the parameters; the range keeps into account the maximum variability of each parameter which is expected to find. All of these parameters are then incremented by a small factor, starting from the lower limit and depending on the accuracy one wants to reach; then, they are used to create the related transformation which is applied to the template image, in order to compute the Mutual Information measure with the target one.

Some other optimization techniques have been also tested. Among the others, the most powerful one is the *fminsearch* MATLAB function [JCL98]. Nevertheless this function often accomplish optimization with good results in many tasks, in the present case it often fails. First of all, it is strongly affected by local minima problems, thus the results obtained by means of it are not guaranteed to be the global minimum of the function. Moreover, several tests demonstrated that it performs quite well as long as the scaling factor is not involved; when the search strategy involves also a scaling factor, often the results this function obtains are divergent up to completely unlikely transformations, whose parameters are completely out the range we expected and as demonstrated by the computation of differences between the transformed template and the target images.

5   Conclusions

In the present work, it has been exploited the use of a known image processing tools in the Cultural Heritage field, in order to become a useful aid for the important role of restorers and curators in the diagnosis task of Cultural goods.

An image registration tool has been exploited. Such a tool is very useful to find the correct alignment among different images of the same good, which could have been acquired in different parts of the light spectrum, in order to highlight some different details. The acquisition of images in different parts of the spectrum and by means of different techniques poses some deformation problems, which can be modeled by a translational displacement, a rotational displacement and a scaling factor. Finding the correct deformation lets the algorithm to invert it, and to align the different images, so as to exactly compare all the particular features shown by each one of them. Note that the Cultural Heritage field poses some very particular problems, due to the particular features of the goods themselves.

Details of the implemented tools and results accomplished over sample images have been also presented.

6   Acknowledgements

We would like to thank Eng. Anna Pelagotti who, during the several months in which this endeavor lasted, provided us with helpful assistance. Without her care and consideration, this work would likely not have matured.

Bibliography

[BJ03]   Zitova B. and Flusser J. Image registration methods: A survey. *Image and Vision Computing*, 21:977–1000, June 2003.

[CF92]   H. Chang and J. M. Fitzpatrick. A technique for accurate magnetic resonance imaging in the presence of field inhomogeneities. *IEEE Transactions on Medical Imaging*, 11:319–329, 1992.

[CMD$^+$95] A. Collignon, F. Maes, D. Delaere, D. Vandermeulen, P. Suetens, and G. Marchal. Automated multimodality medical image registration using information theory. *Proc. 14th Int. Conf. Information Processing in Medical Imaging (IPMI'95), Computational Imaging and Vision*, 3:263–274, June 1995.

[FHJ00]   J. Michael Fitzpatrick, Derek L.G. Hill, and Calvin R. Maurer Jr. *Handbook of Medical Imaging - Volume 2, Medical Image Processing And Analysis*, chapter 8, Image Registration, pages 488–496. SPIE PRESS, Bellingham, Washington, M. Sonka, J.M. Fitzpatrick edition, 2000.

[Fis25]   R. A. Fisher. Theory of statistical estimation. *Proceedings of the Cambridge Philosophical Society*, 22:700–725, 1925.

[JCL98]   M. H. Wright P. E. Wright J. C. Lagarias, J. A. Reeds. Convergence properties of the nelder-mead simplex method in low dimensions. *SIAM Journal of Optimization*, 9(1):112–147, 1998.

[Mas06]   Andrea Del Mastio. *Tools and algorithms for Cultural Heritage Image Processing*. PhD Thesis, February 2006.

[Rez94]   F. M. Reza. *An Introduction to Information Theory*. Dover, New York, 1994.

[SGBA93]   T. S. Sumanaweera, G. H. Glover, T. O. Binford, and J. R. Adler. Mr susceptibility misregistration correction. *IEEE Transactions on Medical Imaging*, 12:251–259, 1993.

[SVM92]   W. E. Smith, N. Vakil, and S. A. Maislin. Correction of distortion in endoscope images. *IEEE Transactions on Medical Imaging*, 11:117–122, 1992.

[VC05a]   A. De Rosa A. Pelagotti A. Piva V. Cappellini, A. Del Mastio. An automatic registration algorithm for cultural heritage images. *Proceedings of ICIP - International Conference on Image Processing 2005, Genova (Italy)*, September 2005.

[VC05b]   A. De Rosa A. Piva A. Nozzoli A. Pelagotti L. Pezzati V. Cappellini, A. Del Mastio. An automatic registration technique for cultural heritage images.

Proceedings of the 8th International Conference on "Non-Destructive Investigations and Microanalysis for the Diagnostics and Conservation of the Cultural and Environmental Heritage", Lecce (Italy), May 2005.

[WHP92]   William T. Vetterling Brian P. Flannery William H. Press, Saul A. Teukolsky. *Numerical Recipes in C - The Art of Scientific Computing.* Cambridge University Press, second edition, 1992.

Digital Speech Watermarking and its Impact to Biometric Speech Authentication

ANDREA OERMANN, ANDREAS LANG, CLAUS VIELHAUER

Contents

Abstract

In this article an approach for connecting biometric speech authentication and digital watermarking is presented in order to integrate metadata into the authentication process without significant quality and performance losses. Different digital audio watermark methods are used to embed metadata as additional information into the reference data of biometric speaker recognition. Metadata in our context may consist ancillary information about the social, cultural or biological context of the owner of the biometric data as well as technical details of the sensor. We perform our tests based on a database taken from 33 subjects and 5 different utterances and a known cepstrum based speaker recognition algorithm in verification mode. The goal is to perform an evaluation of the recognition precision for our selected algorithm in the context of the gender belongings of the persons. The first tests show that the recognition precision is not significantly deteriorated by the embedding of the information. Further, the losses of the performance of the used biometric authentication system are less for female than for male users.

1.   Motivation

Biometric Authentication Systems as well as Digital Watermarking Methods have been developed to fulfill the challenges of IT-Security such as the authenticity and integrity. In an digitally interconnected world where communication is independent from time, localization and culture, the acceptance and success of such a system remain dependent on trustworthy identities.

In order to get access to certain resources, equipment or facilities, users need to be identified or verified. This can be realized through three authentication methods: secret knowledge, personal possession and individual characteristics of a human being (biometrics) [1]. The secret knowledge approach indicates the users knowledge, such as passwords or PINs. Personal possession implies that the user owns something like a physical key, smartcard or special token. Biometrics as an authentication method refers to the user's individual biometrical attributes such as speech and handwriting as behavioral-based modalities and fingerprint, face, iris, retina, or hand geometry as physiological modalities. Hence, instead of identify a person by external information, which can be lost, stolen or handed over, a biometric system identifies a person itself based on its given characteristics. The advantage of biometric user authentication is the unique and reliable identification and verification of a human being's identity. Hence, biometrics improve the level of security in infrastructures and applications.

The goal of biometric user authentication is the determination of similarities based on features derived from sampled signals concerning a particular biometric characteristic. We confine our study to the behavioral-based modality as we base our work on previous evaluations such as [2], [3], and [4], where we found out that the integration of metadata into the authentication process can improve the biometric authentication system. Previous work has shown that for example group discriminatory information such as gender or ethnicity can be derived [5], and also a specific language of a spoken sequence can be identified by biometric features [4]. As [4] and [6] have shown, a local optimization of the authentication process can be achieved by integrating metadata into it.

The focus of our work is to use digital watermarking techniques in order to fulfil biometric challenges as this provides a way to directly connect metadata with the biometric data. In other words, watermarking techniques provide a way to make metadata available for the biometric system. We define metadata as a collection of information the basic audio signal does not provide such as additional biometric information or additional characteristics (e.g. language, culture, ethnicity, gender, condition, age, ...) of the individual or the technical environment (e.g. device).

Based on this, we introduced a basic approach [7] where metadata are embedded by a digital watermarking method into the speaker reference signal in order to measure its impact on the EER of the biometric speaker verification system. In this approach 16 bit quantized speech signals and one LSB watermarking scheme have been applied to demonstrate first results. Further, we have been evaluating different watermark schemes by the application of so called profiles such as biometrics as presented in [8] while in this article we present an evaluation in a gender context. We want to find out if there are differences of quality losses of the performance of a biometric user authentication process regarding the user's different belongings to certain gender groups (male and female). Further, we want to analyze the influence of the length and content (semantics) of the audio signals of user's speech samples and also the influence of audio signal quantization. Here we compare if 16 bit quantized audio signals lead to a decreased distortion of the audio signal caused by the watermarking process and following to an improved performance than 8 bit quantized audio signals.

Digital watermarking has been proposed for a variety of applications, including content protection, authentication, digital rights management and others. Many watermarking techniques have made claims regarding performance, such as transparency, robustness, or capacity. In general, watermarking is an embedding and retrieval process, where hidden or secret information is embedded into or retrieved from digital content like music, image or video [9]. Using digital watermark techniques to embed information in biometric data is an emerging area of research and only a few approaches could be found in the literature such as [10], [11], [12], and [13]. However to date, the impact of watermarks on biometric speech authentication systems has rarely be evaluated. Therefore, and because of the fact that the watermarking procedure always implies changes of the content of information, the subject of our research is to analyze the impact of these changes on the authentication performance of the whole biometric system.

In this article, the same biometric speaker verification system as in [7] is used for feature extraction, which is based on Mel-Frequency Cepstrum Coefficients [6]. Our methodology is as follows. Firstly, the metadata are embedded into the reference signal of the biometric system. Then, the user verification process of the biometric system measures the error rates: false match rate (FMR), false non match rate (FNMR) and the derived equal error rate (EER). This is explained into more detail later in section 2. Different from [7], we now use four selected watermarking schemes working in time, frequency and wavelet domain regarding 16 as well as 8 bit quantized speech signals. Based in this, the evaluation will consider the different watermarking schemes in context with the gender aspect as well as the varying semantics.

This article is structured as follows. In section 2, biometric authentication systems are firstly introduced which includes an explanation of error rates, the speech authentication process, metadata, the cultural context and semantic classes considering the capacity needed to capture the metadata digital watermarks. This is followed by a description of the four used digital watermarking algorithms and the match of biometric authentication and digital watermarks. In section 3, the evaluation set up will be described. Therefor the evaluation methodology, its parameters and goals will be outlined. The evaluation results are presented in section 4. The article closes in section 5 with a summary.

2.   Biometric Authentication Systems and Digital Watermarking

In this section a brief introduction of biometric authentication systems will be provided followed by a description of error rates as quality measures of those systems. Further, a technique for speech authentication will be presented as well as a discussion of four different digital watermarking algorithms. Finally, metadata and their impact on biometric user authentication are elaborated. A description of the harmonization of biometric user authentication, digital watermarks and metadata is closing this section.

2.1.   Biometric Authentication

In biometric systems, user data initially needs to be enrolled which means the biometric parameters of the desired attribute are captured and stored in a database. For this purpose, one or more reference signals are captured from every user at time of registration. In the actual process of authenticating a particular user, again one ore more samples are taken from the subject and compared to the stored reference data. In order to verify or identify a user, new data regarding the same biometric attribute is compared with the stored biometric reference data. If the instances of the biometric data match, the user gets accepted and is allowed to access. Otherwise the user gets rejected.

The authentication can follow two different modes: In one mode a particular identity is declared as known prior the authentication. In this case the biometric system either confirms or declines the declared identity. This process is called verification and implies a comparison of n signal samplings to 1 particular reference storage sampling (1:1 comparison). The other mode refers to the biometric system automatically determining the identity of the actual user, which is called identification. This identification of a particular not known user considers a comparison of 1 signal samplings to n particular reference storage sampling (1:n comparison). Depending on the desired authentication mode, the system parameters may change. Both methods are qualified to bind the biometric data to an identity, thus may be used for authentication.

2.2. Error Rates

Commonly, evaluations of biometric authentication algorithms are based on the Equal Error Rate (EER), the point where False Match Rate (FMR) and False Non-Match Rate (FNMR) are identical. FNMR is the percentage probability of rejections by a biometric system of authentic user while FMR is the percentage probability of acceptances of non-authentic user. Thus, the ERR is one decision measure value at a specific operating point of a biometric system and implies the probability of great similarities. To read more about error rates we refer to [14]. The EER is not necessarily the optimal operating point in every biometric system and measurements such as Receiver Operating Characteristics (ROC) may provide more detailed information about the system's characteristics, but it is an initial clue for comparing recognition capability of biometric systems.

2.3. Speech Authentication

The speech authentication system used for our tests is based on Mel-Frequency Cepstrum Coefficients (MFCC), currently being one of the most popular and widely used feature extraction methods. By applying a mel-frequency scale rather than frequencies themselves MFCC represents a model of the human perception of sounds. Being nearly linear for frequencies below 1,000 Hz and logarithmic above, the mel scale initially has been proposed by S. Stevens, J. Volkman and E. Newman in 1937 [15] as a measure of the perceived pitch. Further, the cepstrum of signals as the Fourier transform or the spectrum of the log spectrum [16] is used.

In our system, all input wave files have a sampling frequency of 44,100 Hz and two different sampling precisions, 16 Bit as well as 8 Bit. Thus, the quality and performance differences of the authentication process can be evaluated. By applying a hamming window function with an overlapping shift of 10ms, the algorithm first justifies the input signal and generates frames of 30ms length. By doing so the influence of the textual content of the utterances, especially how it was spoken, can be limited. In order to reject frames with silence or low noise the total frame energy is compared against a threshold. A filter bank with L=20 mel-spaced triangle bandpass filters l, ranging up to 8,000 Hz was applied to the spectrum of every remaining frame to achieve the corresponding mel-frequency wrapped spectrum Ψ.

By modifying the approach described in [17], our implementation is applying "simple" MFCCs instead of the proposed T-MFCCs, which is based on a Teager Energy Operator. Hence, our frame's acoustic vector is calculated according to the following equation for each cepstrum coefficient k:

$$\text{MFCC}_k = \sum_{l=1}^{L} \log \Psi(l) \cos \left[\frac{k(l-0.5)}{L} \pi \right], \; k = 1, 2, \dots, L \tag{1}$$

Every single acoustic vector is then added to the frame's acoustic vector set. Considering the enrollment mode, the LBG algorithm [18] selects 32 reference vectors (centroids) out of the enrollment's acoustic vectors for each enrollment's reference model. Referring to the verification mode, the score of the verification vector set represents the minimum of all Euclidean distances between each verification vector and each reference vector.

2.4.   Metadata, Cultural Context and Semantic Classes

Embedding metadata regarding individual user information and technical settings into biometric reference data for authentication can be much of a benefit as our previous research [2] and [4] has shown. There we analyzed the impact biological, cultural and conditional aspects can have on a biometric handwriting and authentication system. Results encouraged us to enhance our research in this field. Based on the collected biometric data, both handwriting and speech, we can rely on a solid test set, especially when considering different cultural groups.

In our tests to determine the recognition precision the following information is embedded into the speech reference audio files:

- SampleID
- EventID
- PersonID
- SemanticID
- DeviceID
- LanguageID
- EnvironmentID

The SampleID is the ascending internal number of the speech files in the database. An event (EventID) indicates a collection of samples belonging together due to originator, semantics and action (enrollment, verification or forgery). The internal identification number of the user is stored in the PersonID. The SemanticID encodes the semantics of a speech task. It represents the content and duration of a speech sample. According to a predetermined task list different semantics have been captured from each test subject. Tasks are differentiated in individual, creative and predefined ones. The hardware device for voice recording is defined in the DeviceID. Further, Date and Time of recording is stored as metadata. The LanguageID indicates the spoken language of an utterance, while the environment of the capturing (e.g. soundproof cabin) of the speech recording is stored in an EnvironmentID.

Evaluation regarding the cultural background the PersonID is of importance, since it refers to a particular person. For our tests we have defined certain test sets based on the gender belongings of users with different cultural backgrounds such as Indians, Germans and Italians. Primarily, we focus on the 2 different classes, male and female, for our evaluation, whose particular parameters and goals are described into detail in section 4.

Within this EU-India Culture-Tech project speech and handwriting data has been captured from German, Indian and Italian test users. Further, metadata of all of these participating test users has been acquired. Therefore, we are profiting from an existing database. The collection of speech and handwriting data in our proprietary database followed a defined test plan with 47 different semantics in two languages (English and German). We developed this test set of certain semantics based on individual, creative and predefined tasks in order to be able to analyze its varying influence on the authentication system.

One single task was captured by 10 iterations, where the first 5 are used as reference data and the remaining 5 as authentication data. Audio files are recorded with a sampling frequency of 44,100 Hz and a sampling precision of 16 Bit as well as 8 Bit using a headset microphone in a laboratory environment for a uniform data collection. For our first initial tests, the following listed five out of the set of 47 semantics in English are chosen:

- "Communication"
- "What is your good name?"
- "Where are you from?"
- "She sells sea shells on the shore."
- "Hello, how are you?"

The sentences "She sells sea shells on the shore." and "Hello, how are you?" represent predefined tasks with an average length of 3.08/2.61 (Indians/Germans) seconds (average duration) and 1.83/1.35 seconds (average duration). A predefined semantic with a short duration are the word "Communication" (1.54/1.22 seconds) and the questions "What is your good name?" and "Where are you from?". These semantics represent tasks which encourage the test persons to provide individual answers. They have a short duration at an average of 1.40/1.09 seconds and 1.33/1.10 seconds.

In our test environment we use the verification mode for authentication. During the verification a claimed user identity is confirmed by the biometric system. The person is verified if the confirmation is successful, in the other case the person is rejected from the system.

2.5.   Harmonization of Metadata, Semantic Classes and the Capacity of Digital Watermarks

A specific watermarking payload of audio files, approximately 5,500 bytes per second, is available for embedding our metadata. The metadata, as described above, we have used in our first tests, have an average payload of 215 bytes. It will be embedded repeatedly in the speech data during the watermarking embedding process. Due to the fact that the required space for a watermark's capacity can only be fulfilled by audio signals of a certain length, semantics of speech samples for authentication need to be of a certain length in order to grant the needed capacity. This explains the decision for the five earlier introduced semantics we used for this evaluation.

2.6.   Digital Watermarking Algorithms

Different digital audio watermarking algorithms can be applied, from which we have selected four for our test set. Those four selected watermarking algorithms, implemented by Otto-von-Guericke University, Germany, open source and free available tools such as the one from Microsoft, and their parameters will briefly be introduced.

LSB: This watermarking algorithm works in time domain and embeds the watermark in the least significant bits (lsb's) of the audio sample values by overwriting the original bits [19] and [20]. Depending on the parameters, the message is embedded many times (redundantly) into the audio signal. This algorithm considers the following six parameters:

- The parameter k presents a secret key. The application of k, initializes a pseudo random noise generator (PRNG) which selects the LSB's used for embedding the digital watermark. This indicates the embedder being in scrambling mode and not all LBS's are applied for embedding. If the parameter k is not set, all sample values of the audio signal are applied for embedding, which directly implies the highest embedding capacity.

- The parameter c indicates for the application of an error correction code (ECC) [19] and turns error correction on or off. If an ECC is applied, the length of the embedding message is doubled and errors occurring during the retrieval function can be detected and corrected up to a certain threshold by detecting and retrieving.

- The parameter m specifies the secret message which is embedded into the audio signal.

- The parameter t stands for the mode selection which differs depending on the handling of multiple audio channels. According to the mode, the algorithm handles the audio channels in a naïve (1), identical (2), independent (3), consecutive (4), or random (5) way [20], where the numbers represent the specific value of the parameter.

- The parameter x represents the dynamic synchronization. By applying a PRNG, a different sequence of synchronization flags is generated for each embedded watermark message in order to decrease the risk of watermark detection by a statistical analysis of the audio signal.

- The parameter j describes a number of sample values which are randomly skipped and not used for embedding, preconditioned that parameter k is set and the embedding algorithm works in scrambling mode. The difference between the sample indexes is referred to as the jump length. The default value for this parameter is 9.

Microsoft: This watermarking algorithm works in frequency domain and embeds the watermark in the frequency coefficients by using a spread spectrum technique [20]. This algorithm only applies one single parameter m for the embedding message.

2A2W - AMSL Audio Water Wavelet: This watermarking algorithm works in wavelet domain and embeds the watermark on selected zero tree nodes without applying a secret key. In order to be able to retrieve the watermark information later by a detection function (non blind) the algorithms performs an additional file the marking positions are stored in. This algorithm considers the following parameters:

- The parameter m represents the embedded watermarking message

- The parameter w specifies the watermarking method and currently exclusively limited to ZT (zerotree).

- The parameter c specifies the coding method and currently, only binary (BIN) is possible.

SSWater: This watermarking algorithm works in frequency domain and embeds the watermark in selected frequency bands by using a spread spectrum technique [21]. This algorithm considers the following parameters:

- The parameter k specifies the secret key to initialize the PRNG.

- The parameter l indicates the lowest frequency bound.

- The parameter h indicates the high frequency bound.

- The parameter a defines the embed strength.

- The parameter f defines the frame size used for the FFT transformation.

- The parameter t defines the tolerance value used as threshold by retrieving the watermark.

2.7. Match of Biometric Authentication and Digital Watermarking

In order to analyze and evaluate the usage of digital watermarking algorithms for integrating metadata into speech signals a biometric user authentication is based on, the coordination of all three, digital watermarking, biometric user authentication based on speech and metadata, need to be described. In particular, this will be presented as follows through a description of our test scenario. Basically, the general authentication process consists of two successive steps: The enrollment and the verification/identification, as earlier mentioned in this article. Both steps include the process of watermarking embedding and retrieving. To capture speech data during enrollment each subject is asked to repeat a predefined semantics 10 times. Further, certain metadata from the subjects is collected. In the next step a watermarking algorithm with its default embedding parameters embeds the metadata of a subject as

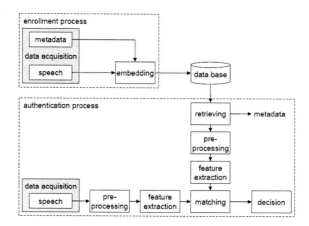

Figure 1.: Biometric user authentication (enrollment and authentication) based on watermarked reference and authentication data (see also [7])

message into all audio signals captured from this particular subject the metadata is related to. The watermarking algorithm embeds the metadata information into the speech file repetitively until the full capacity for each audio signal is reached. The resulting watermarked files are then stored in the reference database of the biometric system. In the authentication process the embedded metadata now gets retrieved from the reference data while the sufficiency of the embedding capacity for the given audio signal is verified at the same time.

The next step is the matching process for biometric user authentication and refers to the comparison of new captured authentication speech data passed though the preprocessing and feature extraction procedure and the stored and watermarked reference data, which also passed through the preprocessing and feature extraction. This matching delivers a value of similarity or dissimilarity (matching score) between reference and authentication data. Based on this score the biometric decision module will be able to make a decision upon the authenticity of the speaker. Thereby, the variable t is used as threshold for tuning the biometric system. Figure 1 demonstrates this test scenario.

For the embedding function in the enrollment process, all four earlier introduced watermarking schemes with their default embedding parameters, which are summarized and shown in Table 1, are applied for embedding. The influence of the different embedding functions on the authentication performance are measured by the occurring biometric error rates FNR and FNMR and the derived EER. Further evaluations will be explained into detail in section 3.

In general, we study the impact of the watermark embedding on the overall authentication performance of our biometric speaker recognition system (MFCC approach), by analyzing the recognition errors for our experimental data collection. Embedding information such as metadata into audio signals is a special case of additional noises within these audio signals.

Watermarking scheme	Embedding parameters
LSB	$k = , c = off, t = 1, x = off$
Microsoft	no parameters
2A2W	$w = ZT, c = BIN$
SSWater	k=1234, l=500, h=10000, a=2, f=1024, t=0.6

Table 1.: Embedding parameters of used watermarking schemes

At the current state of our work, we focus on aspects of quality losses in terms of biometric measurements caused by watermarking embedding schemes and the MFCC approach's noise sensitivity. But also, motivated by approaches for the MFCC method to improve the authentication performance in noisy environments ([22], [23]), we want to consider an optimization of the recognition accuracy of the authentication process as well as we want to support binning strategies in case of identification, both as impacts the direct connection of metadata and biometric data can have in the future.

3. Evaluation Description

In this section, the evaluation process, its parameters and evaluation goals will firstly be outlined followed by a discussion of its results.

3.1. Evaluation Methodology

The evaluation's methodology is based on a test division into two basic test sets: male and female. Further, our tests are always a composition of verification as the authentication mode and random forgery tests.

For each semantics and each user's belonging to either male or female the tests are divided into the following parts: Firstly, based on the previous captured audio data we embed the metadata of each subject of the test sets through all of the four watermarking schemes, LSB, Microsoft, SSWater, and 2A2W into the five different semantic speech samples captured by the same subject. Both, enrollment and verification samples are watermarked with the same metadata information.

In order to compare the impact of embedding metadata in different semantics of subjects belonging to different gender groups, either male or female, using different watermarking schemes we use the well known and earlier introduced biometric error rates.

3.2. Evaluation Parameters

Our evaluations contains of fixed as well as of variable parameters. Fixed parameters can be listed as follows:

a.) database for biometric speech authentication

b.) metadata integrated into the speech signal

c.) number of users

Variable parameters of the evaluation can be listed as follows:

a.) 2 different test sets: male and female

b.) 4 different speech watermarking algorithms: LSB, Microsoft, 2A2W, SSWater

c.) 5 different semantics: see section 2

d.) 2 quantization modes: 8 Bit and 16 Bit

3.3.　　　　Evaluation Goals

The introduced evaluation tests focus on the goal of measuring the quality of watermarking algorithms used for embedding additional information such as metadata into audio signals of a biometric user authentication system based on speech. In particular, we want to measure the influence of the embedding function of four different watermarking schemes on the biometrical user verification in the context of the user's different belongings to certain gender groups (male and female). First test results have shown that embedding additional information into the audio signals seems to always lead to performance losses of the authentication (refs). We now want to find out if there are remarkable differences of quality losses regarding the gender aspect. Further, we want to consider the length and content (semantics) of the audio signals of user's speech samples while the last evaluation goal refers to the influence of audio signal quantization. Here we want to analyze the relation of the quantization of audio signals and the performance of the biometric user authentication process. In detail, we want to find out if 16 bit quantized audio signals lead to a decreased distortion of the audio signal caused by the watermarking process and following to an improved performance than 8 bit quantized audio signals.

4.　　　　Results

In this section, our test results are presented and discussed while considering our earlier declared evaluation goals. Firstly, two tables give an overall representation of the results for all applied watermarking schemes, all semantic classes and the two user groups male and female. Then, two figures illustrate theses results followed by 2 figures concentrating on each watermarking algorithm in order to analyze them separately.

Before starting to discuss the test results performance characteristics of the applied watermarking schemes need to be outlined in order to put the results in relative terms. The LSB watermarking scheme as well as the 2A2W watermarking scheme are able to successfully embed the complete message into all audio files for our test sets while the embedding capacity of the Microsoft watermarking scheme is worse. If a part of message m is embedded, than only the first character of m (e.g. "S") is embedable. Furthermore, the used spread spectrum technique is not able to spread 100% of the first character. It means that for four audio files, only 5.83% and for one audio file 43.33% of the watermark could be spread over the audio signal. The SSWater watermarking scheme is not able to embed the complete message into the audio files. For 16 bit audio signals, the embedding capacity is higher than for 8 bit quantized audio signals. in general, the first characters of a message m can be retrieved directly after embedding.

Table 2 and Table 3 summarize the results for our tests for each of the five semantic classes (left column), where 1 = "Communication", 2 = "What is your good name?", 3 = "Hello, how are you?", 4 = "She sells sea shells on the shore." and 5 = "Where are you from?" and ∅ stands for the average mean of all semantic classes. Test results are represented by the EER for each gender group (male and female) for each applied watermarking scheme (2A2W, LSB, Microsoft and SSWater) and without any watermarking scheme.

As presented in Table 2 and Table 3, the biometric system has an average EER of 0.280 (female) and 0.310 (male) for 8 bit quantized audio signals and 0.280 (female) and 0.289 (male) for 16 bit quantized audio signals without using any watermarking scheme which embeds a message into the reference data. This indicates, that a biometric authentication system works slightly better for female than for male users. Further, considering the average EER for the different watermarking schemes itself and compared to the average EER for not marked biometric data it can be outlined, that the used biometric authentication system continued to work better for female users, no matter which algorithm and which quantization level has been applied to embed the metadata.

In particular, the best performance on an 8 bit quantization level could be achieved for female users by the Microsoft watermarking scheme (0.266) while the lowest EER in the 16 bit quantization level could also be achieved for female users, but by the SSWater watermarking scheme (0.255). This shows, that having a higher quantization level (16 bit) decreases the EER and hence increases the performance of the biometric user authentication. Even though these seem to be the best results, it has to be seen relatively due to the earlier described characteristics of the watermarking schemes, especially the inability of the Microsoft and the SSWater scheme to embed a whole message (metadata) into the audio signals. A first approach to evaluate this is presented in [8].

The results presented in Table 1 and 2 further indicate a remarkable gab between the EER regarding semantic classes. The best possible performance on an 8 bit quantization level could be reached for female users by the Microsoft watermarking scheme and the semantic class "Hello, how are you?" (0.187) while the worst result has been performed for male users by the 2A2W watermarking scheme and the semantic class "She sells sea shells on the shore." (0.409). The best possible performance on an 16 bit quantization level could be reached for female users by the SSWater watermarking scheme and also the semantic class "Hello, how are you?" (0.174) while the worst result on an 16 bit quantization level has been performed for female users by the 2A2W watermarking scheme and the semantic class "She sells sea shells on the shore." (0.391).

	8 Bit	8 Bit	8 Bit	8 Bit	8 Bit	8 Bit	8 Bit	8 Bit	8 Bit	8 Bit
	-	-	2A2W	2A2W	LSB	LSB	MS	MS	SSW	SSW
	female	male	female	male	female	male	female	male	female	male
	EER	EER	EER	EER	EER	EER	EER	EER	EER	EER
1	0,273	0,304	0,304	0,351	0,351	0,253	0,249	0,310	0,293	0,271
2	0,267	0,301	0,333	0,291	0,310	0,311	0,258	0,294	0,291	0,315
3	0,204	0,339	0,297	0,395	0,211	0,381	0,187	0,304	0,198	0,320
4	0,318	0,366	0,311	0,409	0,276	0,385	0,316	0,371	0,302	0,360
5	0,336	0,240	0,373	0,291	0,329	0,256	0,320	0,215	0,286	0,239
∅	**0,280**	**0,310**	**0,324**	**0,347**	**0,295**	**0,317**	**0,266**	**0,299**	**0,274**	**0,301**

Table 2.: Evaluation results based on EER and with a quantization of 8 Bit

	16 Bit	16 Bit	16 Bit	16 Bit	16 Bit	16 Bit	16 Bit	16 Bit	16 Bit	16 Bit
	-	-	2A2W	2A2W	LSB	LSB	MS	MS	SSW	SSW
	female	male	female	male	female	male	female	male	female	male
	EER	EER	EER	EER	EER	EER	EER	EER	EER	EER
1	0,262	0,262	0,276	0,335	0,262	0,263	0,236	0,253	0,249	0,229
2	0,265	0,298	0,324	0,298	0,265	0,298	0,258	0,294	0,298	0,310
3	0,204	0,294	0,283	0,353	0,205	0,294	0,187	0,304	0,174	0,275
4	0,325	0,366	0,391	0,384	0,332	0,366	0,316	0,371	0,262	0,359
5	0,343	0,227	0,356	0,311	0,345	0,228	0,320	0,215	0,291	0,220
∅	**0,280**	**0,289**	**0,326**	**0,336**	**0,282**	**0,289**	**0,263**	**0,288**	**0,255**	**0,278**

Table 3.: Evaluation results based on EER and with a quantization of 16 Bit

The presented figures are underlining our test results. The first two figures (Figure 2 and Figure 3) illustrate the comparison of all watermarking algorithms in the context of the two different gender groups and the five semantic classes. Figures 4-13 represent the specific differences of the EER for each watermarking scheme.

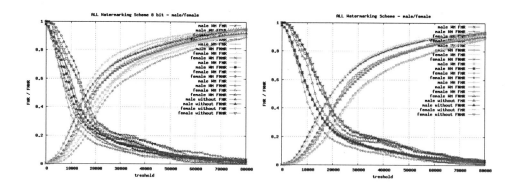

Figure 2.: All 8 Bit   *Figure 3.: All 16 Bit*

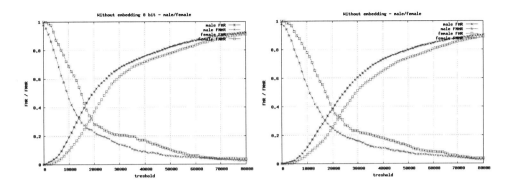

Figure 4.: FMR and FNMR curves for unmarked audio signals and 8 Bit quantization

Figure 5.: FMR and FNMR curves for unmarked audio signals and 16 Bit quantization

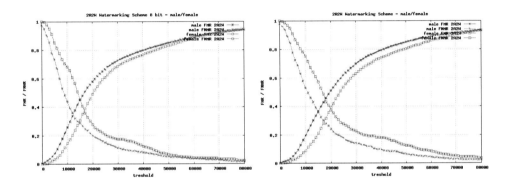

Figure 6.: FMR and FNMR curves for 2A2W watermarking scheme and 8 Bit quantization

Figure 7.: FMR and FNMR curves for 2A2W watermarking scheme and 16 Bit quantization

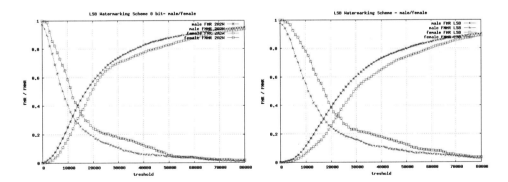

Figure 8.: FMR and FNMR curves for LSB watermarking scheme and 8 Bit quantization

Figure 9.: FMR and FNMR curves for LSB watermarking scheme and 16 Bit quantization

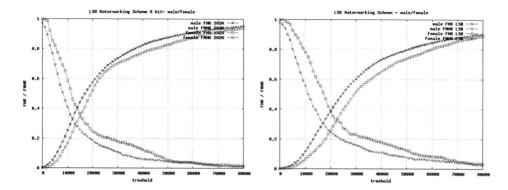

Figure 10.: FMR and FNMR curves for Microsoft
watermarking scheme and 8 Bit quan-
tization

Figure 11.: FMR and FNMR curves for Microsoft
watermarking scheme and 16 Bit quan-
tization

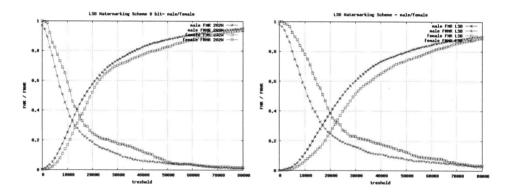

Figure 12.: FMR and FNMR curves for SSWater
watermarking scheme and 8 Bit quan-
tization

Figure 13.: FMR and FNMR curves for SSWater
watermarking scheme and 16 Bit quan-
tization

5.   Summary

The test results have shown that for the selected MFCC approach as biometric user authentication combined with different watermarking schemes such as 2A2W, LSB, Microsoft and SSWater metadata can be embedded in the speech based biometric reference data without remarkable losses of the authentication performance. We have shown that the differences between non-watermarked data, watermarked data with varying capacity are marginal.

Even though knowing that the used data are not sufficient in order to achieve statistic significance, the approach of integrating metadata into biometric reference material may be applied for implementing future biometric authentication systems where metadata contains complementary biometric references. The work presented in this article is an initial investigation, which examines the influence of embedded data on biometric recognition performance. In our current research, the payload of embedded metadata information is not fully exploited, we used in average 215 bytes repeatedly. Therefore it is possible to hide further biometric information such as other modalities as payload into the metadata (see [24]). Hence, a multimodal authentication can be achieved. Also, a knowledge based hash (i.e. password hash) as metadata can be embedded in order to use it in a multi-factor authentication mode. Multi-factor means a combination of biometric based (e.g. handwriting) and non-biometric based (e.g. knowledge, possession) user authentication. In this case the input knowledge can be confirmed by the knowledge retrieved from biometric reference data in addition to the biometric authentication.

Further, our tests have also shown, that applying digital watermarking techniques to embed additional information in biometric reference material and hence, integrate it into the authentication process performs better results for female users than for male. Also, the performance depends on the applied watermarking scheme. In this context our evaluation need to be further developed due to the disadvantageously embedding behavior of certain watermarking schemes, in particular Microsoft and SSWater as they are not able to embed the whole metadata. Therefore, we need to investigate the potential application fields and the required metadata to determine the watermarking parameters capacity, robustness and transparency as well as the required recognition precision.

6.   Acknowledgements

With respect to the cultural aspect and the combination of speech authentication and watermarking as well as its experimental evaluations, this publication has been produced partly with the assistance of the EU-India cross cultural program (project CultureTech, see [26]). The work about the implementation and usage of digital audio watermarking algorithms described in this article has been supported in part by the European Commission through the IST Programme under Contract IST-2002-507932 ECRYPT. The work on developing test methodologies has been supported in part by the European Commission through the IST Programme under Contract IST-2002-507634 BIOSECURE. Our special thanks belong to Tobias Scheidat for many inspirative discussions. The information in this document is provided as is, and no guarantee or warranty is given or implied that the information is fit for any particular purpose. The user thereof uses the information at its sole risk and liability. The content of this publication is the sole responsibility of the University Magdeburg and their co-authors and can in no way be taken to reflect the views of the European Union.

Bibliography

[1] C. Vielhauer: Biometric User Authentication for IT Security, Advances in Information Security. Vol. 18, Springer, New York ISBN: 0-387-26194-X, 2005

[2] F. Wolf, T.K. Basu, P.K. Dutta, C. Vielhauer, A. Oermann, B. Yegnanarayana: A Cross-Cultural Evaluation Framework for Behavioral Biometric User Authentication.: From Data and Information Analysis to Knowledge Engineering. In: Proceedings of 29 Annual Conference of the Gesellschaft für Klassifikation e. V., GfKl 2005, University of Magdeburg, Germany. Springer-Verlag, 2006, pp. 654-661

[3] C. Vielhauer, T. Scheidat: Multimodal Biometrics for Voice and Handwriting. In: Jana Dittmann, Stefan Katzenbeisser, Andreas Uhl (Eds.), Communications and Multimedia Se-curity: 9th IFIP TC-6 TC-11International Conference, CMS 2005, Proceedings, LNCS 3677, Salzburg, Austria, September 19 - 21, 2005, pp. 191 - 199

[4] C. Vielhauer, T. Basu, J. Dittmann, P.K. Dutta: Finding Meta Data in Speech and Handwriting Biometrics. In Proceedings of SPIE-IS&T. 5681, 2005, pp. 504-515

[5] C. I. Tomai, D. M. Kshirsagar, S. N. Srihari: Group Discriminatory Power of Handwritten Characters. In: Proceedings of SPIE-IS&T Electronic Imaging, 2004, pp. 116-123

[6] T. Scheidat, F. Wolf, C. Vielhauer: Analyzing Handwriting Biometrics in Metadata Context. To appear in: SPIE Proceedings - Electronic Imaging, Security and Watermarking of Multimedia Contents VIII, 2006

[7] C. Vielhauer, T. Scheidat, A. Lang, M. Schott, J. Dittmann, T.K. Basu, P.K. Dutta: Multimodal Speaker Authentication - Evaluation of Recognition Performance of Watermarked References. In: Proceedings of MMUA 2006, Toulouse, France, 2006

[8] A. Lang, J. Dittmann: Digital Watermarking of Biometric Speech References: Impact to the EER System Performance. To appear in: Proceedings of IS&T/SPIE Symposium on Electronic Imaging 2007, San Jose, 2007

[9] J. Dittmann, Digitale Wasserzeichen, Xpert.press, Springer Berlin, ISBN 3-540-66661-3, 2000

[10] C. Soutar, D. Roberge, A. Stoianov, R. Gilroy, B.V.K. Vijaya Kumar: Biometric Encryption. R.K. Nichols (Ed.), ICSA Guide to Cryptography, McGraw-Hill, 1999

[11] A.K. Jain, U. Uludag: Hiding fingerprint minutiae in images. Proc. Automatic Identification Advanced Technologies (AutoID), New York, March 14-15, 2002, pp. 97-102.

[12] A.K. Jain, U. Uludag, R.L. Hsu: Hiding a face in a fingerprint image. Proc. International Conference on Pattern Recognition (ICPR), Canada, August 11-15, 2002

[13] A.M. Namboodiri, A.K. Jain: Multimedia Document Authentication using On-line Signatures as Watermarks. Security, Steganography and Watermarking of Multimedia Contents VI, San Jose California, June 22, 2004, pp. 653-662

[14] C. Vielhauer: Biometric User Authentication for IT Security: From Fundamentals to Handwriting. Springer, New York, ISBN: 0-387-26194-X, 2005

[15] S.S. Stevens, J. Volkman, E.B. Newman: A scale for the measurement of the psychological magnitude of pitch. Journal of the Acoustical Society of America, 8, 1937, pp. 185-190

[16] J. W. Tukey, B. P. Bogert, J. R. Healy: The quefrency alanysis of time series for echoes: cepstrum, pseudo-autovariance, cross-cepstrum and saphe cracking. In: Proceedings of the Symposium on Time Series Analysis, 1963, pp. 209-243

[17] H. A. Patil, P. K. Dutta, T. K. Basu: The Teager Energy Based Mel Cepstrum for Speaker Identification in Multilingual Environment. In: Journal of Acoustical Society of India, Nov. 2004

[18] Y. Linde, A. Buzo, R. Gray: An algorithm for vector quantizer design. IEEE Transactions on Communications, Vol. 28, 1980, pp.84-95

[19] H. Klimant, R. Piotraschke, D. Schönfeld: Informations- und Kodierungstheorie. TEUBER, 2. Eddition, ISBN 3-5192-3003-8, 2003

[20] K. Matev: Least Significant Bit Watermarking. Internal report, 2005

[21] S. Dzhantimirov: Spread-Spektrum Verfahren für Wasserzeichen-Markierung von Audiosignalen. Internal report, Otto-von-Guericke University Magdeburg, 2006

[22] Z. Wu, Z. Cao: Improved MFCC-Based Feature for Robust Speaker Identification. Tsinghua Science & Technology, Volume 10, Issue 2, April 2005, pp. 158-161

[23] Q. Zhu, A. Alwan: Non-linear feature extraction for robust speech recognition in stationary and non-stationary noise. Computer Speech & Language, Volume 17, Issue 4, October 2003, pp. 381-402

[24] S. Schimke, T. Vogel, C. Vielhauer, J. Dittmann: Integration and Fusion Aspects of Speech and Handwriting Media. In: Proceedings of the Ninth International Conference Speech and Computer, SPECOM'2004, ISBN 5-7452-0110-x, 2004, pp. 42-46

[25] Andreas Lang, Jana Dittman: Profiles for Evaluation - the Usage of Audio WET. In: Proceesdings of SPIE at Security, Steganography, and Watermarking of Multimedia Contents VIII, IS&T/SPIE Symposium on Electronic Imaging, 15-19th January, 2006, San Jose, USA, 2006

[26] The Culture Tech Project, Cultural Dimensions in digital Multimedia Security Technology, a project funded under the EU-India Economic Cross Cultural Program, http://amsl-smb.cs.uni-magdeburg.de/culturetech/, last requested September 2005

Issues in the Development of an Audio-Video based Person Authentication System

B. Yegnanarayana, C. Chandra Sekhar, S. Palanivel, V. Suresh, Anil Kumar Sao and Dhananjaya N

Contents

Abstract

This chapter deals with some of the issues associated with the development of a person authentication system using audio and visual information. Two kinds of visual information namely the face and visual speech are explored. Motion information is used to localize and track a face in a video, and the face region is further processed in YC_rC_b color space to determine the locations of the eyes. The non-lip region modeled using a Gaussian density function, is used to estimate the coordinates of the center of the mouth. Facial features are extracted relative to the locations of the eyes, and visual speech features are extracted relative to the locations of the eyes and mouth. Acoustic features represented by weighted linear prediction cepstral coefficients are derived from the speech signal. The ability of the autoassociative neural network models to capture arbitrary distributions is exploited to build models of an individual. The evidence from speech, face and visual speech models is combined using a weighting rule, and the result is used to accept or reject the identity claim of a person. The performance of person authentication as well as person identification tasks are evaluated for newsreaders of television news broadcast. The various techniques developed for person authentication are used in the context of news video indexing. The automatic detection of anchorperson frames helps in segmentation of the news video into story units and generation of a visual table of contents. The problems of pose variation in face verification and speaker verification from limited amount of speech data are also addressed.

The results of this work were presented at various meetings and workshops in connection with the CultureTech project of the European Union.

1.   Introduction

The objective of a person authentication system is to accept or reject the identity claim of a person using one or more physiological or behavioral characteristics associated with the person. Person authentication systems make use of one or more biometrics such as speech, face, fingerprint, signature, iris and hand geometry to accept or reject an individual's identity claim. Multimodal person authentication systems have received much attention in recent literature.

The scope of this chapter is confined to some of the tasks and issues associated with the development of an automatic multimodal person authentication system using speech, face and visual speech modalities. Visual speech refers to the physical appearances of the lips and other facial muscles of a person when he/she speaks [Che01]. The various tasks or issues addressed in this chapter are (i) face tracking, (ii) location of the eye and mouth regions, (iii) feature extraction - facial, visual speech and acoustic features, (iv) modeling of the facial, visual speech and acoustic features and (v) combining evidence from the speech, face and visual speech modalities. Some of the desired qualities of the person authentication system are (i) invariance to size and position of the face in the image and its background,

(ii) invariance to orientation and pose of the face to some extent, (iii) enrollment of a person into the system without using any discriminating information from other subjects, and (iv) authentication of an identity claim within a reasonable amount of time. Section 2.1 through Section 2.5 discuss the various issues associated with the above tasks.

The techniques developed for the person authentication system are used to automatically detect and index the anchorpersons in broadcast news video and are outlined in Section 3. The pose problem in face verification is addressed in Section 4. The issue of speaker verification using limited amount of speech data is discussed in Section 5. Finally, the summary and conclusions with directions for future work are presented in Section 6.

2. Audio-video based person authentication system

The development of a person authentication system using three different modalities namely - speech, face and visual speech, is discussed in this section. The motion information is used to localize and track a face in a video, and the face region is further processed in YC_rC_b color space to determine the locations of the eyes. The non-lip region modeled using a Gaussian density function, is used to estimate the coordinates of the center of the mouth. Facial and visual speech features are extracted using multiscale morphological erosion and dilation operations, respectively. The facial features are extracted relative to the locations of the eyes, and visual speech features are extracted relative to the locations of the eyes and mouth. Acoustic features are derived from the speech signal, and are represented by weighted linear prediction cepstral coefficients (WLPCC). Autoassociative neural network (AANN) models are used to capture the distribution of the extracted acoustic, facial and visual speech features. The evidence from speech, face and visual speech models is combined using a weighting rule, and the result is used to accept or reject the identity claim of the subject. The details of the above steps involved in authenticating the claim of a person are discussed in the following sections.

2.1. Face tracking

Automatic person authentication requires a robust method for tracking a face in the video. In this work, a method is proposed for real time face tracking using the motion information between successive frames. As the person walks, the head contour points are extracted from the interframe thresholded difference image. The extracted head contour points are used to generate an ellipse for the head region [FPF99]. This process is repeated for every two consecutive frames in order to track the face in the video. The method requires initial head movement, and assumes that there is no other moving object in the background. If there is no head movement in successive frames, then the coordinates of the previous ellipse are retained. The method is computationally efficient, and is invariant to the size of the face, background and lighting conditions. Figs. 1(a), 1(b) and 1(c) show the thresholded difference image, extracted head contour points and the generated ellipse, respectively.

(a)   (b)   (c)

Figure 1.: Face tracking. (a) Difference image. (b) Contour points. (c) Generated ellipse.

2.2.   Location of eye and mouth regions

One of the main issues in constructing an automatic person authentication system is to extract the facial features that are invariant to size of the face. Most of the existing methods for person authentication assume the availability of cropped face images of a fixed size. The size of the face in the image depends on the distance of the subject with respect to the camera and the actual size of the subject's face. In practice, it is difficult to control the position of the subject with respect to the camera. Hence, the size of the face must be determined for feature extraction. The size of the face can be determined if the locations of two or more facial features are identified. Among the facial features, eyes and mouth are the most prominent features used for estimating the size and pose of the face [HAMJ02]. The face region is processed in YC_rC_b color space to estimate the locations of the eyes. The Y, C_r and C_b values are normalized to the range [0, 255].

The eye regions have low intensity (Y), low red chrominance (C_r) and high blue chrominance (C_b) when compared to the forehead region of the face. Using this fact, the face region is thresholded to obtain the thresholded face image (U), given by

$$U(i,j) = \begin{cases} 255, & \text{if } Y(i,j) < \lambda_1 \text{ and } C_r(i,j) < \lambda_2 \\ & \text{and } C_b(i,j) > \lambda_3 \\ Y(i,j), & \text{otherwise} \end{cases} \tag{1}$$

where λ_1, λ_2 and λ_3 are the average Y, C_r and C_b values of the pixels in the forehead region, respectively. The forehead region is estimated from the extracted head contour points.

Fig. 2 shows the construction of the thresholded face image. The white blobs in Figs. 2(a), 2(b) and 2(c) are the low intensity, low red chrominance and high blue chrominance regions, respectively, when compared to the forehead region of the face. The thresholded face image is shown in Fig. 2(d). Morphological closing operation is applied to the thresholded face image, and the centroids of the blobs are estimated. The blobs whose height or width is greater than $0.25w_1$ are not considered for further processing, where w_1 is the width of the face. The relative positions of the centroids with respect to the rectangular bounding box enclosing the face region and the contrast information in the eyebrow region are used to determine

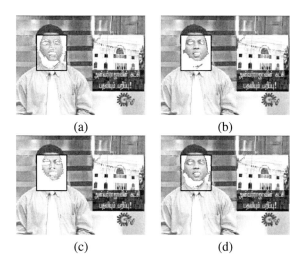

Figure 2.: Construction of thresholded face image. The white blobs in (a), (b), (c) are the low intensity, low red chrominance and high blue chrominance regions when compared to the forehead region of the face, respectively. (d) Thresholded face image.

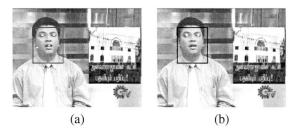

Figure 3.: Estimation of locations of the eyes. (a) Centroids of the blobs. (b) Locations of the eyes.

the locations of the eyes. The eyebrow contrast information is obtained as follows:

$$E(i,j) = \begin{cases} 1, & \text{if } Y(i,j) \geq \lambda_1 \text{ and } Y(i,j+1) \geq \lambda_1 \\ & \text{and } Y(i,j+2) < \lambda_1 \\ 0, & \text{otherwise.} \end{cases} \quad (2)$$

The centroids of the white blobs in Fig. 2(d) are shown in Fig. 3(a). The corresponding locations of the eyes are shown in Fig. 3(b).

The mouth region is estimated from the locations of the eyes and the center of the mouth. For estimating the mouth center, we model the color distribution of the non-lip region of the face using a Gaussian distribution as given by

$$p(\boldsymbol{x}) = \mathcal{N}(\boldsymbol{\mu}, \boldsymbol{\Sigma}) = \frac{1}{\sqrt{(2\pi)^D |\boldsymbol{\Sigma}|}} \exp^{-\frac{1}{2}(\boldsymbol{x}-\boldsymbol{\mu})^T \boldsymbol{\Sigma}^{-1}(\boldsymbol{x}-\boldsymbol{\mu})} \quad (3)$$

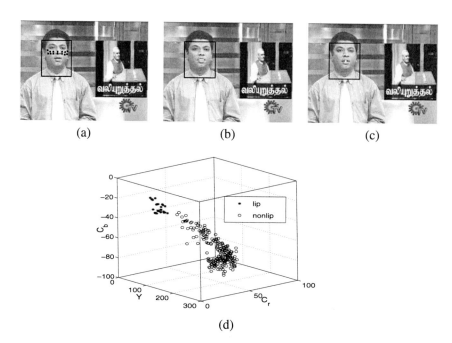

Figure 4.: Estimation of center of the mouth. (a) Non-lip regions, (b) detected lip pixels, (c) center of the mouth and (d) distribution of non-lip and lip pixels.

where x is the feature vector, D is the dimension of the feature vector, μ is the mean vector and Σ is the covariance matrix. The non-lip regions are extracted relative to the locations of the eyes as shown in Fig. 4(a). The Y, C_r and C_b values (feature vector x) of the pixels in these regions are used to estimate the parameters of the Gaussian distribution. The Y, C_r and C_b values of the pixels in the lip region may not fall into the distribution, and hence (3) is used to detect the pixels in the lip region. The detected lip pixels are shown in Fig. 4(b). The distribution of Y, C_r and C_b values of the non-lip and the detected lip pixels are shown in Fig. 4(d). The center of the mouth is estimated using the pixel coordinates of the detected lip pixels. The estimated center of mouth is shown in Fig. 4(c).

2.3.   Feature extraction

This section addresses some issues associated with the extraction of features from the three chosen modalities namely - face, visual speech and speech.

2.3.1.   Facial features

The facial features such as hair, outline of the face, eyebrows, eyes and mouth play an important role in perceiving and remembering faces [ZCRP00]. A cartoonist extracts the required information from these features, and represents them in terms of lines and arcs.

These lines and arcs correspond to the gradient or local extrema (minima and maxima) in an image. The local maxima and local minima are the largest and smallest intensity values of an image within some local neighborhood, respectively. The facial features such as hair, eyebrows, eyes, nostrils and end points of lips are associated with local minima, and shape of the lip contour corresponds to local maxima. The local maxima and local minima can be extracted using the gray scale morphological operations namely, dilation and erosion, respectively [JD96]. In this work, an elliptical grid is placed over the face region, and the multiscale morphological erosion operation is used for facial feature extraction. The face outline or contour can be captured using a rectangular grid which assumes that the training and testing images have the same background. Performance of the person authentication technique must be invariant to the position of the face in the image and its background, and hence we use an elliptical grid instead of a rectangular grid. The length and slope of the line connecting the eyes are used to determine the size and orientation of the grid, respectively. The elliptical grid consists of 73 nodes, and the position of these nodes is determined relative to the locations of the eyes. The multiscale morphological erosion operation is applied at each grid node for extracting the facial features as described below.

The multiscale morphological erosion operation is based on the gray scale morphology, erosion. Let $\mathbb{Z}$ denote the set of integers. Given an image $\mathbf{I}: \mathcal{D} \subseteq \mathbb{Z}^2 \longrightarrow \mathbb{Z}$ and a structuring function $\mathbf{G}_\sigma: \mathcal{G}_\sigma \subseteq \mathbb{Z}^2 \longrightarrow \mathbb{Z}$ at scale σ, the erosion of the image $\mathbf{I}$ by the structuring function $\mathbf{G}_\sigma$ is denoted as $(\mathbf{I} \ominus \mathbf{G}_\sigma)$, and it is defined by

$$(I \ominus G_\sigma)(i,j) = \min_{x,y}\{I(i+x, j+y) - G_\sigma(x,y)\} \tag{4}$$

where $-M_a \leq x, y \leq M_b$, with $1 \leq i \leq W$, $1 \leq j \leq H$. The quantities W and H are the width and height of the image, respectively. The size of the structuring function is decided by the parameters M_a and M_b, and is given by $(M_a + M_b + 1) \times (M_a + M_b + 1)$. The structuring functions such as flat, hemisphere, paraboloid are commonly used in morphological operations [JD96]. The flat structuring function $G_\sigma(x,y) = 0$ is used in this work. For a flat structuring function the expression for erosion reduces to

$$(I \ominus G_\sigma)(i,j) = \min_{x,y}\{I(i+x, j+y)\} \tag{5}$$

where $-M_a \leq x, y \leq M_b$. The erosion operation (5) is applied at each grid node for $\sigma = 1, 2, \ldots, P$ to obtain P facial feature vectors from the face image. The distance d, between the eyes is used to determine the parameters M_a, M_b and P. The values $M_a = \lfloor d/32 \rfloor + \lfloor (\sigma - 1)/2 \rfloor$, $M_b = \lfloor d/32 + 0.5 \rfloor + \lfloor \sigma/2 \rfloor$ and $P = 3$ have been used in our experiments. These parameters are chosen in such a way that $M_a + M_b + 1$ for $\sigma = P$ is less than or equal to the minimal distance between two nodes of the grid. Fig. 5(a) shows the eroded images for $\sigma = 1, 2$ and 3. Fig. 5(b) shows the facial regions used for extracting the feature vectors for $\sigma = 1, 2$ and 3. Each element of the facial feature vector $\mathbf{f} = (f_1, f_2, \ldots, f_{73})$ is normalized to [-1, 1] as follows:

$$y_i = \frac{2(f_i - f_{min})}{(f_{max} - f_{min})} - 1 \tag{6}$$

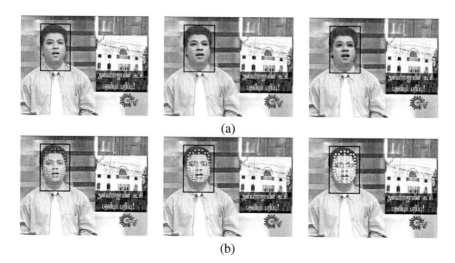

(a)

(b)

Figure 5.: Extraction of facial features. (a) From left to right: Eroded images for $\sigma = 1, 2$ and 3. (b) Facial regions used for extracting the feature vectors for $\sigma = 1, 2$ and 3.

where f_{max} and f_{min} are the maximum and minimum values, respectively, in the feature vector. The normalized facial feature vector $\boldsymbol{y} = (y_1, y_2, \ldots, y_{73})$ is less sensitive to variation in the image brightness.

2.3.2.   Visual speech features

The static nature of the visual speech features in the mouth region such as shape of the lip contour and shape of the moustache play an important role in perceiving and remembering a person. These features are associated with local maxima and they can be extracted using the multiscale morphological dilation operation [JD96]. For visual speech feature extraction, a rectangular grid consisting of 25 nodes is placed over the mouth region. The position of these nodes is determined relative to the locations of the eyes and the center of the mouth. The features are extracted at each grid node using the multiscale morphological dilation operation as described below.

Given an image $\mathbf{I}$: $\mathcal{D} \subseteq \mathbb{Z}^2 \longrightarrow \mathbb{Z}$ and a structuring function $\mathbf{G}_\sigma$: $\mathcal{G}_\sigma \subseteq \mathbb{Z}^2 \longrightarrow \mathbb{Z}$ at scale σ, the dilation of the image $\mathbf{I}$ by the structuring function $\mathbf{G}_\sigma$ is denoted as $(\mathbf{I} \oplus \mathbf{G}_\sigma)$, and it is defined by

$$(I \oplus G_\sigma)(i, j) = \max_{x,y}\{I(i - x, j - y) + G_\sigma(x, y)\} \tag{7}$$

where $-M_a \leq x, y \leq M_b$, with $1 \leq i \leq W, 1 \leq j \leq H$. For a flat structuring function, the dilation can be expressed as

$$(I \oplus G_\sigma)(i, j) = \max_{x,y}\{I(i - x, j - y)\} \tag{8}$$

where $-M_a \leq x, y \leq M_b$. The dilation operation (8) is applied at each grid node for $\sigma = 1, 2, \ldots, P$ to obtain P visual speech feature vectors from the mouth image. The

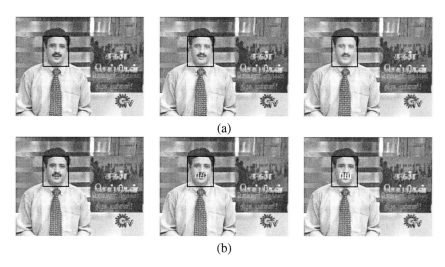

(a)

(b)

Figure 6.: Extraction of visual speech features. (a) From left to right: Dilated images for $\sigma = 1, 2$ and 3. (b) Visual regions used for extracting the feature vectors for $\sigma = 1, 2$ and 3.

distance d, between the eyes is used to determine the parameters M_a, M_b and P. The values $M_a = \lfloor d/64 + 0.5 \rfloor + \lfloor (\sigma - 1)/2 \rfloor$, $M_b = \lfloor d/64 \rfloor + \lfloor \sigma/2 \rfloor$ and $P = 3$ have been used in our experiments. Figs. 6(a) and 6(b) show the dilated images and the visual regions used for extracting the feature vectors for $\sigma = 1, 2$ and 3, respectively. Each element of the visual speech feature vector is normalized to [-1, 1].

2.3.3. Acoustic features

Acoustic features representing the speaker-specific information can be extracted from the speech signal at the segmental level. The segmental features are the features extracted from short (10 to 30 ms) segments of the speech signal. Some of the segmental features are linear prediction cepstral coefficients and mel frequency cepstral coefficients [nis03]. These features represent the short-time spectrum of the speech signal. The short-time spectrum envelope of the speech signal is attributed primarily to the shape of the vocal tract. The spectral information of the same sound uttered by two persons may differ due to change in the shape of the individual's vocal tract system, and the manner of speech production.

The differenced speech signal is divided into frames of 20 ms, with a shift of 5 ms. A 14th order linear prediction (LP) analysis is used to capture the properties of the signal spectrum. The recursive relation between the predictor coefficients and cepstral coefficients is used to convert the 14 LP coefficients into 19 LP cepstral coefficients. The LP cepstral coefficients for each frame are linearly weighted to obtain the weighted linear prediction cepstral coefficients. A 19 dimensional weighted linear prediction cepstral coefficient (WLPCC) vector

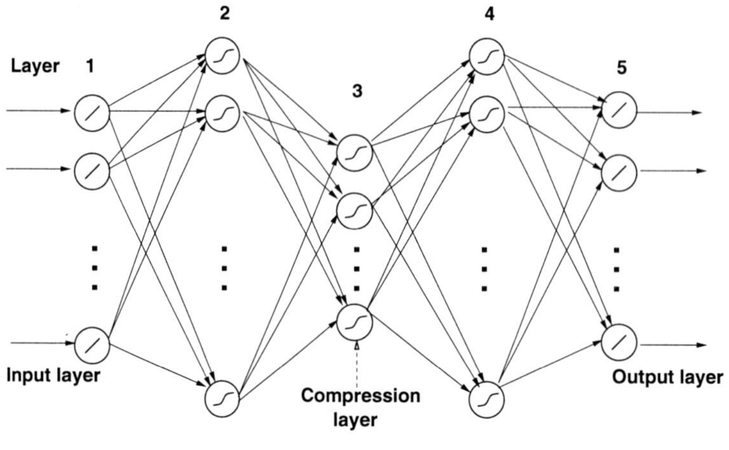

Figure 7.: A five layer AANN model.

for each frame is used as a feature vector.

2.4.   Modeling of acoustic, facial and visual speech features

A five layer autoassociative neural network (AANN) model as shown in Fig. 7 is used to capture the distribution of the acoustic, facial and static nature of the visual speech feature vectors. Autoassociative neural network models are feedforward neural networks performing an identity mapping of the input space, and are used to capture the distribution of the input data [YK02]. The second and fourth layers of the network have more units than the input layer. The third layer has fewer units than the first or fifth. The activation functions at the second, third and fourth layer are nonlinear. The structures of the AANN models used in our study are *19L38N4N38N19L, 73L90N30N90N73L* and *25L40N10N40N25L* for capturing the distribution of acoustic, facial and visual speech features of a subject, respectively, where *L* denotes a linear unit, and *N* denotes a nonlinear unit. The integer value indicates the number of units used in that layer. The nonlinear units use tanh(s) as the activation function, where s is the activation value of the unit. Backpropagation learning algorithm is used to adjust the weights of the network to minimize the mean square error.

2.5.   Performance evaluation of the person authentication system

Performance of the person authentication system is evaluated using the Indian TV broadcast news data (Sun Network: Sun TV and Sun News) for 50 subjects, comprising of 32 females and 18 males. For enrolling (training) a subject, an AVI file of 60 seconds (4 clips, each of 15 seconds) duration at 12 frames per second is recorded with a resolution of 320 × 240. The speech signal is recorded at 8000 samples per second. During news reading, the background around the newsreader is almost constant accompanied by a small motion of the reader in the foreground. Hence, the accumulated difference image is used to estimate the face region as described in Section 2.1. If there is a significant head movement during news-reading, then the thresholded difference image can be used to track the face region. The locations of the eyes and mouth are estimated as described in Section 2.2. The method can detect the locations of the eyes in the presence of eye glasses as long as the eye regions are visible.

The morphological erosion (dilation) is applied on the face (mouth) image for three different scales ($P=3$), and the facial (visual speech) feature vectors are extracted for 300 face images as described in Sections 2.3.1 and 2.3.2, respectively. The distance between the eyes varied from 24 to 33 pixels, and hence the value of $P=3$ is used in our experiment. The acoustic features are extracted as described in Section 2.3.3. The distributions of the acoustic, facial and visual speech feature vectors are captured using AANN models. The extracted acoustic feature vectors are given as input to the AANN model *19L38N4N38N19L*, and the network is trained for 100 epochs as described in Section 2.4 for capturing the distribution. The normalized 900 facial feature vectors are given as input to the AANN model *73L90N30N90N73L*, and the network is trained for 200 epochs. Similarly the distribution of the 900 visual speech feature vectors are captured using an AANN model *25L40N10N40N25L*, and the network is trained for 50 epochs. One epoch of training is a single presentation of all the training data to the network. The network structures are chosen based on empirical studies.

For evaluating the performance of the system, an AVI file of 10 seconds duration at 12 frames per second is recorded, one month after collecting the training data. Most of the person recognition methods described in the literature report identification performance. This work deals with authentication rather than identification. However, for the purpose of performance comparison, the identification performance is also evaluated. For identification, the feature vector is given as input to each of the model. The output of the model is compared with the input to compute the normalized squared error. The normalized squared error (E) for the feature vector y is given by, $E= \frac{\|y-o\|^2}{\|y\|^2}$, where o is the output vector given by the model. The error (E) is transformed into a confidence score (C) using the relation $C = \exp(-E)$. The average confidence score is calculated for each model. The identity of the subject is decided based on the highest confidence score. The identification performance is measured in terms of recognition rate. For authentication, the feature vector is given as input to the claimant model, and the confidence score is calculated. The claim is accepted if the confidence score is greater than a threshold, otherwise the claim is rejected.

In the database of 50 subjects, there will be 50 authentic claims and 49×50 impostor claims. The authentication performance is measured in terms of equal error rate (EER), where the false acceptance rate (FAR) and false rejection rate (FRR) are equal. The identification and authentication performance of the system is evaluated for the single and combined modalities. Performance of the system for single modality is given in Table 1. The EERs are calculated using the unnormalized confidence scores. Score normalization methods such as Z-norm, T-norm and ZT-norm are commonly used for estimating EER in speaker verification studies [nis03]. The EERs are obtained by employing person independent thresholds.

Task	Speech	Face	Visual speech
Person identification (Recognition rate)	90.0%	96.0%	88.0%
Person authentication (Equal error rate)	9.2%	2.5%	8.1%

Table 1.: Person identification and authentication results using individual modalities

Task	Speech + Face	Speech + Visual speech	Speech + Face +Visual speech
Person identification (Recognition rate)	100.0%	94.0%	100.0%
Person authentication (Equal error rate)	1.5%	5.6%	0.45%

Table 2.: Person identification and authentication results for different combinations of the modalities

The confidence scores from speech, face and static nature of the visual speech modalities are combined using (9) to obtain the multimodal confidence score (C^m) as follows:

$$C^m = \frac{1}{M}\sum_{i=1}^{M} w_f C_i^f + w_v(1 - w_f)C_i^v + (1 - w_f)(1 - w_v)C_i^a \qquad (9)$$

where M is the number of frames in the video, and C_i^a, C_i^f and C_i^v are the acoustic, facial and visual speech confidence scores for the ith video frame, respectively. The weight for each of the modality is decided by the parameters w_f and w_v. In our experiment the modalities are combined in three ways: 1) $w_f = 0.5$, $w_v = 0$ (speech and face), 2) $w_f = 0$, $w_v = 0.5$ (speech and visual speech) and 3) $w_f = 0.5$, $w_v = 0.5$ (speech, face and visual speech).

The performance of the system for different combinations of the modalities is given in Table 2. The proposed system achieves about 0.45% EER for 50 subjects using speech, face and visual speech modalities. The performance of the proposed text-independent person authentication system is comparable to or better than the existing text-dependent or text-independent person authentication methods. Most of the existing person authentication methods use models or scores of other subjects in the system, in order to accept or reject the identity claim of a subject (i.e., authentication in terms of identification). In our method, only the claimant model is used for authentication. The proposed method is not sensitive to the size of the face, its position in the image and its background, and orientation of the face. It is also not sensitive to pose of the face as long as the eye regions are visible. The method is less sensitive to variation in the image brightness, and it is sensitive to shadows and other lighting conditions. The face localization and feature extraction techniques are computationally efficient, and the system operates at about 6 frames per second on a personal computer with 2.3 GHZ CPU. As an application of the person authentication system, the task of automatic detection and indexing of anchorpersons in a broadcast news video is discussed in the next section.

3.   Anchorperson detection for news video indexing

With the never ending advances in digital technology, more and more video data is generated every day. As the accessible video collections grow, efficient schemes for navigating, browsing, and retrieving video data are required. A good survey of techniques for automatic indexing and retrieval of video data can be found in [BMM99], [WLH00]. Among the various video categories, news programs are important storing objects, due to the fact that they concisely cover a large number of topics related to society, politics, business, sports, weather, etc. In recent years, several news video indexing techniques have been proposed [BBP01], [GT02], [ATD03]. The news video indexing task has two main subtasks namely video structural analysis and abstraction. Structure analysis is the process of parsing the news video into story units, and video abstraction is the process of extracting representative frames from each story unit which can serve as entries in the table of contents.

3.1.   Video structure analysis

Video structure analysis involves detecting the story boundaries and parsing the complete video into story units. Each news story can be further segmented into an introduction by the anchorperson followed by a detailed report. In general, it can be observed that during the news story introduction by an anchorperson, the background around the anchorperson is almost constant, accompanied by a small motion of the anchorperson in the foreground. Whereas during detailed reporting, motion in the background as well as in the objects of interest is high most of the times. A binary pattern matching method is employed on the motion based binary feature vector derived for the complete video, to segment the complete video into low and high motion segments [SPY04]. Segments of low-motion correspond to the sequence pattern "00...0". These low motion segments are mainly anchorperson segments, and some non-anchor person segments like interviews and graphic objects. Each of these low motion segments is modeled using the visual features extracted after face localization as outlined in [PYV04, PY06]. The segments are categorized as anchorperson segments if more than two segments map onto a single person. The resultant locations of anchorperson segments are then used to construct the story units for video abstraction.

3.2.   Video abstraction

Video abstraction is the process of creating a presentation of visual information about the structure of a video, which should be much smaller than the original video. Key frames play an important role in the video abstraction process. Key frames are still images extracted from original video data, that best represent the content of a story in an abstract manner. Since motion is the major indicator for content change, dominant motion components resulting from camera operations and large moving objects are the most important source of information. So, in an effective approach to key frame extraction, the number of key frames needed to represent a segment of video should be based on temporal variations of video content in the segment.

3.3.   Experimental results

The performance of the anchorperson indexing task is evaluated on more than 6 hours of news video data recorded at 25 frames per second and frame size 320×240 from 4 news channels namely BBC World, CNN, NDTV 24×7 and ETV [SPY04]. The performance is measured in terms of the precision and recall defined as follows:

$$\text{precision} = \frac{\text{number of hits}}{\text{number of hits} + \text{number of false alarms}} \tag{10}$$

$$\text{recall} = \frac{\text{number of hits}}{\text{number of hits} + \text{number of misses}} \tag{11}$$

A precision of 99.35% and a recall of 98.7% for story segmentation is achieved. This method is superior to methods where audio-visual models of anchorpersons are trained offline, as the latter involve manual collection of training data and provide little flexibility. The proposed approach provides for online creation of the anchorperson models without any human supervision. These automatically created models can be used as offline models to detect the appearance of these anchorpersons in a different video.

4.   Pose problem in face verification

It is important for a face recognition system to be able to deal with faces of varying poses, since the test face image is not likely to have the same pose as that of the reference face image. The problem of pose variation has been addressed using two different approaches. In the first approach, a model for each person is developed using face images at different poses of that person. The resultant model is used to verify a given test face image. Such methods are discussed in [DCM03, KJK02]. But, the resultant models may average out some of the information of the face image which is unique to that person. In the second approach, the pose information of the given test face image is extracted, which is then used to synthesize a face image in a predefined orientation (pose) using a 3-D face model. The resultant synthesized face image is matched with a reference face image in the predefined pose. Such methods are discussed in [SBG06, VB98]. In these cases some artifacts may be introduced, or some unique information may be lost while synthesizing the face image, which in turn can degrade the performance of face recognition system.

In this section, a template matching based approach is proposed, which neither synthesizes the face image in a predefined pose, nor derives a model for a person's face. Separate templates of the face image are used for different poses. The template matching is performed

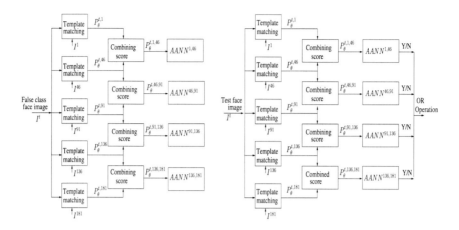

Figure 8.: Block diagram of the face verification system for (a) training phase, and (b) testing phase.

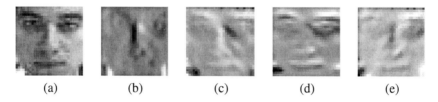

| (a) | (b) | (c) | (d) | (e) |

Figure 9.: (a) Gray level face image. Potential field (u_θ) representation of the face image in (a) for (b) $\theta = 0°$, (c) $\theta = 45°$, (d) $\theta = 90°$ and (e) $\theta = 135°$.

using the edginess-based [Ani03] representation of a face image. The scores obtained by matching a test face image with individual templates are combined in a selective manner. The combined scores are used with an autoassociative neural network (AANN) [YK02] model for classification.

4.1. Template matching approach for pose problem

The block diagram of the proposed approach to address the pose problem for face verification is shown in Fig. 8. This approach consists of training and testing phases shown in Figs. 8 (a) and (b) respectively. The training phase is explained using five reference face images I^1, I^{46}, I^{91}, I^{136}, and I^{181}. Here, I^k denotes the person's face image at pose angle $k°$. This process can be generalized for any number of reference face images. The reference face images are chosen in such a way that their poses are uniformly spaced over the span of $0° - 180°$. Several false class images are chosen and their potential field representations are computed using one-dimensional processing of image [Ani03]. Let u_θ be the potential field representation along θ direction with respect to horizontal scan line. The potential field representation for different values of θ are shown in Fig. 9. It shows that u_θ for different values of θ gives different information about the same face image. Hence, we have performed correlation between the partial evidence (u_θ) of test and reference face image. The partial evidences are computed for four values of θ, namely $0°$, $45°$, $90°$, and $135°$. These representations are correlated with the corresponding representation of each reference face image. The resultant correlation output is used to compute the similarity score Peak-to-Sidelobe Ratio (PSR) [Ani03]. Hence, five sets of four dimensional feature vectors (4 PSR values) are obtained for each false class image. The similarity scores obtained from the reference face images which have adjacent pose are combined, as shown in Fig. 8(a). Let $P_\theta^{t,l}$ be the similarity score (PSR) obtained when the potential field representation along θ direction of the test face image I^t is correlated with the corresponding representation of reference image I^l. The combined similarity score ($P_\theta^{t,l,m}$) for two reference images I^l and I^m is computed as explained in [AY06].

These combined scores are presented to an AANN model for training. The objective of AANN model is to capture the distribution of feature vectors of false class. Hence, if a test face image belonging to the true class is given to AANN model, the resulting score vector does not fall into the cluster of points belonging to the false class. Thus using suitable threshold for the output of the AANN model, a decision can be made whether to accept the claim of the test input or not. The distribution of points due to false class could be different for different reference face images. Hence, we have designed separate AANN models. Let $AANN^{1,46}$ denote the AANN model trained with the combined similarity scores ($P_\theta^{t,1,46}$) obtained using the reference face images I^1 and I^{46}. The structure of the AANN model is $4L$ $8N$ $2N$ $8N$ $4L$, where L denotes a linear unit, and N denotes a nonlinear unit. The AANN model is trained using backpropagation algorithm for 3000 epochs. Similarly we have designed $AANN^{46,91}$, $AANN^{91,136}$ and $AANN^{136,181}$ using the same false class face images. The block diagram of testing phase of face verification system is shown in Fig. 8(b). For a given test face image, the potential field representation u_θ is computed along four directions ($\theta=0°$, $45°$, $90°$, and $135°$). These representations are correlated with the corresponding representation of each reference face image of claimed identity. The resultant similarity scores are combined as in the training phase, and are presented to AANN models as shown in Fig. 8(b). The combined similarity score (4 dimensional feature vector) is used to compute the error in associating the vector with the AANN models corresponding to the reference face images. If the error is above a threshold in any one of the AANN models, the claim is accepted. Here, the threshold value for each AANN model could be different.

The performance of the proposed method is evaluated on the FacePix database [BGK+02, LKBP05]. The results are given in Table 3 for different sets of reference face images along with the performance obtained using existing approaches [LKBP05]. It is seen that the proposed method performs better than the existing approaches. The reason could be that proposed method preserves the unique information about a person's face image in a given pose.

Approaches	Set of reference face images		
	I^{91}	I^1, I^{91} and I^{181}	$I^1, I^{46}, I^{91}, I^{136}$ and I^{181}
PCA	20.74	50.53	71.6
LDA	20.70	56.92	78.63
HMM	31.68	41.27	63.50
BIC	18.42	45.19	69.47
Proposed approach	**49**	**65.45**	**85.83**

Table 3.: Recognition rate (in %) for diferent sets of reference face images by the proposed method, in comparison with the results for different methods given in [LKBP05].

5. Speaker verification using limited amount of speech data

The amount of speech data available for automatic recognition of speakers by a machine is an important issue that needs attention. Popular techniques giving the best possible results require minutes of data, and larger the amount of data, better is the performance [NS04]. But the speaker verification performance is seen to reduce drastically when the amount of data available is only a few seconds of speech [NS04]. This has to do with the features chosen and the modeling techniques employed. Mel-frequency cepstral coefficients (MFCCs), the widely used features, characterize the shape and size of the vocal tract of a speaker and hence are representatives of both the speaker as well as the sound under consideration. Considering the fact that the vocal tract shapes are significantly different for different sounds, the MFCCs vary considerably across sounds within a speaker. Apart from using vocal tract features, the popular techniques for speaker verification also employ statistical methods for modeling a speaker. The performance of these statistical techniques is good as long as there are enough examples for the statistics to be collected. In this direction, exploring the feasibility of using excitation source features for speaker verification gains significance. Apart from adding significant complementary evidence to the vocal tract features, the excitation features can act as a primary evidence when the amount of speech data available is limited. In this section, the problem of speaker verification from limited amount of speech data is treated as computing the similarity between two glottal flow derivative (GFD) signals.

5.1. Correlation-based similarity between two GFD signals

Let $x[n]$ and $y[n]$ be any two glottal flow derivative signals of lengths N_x and N_y, respectively, which need to be compared. Let $z[n] = x[n] + y[n - N_x]$ be the signal obtained by concatenating the signals $x[n]$ and $y[n]$. Let $\mathcal{T} = \{\tau_0, \tau_1, \ldots, \tau_{N-1}\}$ be the approximate locations of the instants of glottal closure (GC) in $z[n]$, chosen such that the first $N/2$ instants

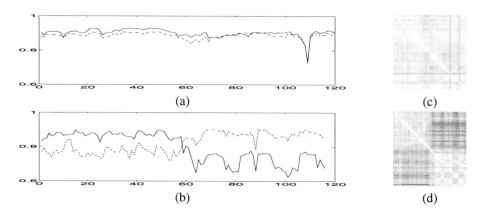

Figure 10.: Average similarity sequences $\bar{c}_x[n]$ (solid line) and $\bar{c}_y[n]$ (dashed line) for a typical (a) genuine and (b) impostor test. Intensity maps of the similarity matrices for a typical (c) genuine and (d) impostor test.

belong to $x[n]$ and the remaining belong to $y[n]$. Let $\mathcal{R} = \{r_0[n], r_1[n], \ldots, r_{N-1}[n]\}$ be the set of signal patterns of length N_r chosen symmetrically around the corresponding GC instants in $\mathcal{T}$. Now, for each signal pattern $r_i[n] \in \mathcal{R}$, the similarity values with all other patterns in $\mathcal{R}$ are computed, to give a set of similarity sequences as follows:

$$C = \{c_i[n]\} \quad i = 0, 1, \ldots, N-1 \tag{12}$$

$$c_i[j] = \max_{-M \le k \le +M} |\rho(r_i[n], z[n - \tau_j + k])| \quad j = 0, 1, \ldots, N-1 \tag{13}$$

where M denotes the search space around the approximate locations specified in $\mathcal{T}$. $\rho(r_1[n], r_2[n])$ is the correlation coefficient value between any two signal patterns $r_1[n]$ and $r_2[n]$ computed as

$$\rho(r_1[n], r_2[n]) = \frac{\displaystyle\sum_{n=0}^{N_r-1} (r_1[n] - \mu_1)(r_2[n] - \mu_2)}{(\displaystyle\sum_{n=0}^{N_r-1} (r_1[n] - \mu_1)^2)^{1/2} (\displaystyle\sum_{n=0}^{N_r-1} (r_2[n] - \mu_2)^2)^{1/2}} \tag{14}$$

where μ_1 and μ_2 are the mean values of $r_1[n]$ and $r_2[n]$, respectively.

The first $N/2$ similarity sequences (or rows) in C belong to patterns from $x[n]$, and hence are expected to have a similar trend (relative similarities). They are combined to obtain an average similarity sequence $\bar{c}_x[n]$. Similarly, the next $N/2$ similarity sequences which belong to patterns from $y[n]$ are combined to obtain $\bar{c}_y[n]$. Figs. 10(a) and 10(b) show typical plots of $\bar{c}_x[n]$ and $\bar{c}_y[n]$ for a genuine (same speaker) and an impostor test (different speakers), respectively. It can be seen that $\bar{c}_x[n]$ and $\bar{c}_y[n]$ have a similar trend when the two utterances are from the same speaker, and have an opposite trend when the speakers are different. The similarity matrix C may also be visualized as a 2-D intensity map. Typical similarity maps for a genuine test and an impostor test are shown in Figs. 10(c) and 10(d),

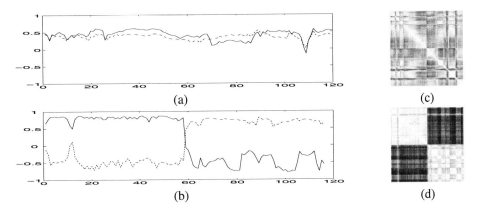

Figure 11.: Second-level average similarity sequences $\bar{s}_x[n]$ (solid line) and $\bar{s}_y[n]$ (dashed line) plots for a typical (a) genuine and (b) impostor test. Intensity maps of the second-level similarity matrices for a typical (c) genuine and (d) impostor test.

respectively. The 2-D similarity matrix can be divided into four smaller blocks as

$$
C = \begin{bmatrix} C_{xx} & C_{xy} \\ C_{yx} & C_{yy} \end{bmatrix}
\tag{15}
$$

where C_{xx} and C_{yy} are the similarity values among patterns within the train and test utterances, respectively, and C_{xy} and C_{yx} are the similarity values between patterns of the train and test utterances. The similarity values in C_{xx} and C_{yy} are expected to be large (more white), as they belong to patterns from the same utterance. The values in C_{xy} and C_{yx}, as compared to C_{xx} and C_{yy} are expected to be relatively low (less white) for an impostor, and of similar range for a genuine speaker. As can be seen from Fig. 10, the similarity values lie within a small range (around 0.7 to 0.9), and hence the visual evidence available from the intensity map is weak. Better discriminability can be achieved by computing a second-level of similarity values $S = \{s_i[n]\}$, $i = 0, 1, \ldots, N - 1$, where $s_i[j] = \rho(c_i[n], c_j[n])$, $j = 0, 1, \ldots, N - 1$. The second-level average similarity sequences $\bar{s}_x[n]$ and $\bar{s}_y[n]$ and the second-level similarity maps are shown in Fig. 11. A final similarity measure between the two signals $x[n]$ and $y[n]$ is obtained as

$$
s_f = \rho(\bar{s}_x[n], \bar{s}_y[n])
\tag{16}
$$

Now, if both the signals $x[n]$ and $y[n]$ have originated from the same source (or speaker), then $\bar{s}_x[n]$ and $\bar{s}_y[n]$ have similar trend, and s_f tends to $+1$. In ideal cases, $s_f = +1$, when $\bar{s}_x[n] = \bar{s}_y[n]$, for all n. On the other hand, if $x[n]$ and $y[n]$ have originated from two different sources, then $\bar{s}_x[n]$ and $\bar{s}_y[n]$ have opposite trends and s_f tends to -1. In ideal cases, $s_f = -1$, when $\bar{s}_x[n] = -\bar{s}_y[n]$, for all n.

5.2.   Experimental results

The performance of the speaker verification task is evaluated on clean microphone speech (TIMIT data), as well as noisy telephone speech (NTIMIT data) [DY06]. The datasets in both cases consisted of twenty speakers with ten utterances (around 2 to 3 secs) for each, giving rise to a total of 900 genuine tests and 18000 impostor tests. Equal error rates (EERs) of 19% and 38% are obtained for the TIMIT and NTIMIT datasets, respectively. The performance is also evaluated when more number of utterances (three train and three test utterances) are used per claim. The nine different similarity scores available for each verification are averaged to obtain a consolidated score. The EERs improve to 5% for TIMIT and 27% for NTIMIT datasets, respectively. The results are illustrative and the performance needs to be evaluated on a large dataset like NIST which has significant channel and noise variations.

6.   Summary and conclusions

The studies presented in this chapter addressed some issues related to the development of an automatic multimodal person authentication system using speech, face and visual speech modalities. The acoustic features were represented by WLPCC and the facial and visual speech features were extracted using the multiscale morphological operations. The distribution capturing ability of the autoassociative neural network models was exploited to capture the distribution of feature vectors describing each of the biometric modalities such as speech, face and visual speech. The method is invariant to size of the face, its position in the image and its background. The face localization and feature extraction techniques are computationally efficient, and the system test the identity claim of a subject within a reasonable time. While the performance of the person authentication system is good in the laboratory conditions, the same need to be evaluated in outdoor conditions, where the environmental noise and the fluctuations in the lighting conditions is high. The robustness of the system can be further enhanced by introducing more modalities into the system like finger print, iris, retina, signature, etc. Also, not all the person specific information in speech, face and visual speech modalities is utilized in the current person authentication system. It is necessary to explore other complementary features which can be extracted from these modalities and combine them with the existing features.

Some issues in automatic detection of anchorpersons in broadcast news video for indexing application were addressed. The facial features extracted from the localized face, as proposed by the person authentication system, were used for the detection of anchorperson segments in the news video. The proposed approach provided for online creation of the anchorperson models without any human supervision. As of now, only the visual information is used for segmenting the news clip into possible story units. The analysis of audio in conjunction with either a reasonable speech recognizer or a simple keyword recognizer, can help in the generation of a better video table-of-contents.

Some specific issues like the pose problem in a face verification system and speaker verification from a limited amount of speech data were also addressed. A solution to the pose problem was proposed by using separate templates for different poses of a person. The edginess-based representation of a face image was used for template matching. An AANN model was further used to characterize an impostor or false class based on the combined evidence obtained by matching a test face with different templates. The excitation source features, which have less variations within a speaker as compared to the commonly used vocal tract features, were used for verifying the claim of a speaker when the amount of speech data available is limited. The correlations in the glottal flow derivative signal were exploited to compare any two short segments of speech for speaker verification. The incorporation of the these modules into the person authentication system can make it more flexible and robust.

The results of this work were presented at various meetings and workshops in connection with the CultureTech project of the European Union.

7.   Acknowledgements

This publication has been produced partly with the assistance of the European Union (project CultureTech, see [EUI]). The content of this publication is the sole responsibility of the authors and can in no way be taken to reflect the views of the European Union.

Bibliography

[Ani03]   Anil Kumar Sao. Significance of image representation for face recognition. Master's thesis, Department of Computer Science and Engineering, Indian Institute of Technology, Madras, Sep. 2003.

[ATD03]   Alberto Albiol, Luis Torres, and Edward J. Delp. The indexing of persons in news sequences using audio-visual data. In *Proceedings of the International Conference on Acoustics, Speech and Signal Processing*, Hong Kong, Apr. 6-10, 2003.

[AY06]   Anil Kumar Sao and B. Yegnanarayana. Template matching approach for pose problem in face verification. In *Int. Workshop on Multimedia Content Representation Classification and Security (MRCS-06)*, Istanbul, Turkey, September 2006.

[BBP01]   M. Bertini, A. Del Bimbo, and P. Pala. Content-based indexing and retrieval of TV news. *Pattern Recognition Letters*, 22(5):503–516, Apr. 2001.

[BGK+02] J Black, M Gargesha, K Kahol, P Kuchi, and S Panchanathan. A framework for performance evaluation of face recogniton algorithm. In *Internet Multimedia System*, Boston, July 2002.

[BMM99] R. Brunelli, O. Mich, and C.M. Modena. A survey on the automatic indexing of video data. *Journal of Visual Communication and Image Representation*, 10(2):78–112, 1999.

[Che01]   T. Chen. Audiovisual speech processing. *IEEE Signal Processing Magazine*, pages 9–21, January 2001.

[DCM03]   O. Deniz, M. Castrilon, and Hernandwez M. Face recognition using independent component analysis and support vector machine. *Pattern Recognition Letters*, 22:2153–2157, 2003.

[DY06]   N. Dhananjaya and B. Yegnanarayana. Correlation-based similarity between signals for speaker verification using limited amount of speech data. In *Int. Workshop on Multimedia Content Representation, Classification and Security (MRCS-06)*, Istanbul, Turkey, Sept. 2006.

[EUI]   Cultural dimensions in digital multimedia security technology. In *EU-India Economic Cross Cultural Programme*, http://amsl-smb.cs.unimagdeburg.de/culturetech/.

[FPF99]   A. Fitzgibbon, M. Pilu, and R.B. Fisher. Direct least square fitting of ellipses. *IEEE Trans. Pattern Anal. Machine Intell.*, 21(5):476–480, May 1999.

[GT02]   Xinbo Gao and Xiaoou Tang. Unsupervised video-shot segmentation and model-free anchorperson detection for news video story parsing. *IEEE Trans. Circuits, Systems, Video Technology*, 12(9):765–776, Sep. 2002.

[HAMJ02]   R. Hsu, M. Abdel-Mottaleb, and A.K. Jain. Face detection in color images. *IEEE Trans. Pattern Anal. Machine Intell.*, 24(5):696–706, May 2002.

[JD96]   P.T. Jackway and M. Deriche. Scale-space properties of the multiscale morphological dilation-erosion. *IEEE Trans. Pattern Anal. Machine Intell.*, 18(1):38–51, January 1996.

[KJK02]   K. I. Kim, K. Jung, and K. Kim. Face recognition using support vector machine and with local correlation kernels. *Int'l Journal Pattern Recognition and Artifical Intelligence*, 16(1):97–111, 2002.

[LKBP05]   G Little, S Krishna, J Black, and S Panchanathan. A methodology for evaluating robustness of face recognition algoritms with respect to change in pose and illumination angle. In *ICASSP*, Philadelhia, March 2005.

[nis03]   *National Institute of Standards and Technology (NIST)- Speaker Recognition Workshop Report*. University of Maryland, Baltimore, 2003.

[NS04]   NIST-SRE-2004. One-speaker detection. In *Proc. NIST Speaker Recognition Evaluation Workshop*, Toledo, Spain, June 2004.

[PY06]   S. Palanivel and B. Yegnanarayana. Multimodal person authentication using speech, face and visual speech. *to appear in Computer Vision and Image Understanding*, June 2006.

[PYV04]   S. Palanivel, B. Yegnanarayana, and B. V. K. Vijaya Kumar. Person authentication using acoustic and visual features. In *Proc. Workshop on Biometric Challenges arising from Theory to Practice (BCTP)*, pages 63–66, Cambridge, UK, August 2004.

[SBG06]   Conrad Sanderson, Samy Bengio, and Yongsheng Gao. On transforming statistical models for non-frontal face verification. *Pattern Recognition*, 39:288–302, 2006.

[SPY04]   V. Suresh, S. Palanivel, and B. Yegnanarayana. Anchor person indexing and visual table of contents generation for tv news. In *Proc. Workshop on Biometric Challenges arising from Theory to Practice (BCTP)*, pages 59–62, Cambridge, UK, August 2004.

[VB98]   T. Vetter and V. Blanz. Estimating coloured 3D face models from single images: An example based approach. In *Proceedings of Conf. Computer Vision ECCV'98*, 1998.

[WLH00]   Yao Wang, Zhu Liu, and Jin-Cheng Huang. Multimedia content analysis using both audio and visual clues. *IEEE Signal Processing Magazine*, 17(6):12–36, Nov. 2000.

[YK02]   B. Yegnanarayana and S.P. Kishore. AANN: an alternative to GMM for pattern recognition. *Neural Networks*, 15:459–469, January 2002.

[ZCRP00]   W. Zhao, R. Chellappa, A. Rosenfeld, and P.J. Phillips. *Face recognition: A literature survey*. UMD CAFR, Technical Report, CAR-TR-948, October 2000.

Verification and Watermarking Schemes of Biometric Signatures

KAR BISWAJIT, KATIYAR DEVESH , DUTTA P. K. , BASU T. K.

Contents

Abstract

Each person's signature is unique as evidenced by the long history of its usage for authentication. Signature verification can be classified in two categories according to the available data in the input. Offline (static) signature verification takes the image of a signature as input. The major advantage of static signature verification is that the signature owner need not be present for the verification to take place. The major drawback of this type of signature verification is that the signature image alone constitutes a limited database for analysis, making it difficult to effectively determine the validity of the signature. This study was taken keeping in mind the wide acceptance of signature as a method for person authentication and that in case of dynamic signature verification scenario it can easily be put as active biometric. Because of increase in biometric authentication, it is important to maintain the security of the biometric samples. It is here where watermarking comes into play, empowering the biometric authentication system and securing biometric data stored in the databases. A new application of watermarking is presented here to secure electronic biometric signatures using digital watermarking techniques. Section one presents an implementation of a novel signature verification algorithm and section two presents a watermarking scheme to protect the biometric signature.

1.   Signature Verification

Here a new verification methodology is proposed where stoke point matching by DTW and strokes wise segment alignment by using spline interpolation for time and coordinate signals. In this system both the features and signal based verification methodologies applied. The first stage of the verification System will eliminate random, simple and certain level of expert forgeries rapidly and accepted the certain level of consistence signer by statistical feature based verification method. In this stage we normalize the feature by setting mean zero and standard deviation one. And in the enrollment stage we evaluate the weight age of the individual feature for individual person by calculating the inverse of the Euclidean distance. And in verification stage we measure the weighted Euclidean distance. The top-level in signature representation deals with the global geometric shape. This method will verify not only the signature shape but also some other property like sequence of writing segments, start to end writing direction of every segment. Signature shape verification is given top priority in a signature verification system. Simultaneously, for improving robustness against forgery signer, online property of a signature needs to be considered. Therefore in the second stage, we will verify time profile and coordinate signals of the signature by segment wise warping functional approach. The decision about the authenticity of the specimen is influenced by correlation measurements and statistical distance measurements. The on-line data has been acquired with the help of a tablet PC. Also we verify our algorithm using SVC 2004 database. The commonly used warping technique is dynamic time warping (DTW). It was originally used in speech recognition and has been applied in the field of signature verification with some success in the last two decades. Extreme points warping (EPW) technique have been introduced by Hao Feng [HC03]. For a signal function (e.g. x(i), y(i), p(i), t(i)etc. i is index), it has been generally observed that the signal duration changes for different samples even from the same signer. In addition, for different signings, local shifts occur in a non-linear fashion within the signals. An established warping technique used in speech recognition is dynamic time warping, or DTW. For the past two decades, the use of DTW has also become a major technique in signature verification [V.S97]. Though DTW has been applied to the field with some success, it has some drawbacks. The DTW technique is based on the dynamic programming (DP) matching algorithm to find the best matching path, in terms of the least global cost, between an input signal and a template. The DTW takes a signature sample as the input and aligns it nonlinearly with respect to the stored reference signature. DTW match the signal duration but the local shift remains. The process changes the input signal waveform in two aspects:

1. The end of the input waveform will be aligned with that of the reference

2. Peaks and valleys will be shifted to align with those of the reference.

Most of the local shifts occur at the time of stroke point. The new starting point after the stroke, create the local shift in the signal function. To minimize the local shift in the signal function we propose a new stroke based warping technique before comparing the two signatures. The distortion, during pen down is treated as fault. The EPW technique aligns the input signal with the reference by peak and valley matching. This technique has some drawbacks. A small peak and valley may become a ripple which is less that the predefined threshold height in one signature signal or a valid peak and valley in another signature signal for a same signer. Threshold selection is difficult.

1.1.   Proposed model for Signature verification

The model of signature verification system has shown in Fig. 1. The whole system is divided into two sections, enrollment section and verification section.

1.2.   Enrollment Procedures

The enrollment procedure is part of a biometric system during which a set of biometric samples are taken from the user and a biometric template is chosen from the given set of biometric samples. First stage of enrollment procedure is data acquisition. We have taken 10 signatures from each user during enrollment. All the signature samples were taken using PLATASIGN software in a tablet PC. After the data acquisition, the input signature signal undergoes preprocessing procedures including smoothing, rotation, shifting and size normalization. At the time of enrollment the system will take ten signatures from the enroller. From the ten signatures two signatures having lower correlation among the ten will be rejected by the system. Also at the time of enrollment, the user is permitted to delete two

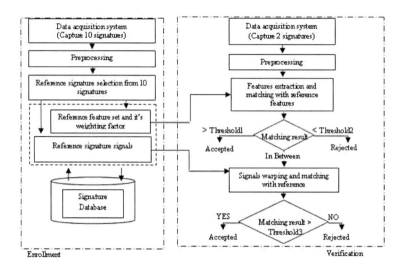

Figure 1

of his signatures from the ten and resign again. This is done for clarity purpose. The system will calculate correlation value of one signature with respect to each of the other nine signatures. Here we need to calculate 45 correlation values out of 100. Before correlation calculation, system will normalize the vector length of the signature signals based on our stroke based warping method. Ten correlation values will be having value 1(i.e. correlation between signature serial number n with signature serial number n). After the 45 correlation calculation, we will take the average correlation values for every corresponding signature. For ten signatures there will be ten resulting average values. The signature corresponding to the highest value will be considered as reference signature. The signatures corresponding to the lowest and the second lowest average value will be deleted from the list. Remaining eight signatures (including reference) will pass on to the next stage where the reference feature will be extracted.

A feature vector is extracted for each signature. Out of the 8 signatures the one which is at a minimum distance is used as the template feature vector.

1.3.   Preprocessing

After data acquisition, preprocessing is necessary to enhance the input data. The preprocessing of an on-line signature generally consists of filtering, in order to remove spurious signals from the signature. Subsequently, a normalization procedure is used to standardize the signatures in time-duration and size domain. We observed noise in the data, due to quantification, and also because of the high sampling rate of the digitizer. Different filtering strategies were thus chosen according to each parameter. For each coordinate, an analysis

	1	2	3	4	5	6	7	8	9	10
1	100	97	98	97	97	96	96	91	94	92
2	97	100	97	97	96	94	95	93	93	92
3	98	97	100	96	97	95	96	91	94	94
4	97	97	96	100	97	95	97	91	95	94
5	97	96	97	97	100	94	96	90	95	95
6	96	94	95	95	94	100	98	86	97	95
7	96	95	96	97	96	98	100	88	98	96
8	91	93	91	91	90	86	88	100	85	83
9	94	93	94	95	95	97	98	85	100	96
10	92	92	94	94	95	95	96	83	96	100

Table 1.: Correlation measure between ten enrolled signatures (each other)

Sinatures No.	Average correlations	Status
4	96.0	Reference
7	95.9	Pass
3	95.9	Pass
5	95.9	Pass
1	95.8	Pass
2	95.5	Pass
6	94.9	Pass
9	94.7	Pass
10	93.6	Delete
8	90.1	Delete

Table 2.: Reference Signature Selection Based on Correlation Measurements

of its spectrum on several signatures of the database showed that more than 95 of the signal's power is represented by frequencies below 10 Hz. This confirms that low frequencies are the most informing ones in signatures, high frequencies indicate involuntary oscillations of the pen during the signing process. We therefore used a low-pass filter of order 3 with cut off frequency 10 Hz. As for pressure, we deemed it essential to keep pen-lifts (when pressure is zero), since it is a very signer-dependent information. Therefore, a binary signal was chosen to describe pressure, in order to oppose pen-lifts to pen-downs. Before pre-processing, signatures have in average 300 points. One point out of two was kept in the following. Finally, pen-tilt has few sharp variations during the signing process. Our goal was to keep this information while removing oscillations. A median filter of window size 5 was judged as the best compromise. A very difficult preprocessing task concerns signature segmentation, since different signatures of one writer can differ from each other by local stretching, compression, omission or additional parts. The simplest on-line signature segmentation determines the components of the signature. [GSG92], [JEJ98] defines a component as a piece of the written trace between a pen down and a pen up movement.

This approach is based on the consideration that the signature can be regarded as a sequence of writing units delimited by abrupt interruptions. Writing units are the regular parts of the signature, while interruptions are the singularities of the signature.

1.4.   Feature vectors

Following are the dynamic features which have been extracted from the signature.

1. Number of continuous pen-down sequences (strokes).

2. Duration of the complete writing process in ms.

3. Number of samples for the complete writing process.

4. Sum of all local minima and maxima in writing signals x (t) and y (t).

5. Sum of all local minima and maxima in writing signals x (t) and y (t).

6. Aspect ratio of x/y bitmap.

7. The ratio of pen down time and total time duration in the signature.

8. Ratio of pen-down and pen-up duration for the complete writing process.

9. Integrated distance covered by the x-writing signal for the complete writing process.

10. Integrated distance covered by the y-writing signal for the complete writing process.

11. Average of the absolute writing velocity in x-direction.

12. Average of the absolute writing velocity in y-direction.

13. Average writing velocity.

14. Average of the absolute writing acceleration in x-direction.

15. Average of the absolute writing acceleration in y-direction.

16. Effective average writing velocity in x-direction.

17. Effective average writing velocity in y-direction.

18. Average pen pressure for the entire signature.

19. Maximum pen pressure through out the signature.

20. Minimum pen pressure through out the signature.

21. Standard deviation of the pen pressure through out the signature.

22. Average of absolute turn angle.

23. Standard deviation of the absolute turn angle.

24. Standard deviation of the turn angle.

25. Maximum velocity in positive x direction.

26. Maximum velocity in positive y direction.

27. Maximum velocity in negative x direction.

28. Maximum velocity in negative y direction.

29. The ratio of horizontal distance traveled to total distance covered by the signature.

30. The ratio of vertical distance traveled to total distance covered by the signature.

1.4.1.   Results and Discussion on Signature Verification

Sl No.	Feature no.	Mean	Standard deviation	Wt. Factor		Sl No.	Feature no.	Mean	Standard deviation	Wt. Factor
1	19	822.2	1.5	9.68		17	10	11.0	5.7	2.47
2	20	1012.3	1.5	9.47		18	2	6231.0	6.0	2.36
3	21	911.5	1.7	8.41		19	17	806.4	6.1	2.31
4	24	65.9	1.7	8.16		20	13	3.2	6.7	2.09
5	25	102.3	2.1	6.82		21	6	0.3	7.6	1.85
6	22	223.3	2.2	6.30		22	11	1338.3	7.9	1.78
7	23	78.2	3.0	4.69		23	15	0.0	9.2	1.54
8	23	78.2	3.0	4.69		24	18	209.9	9.5	1.48
9	9	1.8	3.6	3.97		25	29	18.1	9.6	1.478
10	7	0.7	3.7	3.87		26	8	2.5	11.1	0.00
11	31	0.9	4.3	3.31		27	4	48.2	11.3	0.00
12	5	54.3	4.4	3.18		28	16	0.0	14.4	0.00
13	1	10.7	5.0	2.80		29	26	10.5	18.4	0.00
14	30	2.3	5.1	2.79		30	28	10.5	23.5	0.00
15	12	2.0	5.5	2.56		31	27	24.9	49.5	0.00
16	14	1894.2	5.7	2.49						

Table 3.: Feature and its weighting factor selection based on consistency

In the first stage of our verification system we successfully managed to verify 90% of the signatures, based on feature based verification methodologies. The ambiguous signatures were transferred to the second stage of verification. In this stage we had applied a new stroke wise warping method and after the test signature was warped with the reference signal we measured the correlation between the two. We tested the algorithm on our collected original

	1	2	3	4	5	6	7	8
1	97	96	97	96	95	98	94	96
2	95	96	96	95	96	97	92	96
3	95	94	96	94	96	98	93	96
4	96	96	97	97	95	98	95	97
5	94	94	97	95	95	98	96	98
6	95	92	94	97	91	95	95	95
7	94	92	95	97	92	96	95	96
8	93	90	93	97	90	95	95	96

Table 4.: Correlation between genuine signatures' horizontal coordinate

	1	2	3	4	5	6	7	8
1	54	38	41	31	46	49	38	45
2	56	40	44	36	49	52	43	47
3	59	45	44	35	49	51	41	47
4	55	38	41	34	46	50	40	45
5	58	46	44	31	48	49	40	44
6	53	36	45	34	50	55	45	48
7	56	39	44	32	50	54	47	47
8	55	36	35	28	41	45	35	40

Table 5.: Correlation between genuine and forge signatures' horizontal coordinate

and forge signatures. The success rate was 97%. The test data base, however, need to be much larger for better inference.

2.   Watermarking of Biometric Signature

Biometric identification system has inherent advantages, but ensuring the security and authenticity of biometric samples is very important and critical. Our work is a step in the direction to nullify the attacks, such as tampering, on the biometric template stored in the database, attack on which can compromise the whole credibility of the biometric system [NJR01] and Martens and [RL96] identify eight basic sources of attacks that are possible in a generic biometric system. We try to nullify these attacks especially the sixth type of attack (the attack on the templates stored in databases) and the seventh type of attack (where the channel between the database and matcher could be compromised to alter transferred template information) as shown in fig. 2, by empowering the matcher with watermarking technique to identify such attacks. This section is divided into 6 subsections. In the subsection 2, the common Online Signature Verification algorithm is discussed. The third subsection presents the algorithm and the performance of the watermarking algorithms. The first is the basic LSB watermarking technique [http://www.cs.ust.hk/svc2004/download.html].

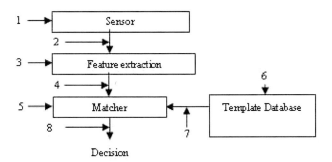

Figure 2

The second is a modified version of the first technique named SD_LSB F. [FM99]. The third technique is a more robust technique using the idea of Fourier descriptor watermarking [AU03]. Here we also compare these watermarking techniques using the signature verification algorithm.

2.1. Online Signature Verification Algorithm

The algorithm used here is proposed in [Kra05]. The algorithm is based on the features Δx and Δy of the dynamic signature. The major aspects are the user dependent normalization and the training algorithm based on Principal Component Analysis (PCA). The performance evaluation is done in terms of False Acceptance Rate (FAR) v/s False Rejection Ratio (FRR) curve or simply ROC curve (see section 3.5.3 for results)

2.1.1. Digital Watermarking of Electronic Signatures

This section presents three watermarking schemes. The first two watermarking schemes watermark the $\{\Delta x, \Delta y, \Delta t\}$ vectors and the third one watermark only $\{\Delta x, \Delta y\}$. The reason for our choice is three fold. Firstly, according to a study done on the consistency of features of the online signature samples Lei [LG05], features like velocity $\{V_x, V_y\}$ which can be considered same as $\{\Delta x, \Delta y\}$ because of the equal spaced time stamps 't', scored the highest. Secondly, we found out that watermarking of these vectors gave better result than normal watermarking $X, Y or T$ vectors. Thirdly, our online signature verification algorithm as discussed in chapter 2 is based on $\{\Delta x, \Delta y\}$ feature vectors only. Hence, the effect of watermarking on the performance of verification algorithm is direct. Also, all the watermarking schemes have an inherent round off attack at the end of the embedding procedure due to rounding of floating point value to integer values. This has to be done since our signature database is originally stored in the integer domain.

2.1.2.   Motivation

The motivation behind watermarking biometric samples or data is just to provide another level of security to the biometric authentication systems which are widely used due to convenience and accuracy. Some security aspects regarding biometric data have been discussed in [SSCT05]. They have pointed out that error in judging the genuine signature (EER) significantly increases (by the order of one magnitude), if signature verification systems are exposed to skilled forgeries. In [AU03], they have suggested that watermarking, steganography, encryption or a combination can be used to protect the biometric authentication system against possible attacks at various stages N.K. [NJR01]. They have used steganography or hiding of biometric data inside another data having a large data payload capacity. Although steganography and encryption have been tried before, no past work has been done in regard to the watermarking of the biometric data (such as electronic biometric signature) itself. But watermarking of images and audio signals has been researched heavily in the past decade or so. Different watermarking schemes are available on the basis of

1. robust/ fragile

2. spatial / DCT / DFT / DTW

3. reversible / irreversible

The basic overview of the watermarking technique is shown in fig. 3. Let there be N sample points in the signature,

$$S_k = \{x_k, y_k, t_k\} for k = 1 to N \tag{1}$$

Where set S is the set of all the sample points, We also define

$$\Delta x_k = x_k - x_{k-1} \tag{2}$$

The equation (3.2) also holds well for Δy. The watermark embedding algorithm is broadly divided into four steps A, B, C and D as shown in the fig. 3. These steps are further discussed in the following sections.

2.1.3.   Step A (Pre-processing)

We first calculate the first differences (as given in equation 3.2) for each vector X, Y and T and get vectors $\{\Delta x, \Delta y, \Delta t\}$ respectively. These vectors are then normalized between values [0 1] using the transformation.

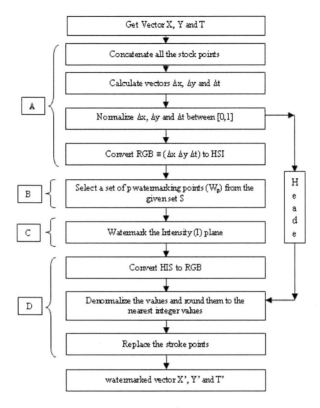

Figure 3

$$\Delta x_{normalized} = \frac{\Delta x - min(\Delta x)}{max(\Delta x) - min(\Delta x)} \qquad (3)$$

In the same manner Δy and Δt can also be normalized. The information to de-normalize the difference vectors as well as to convert the difference vector to the original vector form is stored in the header. After normalization, we consider the normalized $\Delta x, \Delta y$ and Δt vectors as R, G and B vectors respectively as shown in fig. 4. We then apply a RGB to HSI transformation on the vectors. As in image watermarking we then choose I^{th} vector for watermarking.

2.1.4.   Step B (Selection of watermarking points)

Selection of the watermarking points W_p from the set S is very critical in a sense that not all the points in set S can be watermarked. The reason for above is two folds. Firstly, it can be seen that while watermarking all the points will result in change of max, min and start-

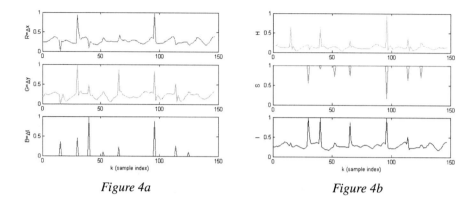

Figure 4a   *Figure 4b*

ing values stored in the header during detection and henceforth change in all the Intensity values resulting in the loss of the watermark e.g. suppose intensity value during embedding after normalization is 0.999, then if a bit '1' is embedded to this value it will become greater than 1, so during de-normalization the maximum values of each vector Δx, Δy and Δt will change. In this case, during detection the values of vectors R, G and B after normalization will be absolutely different and our watermarking will be lost. Secondly, the recovery of the watermark during decoding process is not complete at higher payload, since a rounding off attack inherently exists in the watermark embedding algorithm.

We propose two ways of selecting of watermarking points:

1. We can choose the points randomly i.e. we can generate 'n' random integer values between 1 to N using a key and use these n samples points as the watermarking point set W_p.

2. We can also use the parameter p (pressure) to help us choose the watermarking points e.g. n points can be chosen from the sample points where the vector $(\Delta p/\Delta t)$ is maximum or minimum.

The second scheme proposed above also incorporates the dynamic parameter 'p' into the watermarking scheme. Any tampering with 'p' will result in the selection of different sample point during detection and hence the bits will be extracted incorrectly. Although this scheme has an inherent advantage over the first scheme, we decided to use the first scheme because it helps in better study of the effect of choosing different sample points on the watermarking scheme as a whole. Also the sample points chosen in the second case can be invariably said as one of the cases of the first scheme.

Finally, in our case, we watermarked all the intensity values except those whose values were greater than 0.998.

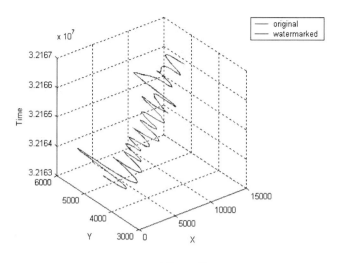

Figure 5

2.1.5.   Step C (Fragile Watermarking scheme)

We have used two types of fragile watermarking schemes to watermark the Ith vector. The scheme is the basic LSB [FM99] watermarking scheme where we generate a random binary watermark 'w' of length n using a key and replace the LSB of I_k, where $k \in W_p$ with the watermark bit 'w'. During the detection, we generate a random binary watermark using the same key and extract the LSB's of the watermarked points and check whether extracted LSB vector and watermark are same or not.

2.1.6.   Step D (reverse of step A)

The step is just the reverse of step to convert the watermarked I vector to the original signature form. The watermarked I', original H and S are first converted to R', G' and B' using HSI to RGB transformation. Then the values are de-normalized to get $\Delta x'$, $\Delta y'$ and $\Delta t'$. Then the watermarked difference vectors are converted to X', Y' and T' and then these vectors are rounded off to closest integer values since the signature values originally were in integer domain. In the final step, the removed stroke points are inserted back. Now we get our watermarked signature.

During detection only step A, B and C are performed. The step D is not required during detection of the watermark. An example of the watermarking scheme is shown in fig 5.

This is the second watermarking scheme that we used. In this scheme, apart from part C, the entire steps are same as LSB algorithm as explained in section 3.2. In step C, we have used the fragile watermarking scheme proposed in [YC04]. In this scheme, embedding of bit at sample point belonging to set W_p is dependent on the 'm' neighboring points. We generate two random binary watermark 'w1'of length n and 'w2' of length n x (2m). The random binary bit for each sample point in the set W_p comes from 'w1' and the random bit for the neighboring points comes from 'w2'. Then we find the secret deterministic factor Sdi for the ith sample point in set Wp , as follows

$$q = W p_i \quad for i = 1 ton \tag{4}$$

$$Sd_i = | \sum_{j=-m}^{m} (w1_i \times w2_{2mi-2j+1} \times I_{q+j}^{M})| \tag{5}$$

Here I_{q+j}^{M} is the value of the first 7 MSB's of I_{q+j}. Then we change the LSB of the I_q such that

$$parity(sd_i \bigoplus I_q) = w1_i \quad \forall i = 1 ton \tag{6}$$

During the detection part we generate w1 and w2 using the same key, then calculate Sd and find out the parity using equation 3.5. If the parity bit vector is not same as the watermark w1, we conclude that signature has been tampered with.

2.2.   Fourier Descriptor Watermarking scheme (FDWM)

This scheme is based on the Fourier descriptor watermarking scheme for polygons proposed in [SP04]. Our scheme is entirely same as this scheme except for the fact that we do not watermark the exact X and Y coordinates but the $(\Delta x, \Delta y)$ coordinates. The signatures cannot be regarded as polygons but we have just tried making a step forward in using this scheme to watermark the biometric signature samples.

2.2.1.   Fourier Descriptor Watermarking algorithm (FDWM)

In this scheme, we watermark only Δx and Δy.

Let define $\Delta z = \Delta x + i\Delta y$; A complex DFT is performed on this signal, producing the Fourier Descriptors $X : \Delta X[k] = \Delta X_R[k] + i\Delta X_I[k]$ for $k = 0, 1, N - 1$. The representation of a polygonal line in terms of its Fourier Descriptors has some interesting geometric invariance properties [AU03] that can be exploited to devise a robust watermarking method. More specifically, the Fourier Descriptors magnitude remains the same after several geometrical transformations of the polygonal line, so it has been chosen to host the watermark. The Watermark is embedded by modifying the magnitude of the Fourier Descriptor in the following way

$$|\Delta X_k| = |\Delta X_k|(1 + sW(k)) \qquad for \quad k = 0, 1, ..., N-1 \tag{7}$$

Where the scalar s controls the watermark power (0<s<1), and W[k] is a sample of the watermark. The phase of the Fourier Descriptors is not affected by the watermark W. The watermark is a pseudorandom signal generated from a seed integer K, which is the watermark secret key. More specifically, samples W[k]; k=0,1Ě., N-1 take randomly the values +1 and -1 with equal probability, whereas the samples with W[k]=0 are used for low and high frequency Fourier descriptors. In other words, the watermark is not embedded in the low frequencies to avoid severe contour distortions. And it is not embedded in the high frequencies either, so that it is robust to low-pass attacks. Thus, the watermark has the form:

$$W[k] = \begin{cases} 0 & \text{if } k < aN \text{ OR } k > (1-a)N \text{ OR bN<k<(1-b)N;} \\ \pm 1 & \text{else.} \end{cases} \tag{8}$$

Where, 0<a<b<0.5. The parameters a and b control the range of frequencies that will be affected by the watermark. After watermark embedding, the inverse DFT is calculated to produce the new watermarked signature. During detection, first we tried using a simple correlation detector. We also tried second type of detector known as a differential correlation detector to enhance the detector performance. In this type of detector the correlation values are calculated as discussed in section 1.6 for the pseudo random watermark generated using the known user key and also with dummy watermarks (Pseudo random watermarks generated using other than the known key). Then these values are normalized using the maximum correlation value found among them as shown.

Suppose correlation values are $C = \{c_d(-k), c_d(-k+1), ..., c_o(0), ..., c_d(k-1), c_d(k)\}$
In our case we have taken K= 50. Now these values are normalized as in equation

$$C = C/(maxC) \tag{9}$$

After this a threshold of is taken to decide whether a watermark is detected or not as shown. Suppose

$$\{C : C \geq Th\} \, if \, d = \frac{C_o}{maxC} \, then \, detected \, else \, not \, detected \tag{10}$$

The example figures of our differential correlation detector are shown in fig. 6 and 7.

2.3.   Performance Evaluation and Comparison

All the watermarking schemes were used to watermark 1600 signature from 40 different users and the statistic are based over these 1600 signatures.

- Embedding capacity = no. of bits embedded / Total length of a signature(N)
- Bit Error Rate = no. of bits incorrectly detected / no. of bits embedded

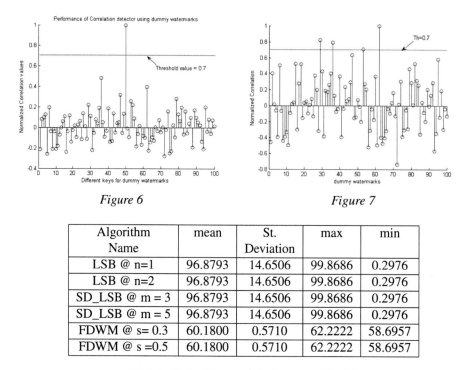

Figure 6   Figure 7

Algorithm Name	mean	St. Deviation	max	min
LSB @ n=1	96.8793	14.6506	99.8686	0.2976
LSB @ n=2	96.8793	14.6506	99.8686	0.2976
SD_LSB @ m = 3	96.8793	14.6506	99.8686	0.2976
SD_LSB @ m = 5	96.8793	14.6506	99.8686	0.2976
FDWM @ s= 0.3	60.1800	0.5710	62.2222	58.6957
FDWM @ s =0.5	60.1800	0.5710	62.2222	58.6957

Table 6.: Embedding capacity in terms of % of N

- n = Least significant bit plane depth in LSB algorithm
- m = size of neighborhood as discussed in SD LSB algorithm
- s = strength of watermark in FDWM algorithm

2.3.1.   Embedding Capacity

We define the embedding capacity as a percentage of the total no. of points N in the signature.

2.3.2.   Detector's Performance

For the algorithm LSB and SD_LSB, the Bit Error Rate (BER) statistic is as follows.

The detector performance is best identified in terms of the ROC curve. The ROC curves for algorithm LSB and SD_LSB are shown in fig 8. The threshold parameter in this case is the BER which ranges from 0 to 1. So in order to construct the ROC curve, we first calculated the BER values for 1600 un-watermarked signatures. Secondly we found the BER values

Algorithm Name	mean	St. Deviation	max	min
LSB @ n=1	1.6475e-002	7.0898e-002	9.8496e-001	0
LSB @ n=2	1.6013e-002	7.2341e-002	8.7970e-001	0
SD_LSB @ m = 3	1.5514e-004	6.7273e-004	6.9959e-003	0
SD_LSB @ m = 5	1.5593e-004	6.6492e-004	6.0150e-003	0
all algorithms	18.875%	15.9%	50%	0

Table 7.: Statistics of BER for LSB and SD_LDB algorithm

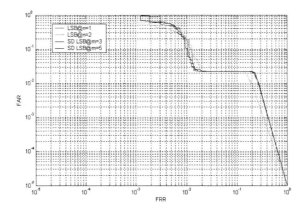

Figure 8

using 1600 signatures watermarked using the two watermarking schemes. Both set of BER values were then used to construct the ROC curve. The EER values found from the ROC curve shown in fig. 8 are as shown in table 7.

Detector performance for the algorithm FDWM can be judged in terms of Probability density function of Correlation values (as in section 3.4) shown in Fig. 9. The performance of the correlation detector is not very good as evident from the low correlation values in fig. 9. This performance was enhanced using 100 dummy watermarks and normalizing the correlation values with the max correlation value over these 100 watermarks as shown in

Algorithm Name	EER value
LSB @ n=1	2.25%
LSB @ n=2	2.25%
SD_LSB @ m = 3	2.31%
4SD_LSB @ m = 5	2.25%

Table 8.: EER values for theROC curve shown in fig 8

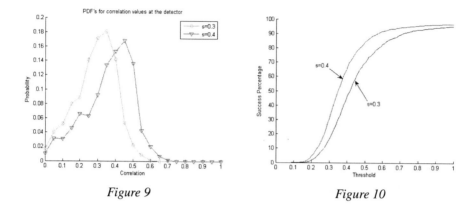

Figure 9   Figure 10

fig. 6. Then a threshold of 0.7 is used for the judging the right key with which the signature was watermarked. Success Percentage of FDWM at various threshold levels is shown in fig 10.

2.3.3. Performance Evaluation using Signature Verification Algorithm

This section deals with the performance evaluation of the signature verification algorithm due the watermarking of the signature template and the input signature Y. Since there is training involved in the verification algorithm, therefore there are two ways to judge the performance after watermarking as shown

I. Watermark Verification (using matcher trained with non watermarked Signatures) II. Watermark Training (using watermarked signatures) Verification With our experiments we found out that all the watermarking very slightly perturb the matching performance found without any watermarking of templates. The Equal Error Rate (EER) statistics remain unchanged for both cases.

2.4. Discussion

- The watermarking schemes presented here are a novel way of watermarking biometric signatures. Although the idea of watermarking biometric signature can be closely related to audio watermarking but no exact past research has been made in this particular application of digital watermarking technology. The peculiar behavioral characteristics of biometric signatures make it mandatory to study the watermarking schemes over large number of signatures from different users. Hence, all our watermarking schemes were checked over 1600 signatures both skilled and forged from 40 different users

- We studied the Payload Capacity for different watermarking algorithms. For the first two schemes very high payload capacity is found while for the FDWM scheme the payload capacity goes down because we embed watermark only in middle frequencies Fourier descriptors

- The most important aspect of combining Watermarking and Biometrics is that watermarking should not affect the performance of the any biometric system. Hence apart from studying the individual performances of the watermarking schemes, the effect of watermarking on the performance of signature verification algorithm was studied. The results suggest that if the perturbation of the original signature due to watermarking is kept within limits then the ROC curve of the verification algorithm does not change.

- Variation of different parameters in the watermarking scheme were also studied

  - In case of LSB, the effect of embedding at different bit planes 'n' was studied. The result suggested that watermarking at higher bit planes as expected improved the robustness of the algorithm. But an optimum level of n has to be decided keeping in mind the perturbation to the signature and the robustness of the watermarking scheme.

  - In case of SD LSB, effect of the neighborhood size 'm' was studied. The results suggest that increasing the value of m does not improve the performance and also make the algorithm much more time consuming compared to m = 3. Hence, m =3 can be chosen as size of the neighborhood.

  - In case of FDWM, effect of the strength of watermark 's' was studied. The increase of value of s improves the performance of the watermarking scheme and at this value the signature verification scheme is also not affected. Even higher values of s can be studied and an optimal value can thought of.

- A minor but very critical aspect that has deteriorated the performance of all watermarking scheme is the inherent round off attack in the end of the watermark embedding algorithms. This inherent attack causes some of loss of watermark information so it becomes mandatory that all the watermarking schemes must be at least robust enough to counter this attack otherwise most of the information will be lost at the embedding time itself. E.g. during the study of watermarking scheme FDWM, we found that at a watermark embedding strength of s = 0.15, the detection of watermark was absolutely not possible. But with a slight increase of strength to s = 0.3 the performance improved drastically, suggesting that a certain minimum strength of watermark is required to take care of the inherent round off attack.

Some Reversible watermarking schemes can be developed where both watermark and the host signal is fully recoverable. Such type of watermarking schemes will definitely find great application in securing biometric data, keeping in mind the accuracy and security restriction on the biometric authentication system. On one hand, this type of watermarking schemes will not hamper the performance of the biometric authentication algorithm and on the other hand, they will provide an excellent way of securing the biometric data. Some prior research done on reversible watermarking of GIS data [VYB04] can be directly applied to this field also.

3.   Acknowledgements

The authors would like to thank the authorities of IIT Kharagpur, EU-India CultureTech Project their support to carry out this research work. They also thank Prof. Jana Dittmann, Dr. Claus Vielhauer, for their kind help during manuscript preparation for various research publications during EU-INDIA CultureTech project. The content of this publication is the sole responsibility of the authors and can in no way be taken to reflect the views of the European Union.

Bibliography

[AU03] Anil K. Jain and Umut Uludag. Hiding biometric data. *IEEE Transactions on pattern analysis and machine intelligence*, 1 2003.

[FM99] F. Hartung and M. Kutter. Multimedia watermarking techniques, pp. 1079-1107. *Proc. IEEE*, 1 1999.

[GSG92] G.Dimauro, S.Impedovo, and G.Pirlo. A stroke-oriented approach to signature verification", in from pixels to features iii Ű frontiers in handwriting recognition, pp. 371-384. *Elsevier Publ.*, 1April 1992.

[HC03] Hao feng and Chan Choong Wah. Online signature verification using a new extreme points warping technique. *pattern recognition letter)*, 16December 2003.

[JEJ98] J. Dolfing, E. Aatrs, and J. Osterhout. On-line signature verification with hidden markov models, pp 1309Ű1312. *ICDAR*, 1April 1998.

[Kra05] Krawczyk, S. User authentication using on-line signature and speech. *Master's the-sis, Michigan State University*, 1April 2005.

[LG05] Lei Hansheng and Govindaraju Venu. A comparative study on the consistency of features in on-line signature verification, pp. 2483-2489. *pattern recognition letter*, 1 2005.

[NJR01] N.K. Ratha, J.H. Connell, and R.M. Bolle. An analysis of minutiae matching strength, pp. 223-228. *Proc. Third IntŠl. Conf. Audio- and Video-Based Biometric Person Authentication*, 1 2001.

[RL96] R. Martens and L. Claesen. On-line signature verification by dynamic time-warping, pp. 38-42. *In the 13th International Conference on Pattern Recognition*, 1April 1996.

[SP04] Solachidis, V and Pitas, I. Watermarking polygonal lines using fourier descriptors, pp 44- 51. *Computer Graphics and Applications, EEE*, 1June 2004.

[SSCT05] S. Schimke, S. Kiltz, C. Vielhauer, and T. Kalker. Security analysis for biometric data in id documents, pp. 474-485. *Proceedings of the SPIE*, 1April 2005.

[V.S97] V.S. Nalwa. Automatic on-line signature verification, pp 215Ű239. *Proc. IEEE*, 1 April 1997.

[VYB04] Voigt M, Yang B., and Busch C. Reversible watermarking of 2d-vector data. *Multimedia and Security Workshop, MM&SEC*, 1 2004.

[YC04] Yinyin Yuan and Chang-Tsun Li. Fragile watermarking scheme exploiting non-deterministic block-wise dependency. *ICPR*, 1April 2004.

Cross-Cultural Analysis of Digital Media: From Fundamentals over Feature Extraction to Inter-Feature Fusion

ANDREA OERMANN

Contents

Abstract

In this article, a general methodology is presented in order to analyze information presented by digital media. This provides a framework to evaluate digital applications such as biometric user authentication systems in a cross-cultural context. Further, the impacts of cultural aspects on specific approaches applied in digital communication systems are elaborated. This article will show that applying additional knowledge to approaches like biometric user authentication systems can improve the performance on the on hand, and deriving additional knowledge such as metadata which is not directly contained in the basic captured signals on the other hand can be of benefit in different application fields such as forensics or digital rights management systems. In particular, the needs for a semantic fusion of information will be outlined and demonstrated. By the presented methodology information is classified in different levels focussing two domains, the syntactic and semantic domain. Hence, data can be analyzed in any kind of context such as cultural societies, its individual values, legal aspects, specific experiences and skills. As the methodology differentiates between representation (syntax) and content (semantics) of information, changes can more reliably be detected and localized. In particular, these are changes or manipulations which otherwise would not have been noticed, as information changes in representation domain not necessarily result in changes on content domain. This article demonstrates that making semantic information available to digital applications has to be seen as the key in order to develop future trustworthy systems, which are trusted and accepted by different cultures at the same time.

1.   Motivation

Digital Rights management is going to play an extremely important role in the next wave of e-solutions. A general method of digital verification has to include multiple levels of authentication under various possible modalities in a flexible manner. Data authentication in the multimedia scenario can be done by validating speech, image, handwriting, digital key, watermark etc. Convergence of these validation procedures will give better selectivity and discriminating power, in particular when the sample is large. In a large sample multimodal authentication procedures may improve the resolution several times than the unimodal procedure. The resulting resolution of a composite authentication procedure depends on efficient selection of feature vector of each mode and also statistical nature of the inter-modal dependencies. Efficient fusion of e.g. image, handwriting and speech processing can be done by taking into account these aspects.

In this article a new methodology is presented in order to fuse any kind of information not only on a syntactical level but also on a semantic level. This can be of a benefit considering DRM systems, where information usually is represented by different types of media, e.g. image, text or audio, which then needs to be connected. Further, in authentication scenarios such as multimodal biometric user authentication systems, a better performance can be achieved by applying our methodology.

In particular, a model for classifying information is presented as it is described into detail later in section 2. Six different levels are defined referring to certain features of the information. Hence, the whole information can be captured. Further, information changes can be detected, which otherwise would not have been noticed. While developing the model, two different goals are followed:

1. applying additional knowledge

2. deriving additional knowledge

The framework enables to interpret data in any kind of context such as for example the cultural background of a person which wants to be authenticated by a biometric user authentication system. There certain questions may be answered: What can be achieved by the methodology? Which type of features can be culturally analyzed? In how far additional knowledge can be integrated into an authentication process? Within this EU-India CultureTech programme (see [1]) the methodology could be evaluated, especially the consideration of different cultural backgrounds: Indians, Germans, Italians. The authentication always implies an exploration of legal and cultural consequences and aspects regarding the acceptance of multimedia technologies. Especially when considering biometrics, individuals need to provide personal information which might belong to their privacy. There the cultural background of users plays a significant role and has a direct impact on the technology. Some cultural groups don't have any problem with offering this biometric information while others do. While common European citizens for example may find it deterring to use a fingerprint for automated authentication purposes, as it resembles treatment of suspects in crime. This view may be significantly different in cultures, where fingerprints are not only used in forensic context, but also in other daily processes like authentication for election votes. Further, multimedia technologies allowing the reproduction of digital goods which has triggered a lot of legal activity in the area of copyrights. Hence, it is always necessary to take aspects of the legal and cultural nature of a society into account when developing or analyzing approaches of digital techniques.

Our research investigations are targeting to fulfill the aspects of IT-Security. As defined in the section "Definitions" in this article those aspects are:

- Availability
- Integrity
- Authenticity
- Confidentiality
- Non-repudiation

The goal of today's communication systems, where authentication plays a key role in order to provide trustworthy identities [2], is a cross-cultural acceptance. The main problem which has to be faced is to create a homogenous and global concept and design of authentication systems at the same time, independent of different cultures. Therefore, a culture's needs, habits and values has to be estimated while considering security aspects such as integrity, authenticity and privacy and apply security mechanisms. In doing so transparent and trustworthy systems can be achieved by integrating domestic standards due to trust has to be seen as a condition of the acceptance of digital communication systems which are a target for attacks and forgeries.

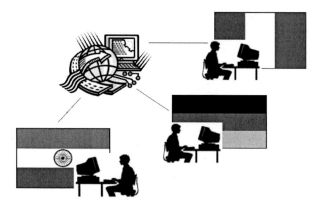

Figure 1.: Different users participating digital communication systems

Trust plays a significant role when elaborating digital technologies in a cultural context. In the age of globalization trust is particularly important when operating in the areas of E-Technologies as we have examined in [3]. Developing digital communication systems conditionally implies touching the interface between technical innovation and its applicability by users. Users live and work in a certain social context which means that

- different legal systems
- different values
- different cultural contexts
- different experiences and
- different skills

need to be considered. This necessarily has consequences for IT-Solutions and IT-Security which needs to keep in mind when designing IT-systems. Especially authentication systems need to be contextualized, harmonized and culturally adapted in order to be accepted by different cultures.

This article is about to present a framework, a methodology which enables to not only additionally consider cultural information and integrate it into approaches of digital communication systems such as biometric user authentication or digital rights management systems but also to show its impacts on modern technologies.

This article is structured as follows. In section 2, the syntax and the semantics regarding digital media are explored. This is followed by a exemplary demonstration of feature cluster collections for handwriting, speech and face as types of digital information. In section 3, determining perusable features will briefly be introduced. In section 4, the inter-feature fusion function and specific semantically fused features are presented. Therefor, its needs will be outlined. This is followed by a description if biometrics as an specific application field in section 5. The article closes in section 6 with a summary.

2.   Syntax and Semantics regarding Digital Media

The methodology for classifying syntax and semantics regarding digital media has been initially introduced as a so-called *Verifier-Tuple* in order to measure information changes in the field of forensics [4]. By following this methodology not only specific information features can be clustered, but also changes as for example forgeries or counterfeitings can be detected and precisely localized. The reason for developing a new classification model for digital information is the gab between representation and content. Information represented by digital media are easier to manipulate than information represented by analogue media. Unpredictable changes of information or negatively target-oriented manipulations are often not perceived due to the representation of digital media. A picture for example can be digitally represented through different formats but still the same content of the picture is perceived while the changes of the representation remaining undetected. This indicates that especially in the fields of authentication and digital rights management this can either be a benefit or it can be disprofiting. A benefit as well as a nightmare in so far, that there are channels existing where secret information can be hit. This unfortunately is supporting criminals as it provides an alternative of secretly exchanging, attacking and accessing information. But it is also the key for digital watermarking techniques which today are increasingly applied in order to ensure the integrity of information [5].

The *Verifier-Tuple* is derived from a general concept of the explanation of programming languages as it is presented in [7]. It describes a combination of syntax and semantics, as introduced in [4] and further applied in [8] and [9]. According to [10], we now additionally differentiate between three interdependent levels of syntax as an extension of our basic *Verifier-Tuple*. Instead of four levels of information we now distinguish between six levels of information, as it can be seen in equation 1.

$$V = \{SY_P, SY_L, SY_C, SE_E, SE_F, SE_A\} \qquad (1)$$

Following our invented methodology, the whole information consists of six levels, three levels belonging to the syntactic domain and three levels belonging to the semantic domain:

Syntactic domain SY:

1. Syntax (SY_P) - physical level (location and characteristics of storage)

2. Syntax (SY_L) - logical level (bit-streams, formats)

3. Syntax (SY_C) - conceptual level (information, signal characteristics)

Semantic domain SE:

1. Semantics (SE_S) - structural level

2. Semantics (SE_F) - functional level

3. Semantics (SE_A) - analytical level

The syntax is defined as the composition of certain signs within a selected alphabet. It is a systematic, orderly arrangement whose description is rooted in linguistics. In order to analyze the syntax of languages, formal logic can be applied as presented in [11] and [12]. The syntax determines the composition of elements associating with an alphabet by following certain rules, structures and regulations. The syntax defines valid and permitted constructs within an alphabet.

The three defined levels of the syntactic domain are required for analyzing digital information. The structural level refers to the location of the stored information and its characteristics, such as sectors on a harddrive or further pitchs regarding a CD-ROM or DVD. The logical level implies the bit stream and the type of storing, in other words the formats and how information is digitally coded. The conceptual level represents the "raw data" of the information, the signals and its specific constituents and properties. These three levels are interacting with each other. Changes on one level can result in changes on either one or both other levels. But it does not necessarily need to. Further, it can effect the semantic domain while it can also be out of any impact on the semantic domain as digital watermarking techniques can prove.

Semantics is the study or science of the meaning in language and refers to the content of information. Semantics defined as the connection of characters, tokens or symbols and their relation to the meant object or information [13]. Semantics is implying the interpretation of the facts given by the syntax. Thus, considering semantics conclusions about the author of information and his or her intention can be drawn. The interpretative characteristic of semantics need to be differentiated. Therefore, semantics is subdivided into three levels, the structural level, the functional level and the analytical level.

The structural level can be defined as applying particular operations in order to determines a specific process sequence. Starting with a certain input, the applied operations effectively generate an output [7]. This level of semantics connects abstract syntactic elements. The functional semantics indicates a semantic algebra and specific evaluation functions as an additional interpretative enhancement [7]. On the functional level the impact of allocations of variables is analyzed. This is achieved by functions specifying measurement categories

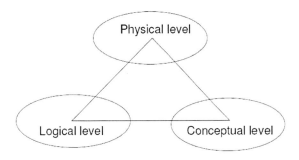

Figure 2.: Syntactical domain and the relation of its levels

for analyzing the content of an information presented by the medium. The analytical level is mostly supported by a human being but can also be integrated in a digital, automatic system. It is based on background knowledge and can be abstractly explained using methods of formal logic as presented in [7].

This *Verifier-Tuple* enables a more detailed analysis and classification of information. Hence, not only particular features can be extracted, but also manipulations or attacks can be recognized and localized. Further, it allows drawing conclusions about the context of an information. Additional information which is not directly presented within the analyzed information such as metadata ([14], [15], and [16]) can be derived.

According to equation 1, the extraction of features on the different syntactic and semantic levels of an arbitrary information i_j can be formally represented in vectors as follows:

$$\vec{sfv}_{i_j} = \{\vec{sfv}_{SY_P}, \vec{sfv}_{SY_L}, \vec{sfv}_{SY_C}, \vec{sfv}_{SE_S}, \vec{sfv}_{SE_F}, \vec{sfv}_{SE_A}\} \tag{2}$$

$j = 1, ..., k, k \in \mathbf{N}$

A feature vector represents a collection of specific features, which can be represented as follows in equation 2:

$$\vec{sfv}_{i_j} = \{ \begin{pmatrix} psy_1 \\ ... \\ psy_a \end{pmatrix}, \begin{pmatrix} lsy_1 \\ ... \\ lsy_b \end{pmatrix}, \begin{pmatrix} csy_1 \\ ... \\ csy_c \end{pmatrix}, \begin{pmatrix} sse_1 \\ ... \\ sse_d \end{pmatrix}, \begin{pmatrix} fse_1 \\ ... \\ fse_e \end{pmatrix}, \begin{pmatrix} ase_1 \\ ... \\ ase_f \end{pmatrix} \} \tag{3}$$

$a, b, c, d, e, f \in \mathbf{N}$

where $\vec{sfv}_{SY_P}$ represents the vector of features on the physical syntactic level and $\{psy_1, ..., psy_a\}$ is the set of specific features, $\vec{sfv}_{SY_L}$ represents the vector of features on the logical syntactic level and $\{lsy_1, ..., lsy_b\}$ is the set of specific features, $\vec{sfv}_{SY_C}$ represents the vector of features on the conceptual syntactic level and $\{csy_1, ..., csy_c\}$ is the

set of specific features, $\overrightarrow{sfv}_{SE_S}$ represents the vector of features on the structural semantic level and $\{sse_1, ..., sse_d\}$ is the set of specific features, $\overrightarrow{sfv}_{SE_F}$ represents the vector
of features on the functional semantic level and $\{fse_1, ..., fse_e\}$ is the set of specific features and $\overrightarrow{sfv}_{SE_A}$ represents the vector of features on the analytical semantic level and
$\{ase_1, ..., ase_f\}$ is the set of specific features. Vectors can have varying dimensions, which
is indicated through $a,b,c,d,e,$ and f. For analyzing information not necessarily all information levels need to be integrated or can be considered in the fusion levels. In this case the
elements of the corresponding vector will be set to 0.

3.   Feature Extraction exemplarily for Handwriting and Speech and Face

In this section, specific features are exemplarily listed regarding their belongings to the
defined level of information. Listings are presented for information related to biometric
user authentication system. In particular, biometric data for handwriting (see Figure 1) and
speech (see Figure 2) as behavioral biometric modalities [17] as well as face (see Figure 3)
as a physical biometric modality [17] is classified by applying our invented methodology.

Syntactic Domain SY	
Syntax - Physical Level	
	- location within the storage, - e.g. sectors, of hardware (medium) - its characteristics
Syntax - Logical Level	
	- bit stream - bits per sample - formats: sample in a database
Syntax - Conceptual Level	

	- Horizontal pen position signal $x(t)$
	 - Vertical pen position signal $y(t)$
	 - Pen tip pressure signal $p(t)$
	 - Pen azimuth signal $\Theta(t)$
	 - Pen altitude signal $\Phi(t)$
	
	 - Horizontal pen acceleration signal $a_x(t)$
	   (via horizontal pen force)
	 - Vertical pen acceleration signal $a_y(t)$
	   (via vertical pen force)

Semantic Domain SE	
Semantics - Structural Level	

	- Dynamic Time Warping (DTW)
	 - Hidden-Markov-Models (HMM)
	 - Neural Networks
	 - Multi Level Approaches
	 - BioHash with distance measures for extracting
	    certain statistical parameters
	 - Set of k statistical parameters
	    derived from the syntax

Semantics - Functional Level	
	- Word + its individual shape - Passphrase + its individual shape - Symbol + its individual shape - Number + its individual shape - Signature + its individual shape
Semantics - Analytical Level	
	- Tablet - Pen - Device - Environment - Emotions - Metadata [18], [17] or Soft Biometrics [15], [16] - Acceptance
$i = 0, ..., n, n \in \mathbf{N}, n = 0$	

Table 1.: Classification of handwriting features (similar to [8])

Syntactic Domain SY	
Syntax - Physical Level	
	- location within the storage, - e.g. sectors, of hardware (medium) - its characteristics
Syntax - Logical Level	
	- bit stream - bits per sample - formats and audio models: saved digital audio signal S_{ds} - MP3, WAVE, ...

Syntax - Conceptual Level	
	- analog audio signal S_a or digital audio signal S_d - discrete samples $s = (a_i, t_i)*$ - time t_i* - continuous acoustic pressure a_i* of a wave in db (volume and amplitude) - phase - frequency spectrum (FFT) wavelets - sample rate - impulse signal - pitch
Semantic Domain SE	
Semantics - Structural Level	
	- data rate - signal shaping - size of audio stream, sample size - channels - histogramm
Semantics - Functional Level	
	- sound, tone, vocal tone, fundamentals - speech, language, music, noise (type of noise) - sound source location and orientation (distance to sensor, microphone) - voice and language - foreground and background sounds
Semantics - Analytical Level	
	- understanding of speech, tone, signal, sound, noise, impulse - understanding of voice and spoken information - male or female speaker - voiced or voiceless - Emotions - used device -> microphone or sensor - room and background characteristics - speech disorder - Metadata [18], [17] or Soft Biometrics [15], [16] - Acceptance
$i = 0, ..., n, n \in \mathbf{N}, n = 0$	

Table 2.: Classification of voice features

Syntactic Domain SY	
Syntax - Physical Level	
	- location within the storage,
	- e.g. sectors, of hardware (medium)
	- its characteristics
Syntax - Logical Level	
	- bit stream
	- bits per sample
	- bits per color
	- formats: saved digital signal Sds
	- MPEG, M-JPEG (MotionJPEG), AVI, Quicktime, Real, or
	- JPEG, BMP, SVG, ...
Syntax - Conceptual Level	
	- spatial domain coordinates x_{ij}
	- frequency domain coordinates
	- sequence of single images/frames
	$f_i (i = 0...n, n \in R, n \geq 0)$
	- wavelets (JPEG2000)
	- analog continuous image signal s_a or
	digital discrete image signal s_d
	- λ - wavelength
	- sample rate
	- pixels, number of pixels
	- RGB, CMY, YUV
	- HSV (hue, saturation, intensity (brightness))
	- chrominance, luminance, contrast
Semantic Domain SE	
Semantics - Structural Level	
	- data rate and image stream
	- pixel or frame level
	- signal shaping
	- frame (image) size and number of pixels
	- color depth, resolution
	- black and white, grayscales, color
	- quantity of gray values, quantity of color values
	- channels
	- histogram

Semantics - Functional Level	
	- foreground and background objects - positions of objects - face recognition - shadows, segments - lighting and illumination - shapes, characteristics of face, textures - point of view - physical surface characteristics - overlaying, transparency - motion blurring
Semantics - Analytical Level	
	- who can be seen - interpretation of objects, scene in combination with background knowledge - mouth and lip movements - emotions (see condition) - male or female speaker, child or adult - determination of the used device - object and scene characteristics - metadata such as cultural and ethnical background of person or condition of person - Metadata [18], [17] or Soft Biometrics [15], [16] - Acceptance
$i = 0, ..., n, n \in \mathbf{N}, n = 0$	

Table 3.: Classification of face features

4.   Perusable Features: Succession of a Fusion

Considering a fusion of information represented by two different media, not necessarily all features can be considered and hence, they are not perusable for an evaluation. Especially, information clusters on the conceptual syntactic level and the structural semantic level are almost impossible to compare. An audio signal consists of different characteristics than e.g. handwriting signals. Those signals are rarely to compare. Therefore, being able to consider semantic information, which in this case can better be compared is advantageous.

Before analyzing information features perusable features need to be specified. This can be done by e.g. a boolean operation which differentiates perusable features (1) from non-perusable features (0). Considering equation 3, each vector element will be multiplied by either 1 or 0.

		Semantic Domain – Voice
Semantic Domain - Video		Functional level
	Functional level	– a person speaks in a noisy environment (street) – car is honking in the background – a person is close or far away to the sensor (microphone, camera) – many people are speaking – a certain language is spoken
		Analytical level
	Analytical level	– a person is wearing a hearing device – a male speaker of a certain age is saying "Hello, how are you." with happy emotions – visual mouth and lip movements of a person validate voice – visual mouth and lip movements of a person lead to assumptions about disorder or identify distortions of speech – an person of a certain culture and ethnical background is speaking (Indian, German, Italian) – a person of a certain condition (in a hurry, nervous) is speaking – a person is whispering – ..

Table 4.: Semantic fusion of information

5. Inter-feature Fusion Function and Specific Semantically Fused Features

Similar to [9], a so-called inter-feature fusion function $\overrightarrow{FFF}$ with the fusion operator $\odot$ consolidates specific feature vectors regarding the functional and analytical semantic level of information represented by two different types of media, as shown in equation 3.

$$\overrightarrow{FFF} = \overrightarrow{sfv}_{m_1} \odot \ldots \odot \overrightarrow{sfv}_{m_k} \tag{4}$$

An exemplary outcome of the inter-feature fusion function $\overrightarrow{FFF}$ with the fusion operator $\odot$ is shown in Table 4. There it can be followed, that information represented by different media can be compared and consolidated on the functional and analytical semantic level. If an information is represented by the same media but in two different formats such as in JPEG, BMP or GIF regarding the media image, the syntactic domain and the structural semantic level is firstly preferably be considered to be analyzed in order to detect information changes which are not affecting the content.

This inter-feature fusion function has been initially invented in a biometric scenario in [9] in order to demonstrate its applicability. Goal of our work was to show that making semantic information available to a biometric fusion process [19], [20], or [21] the performance might be improved as first test results in an earlier work have pointed out this tendency [8].

6.   Biometrics as an Application Scenario

The field of biometrics offers evidently promising techniques in order to determine an individual's identity and authorize an individual. Instead of relying on external knowledge such as PINs or Smartcards which can be lost, as classical authentication systems do, biometric systems consider given biological characteristics, also known as traits or modalities, which identify an individual's uniqueness.

Biometric techniques are either based on passive (e.g.iris, face and fingerprint) or active modalities (e.g. voice and handwriting). Passive modalities refer to physiological whereas active modalities indicate behavioral characteristics of an individual, which is learnt and acquired over time. Unimodal biometric systems only consider one source of information for authentication. However, unimodal systems are associated with several problems such as noisy data, attacks, overlapping of similarities, and non-universality of biometric characteristics [19] due to a modality contains several aspects: multiple sensors, multiple representations, multiple instance and multiple samples are existing. Hence, the development of multimodal biometric systems [19], [22], which consider multiple sources of information, is focus of recent research investigations.

Multimodal biometric systems fuse several biometric subsystems considering different modalities [22]) while different strategies such as described in [20] and [21] when, how, and where to apply a fusion can be followed. Thus, the performance of a biometric user authentication process in a multimodal biometric system can be increased as test results have shown [21]. Basically three fusion levels can be applied: feature level, matching score level or decision level [20]. In addition to these three fusion levels, two fusion levels, sensor level and rank level have been introduced by [23] and [24].

With the invented methodology and inter-feature fusion function the fusion performance might be improved independently of its application level. By extracting and merging certain semantic information and providing it as additional knowledge (e.g. metadata) to the process the fusion and its decision outcome can be controlled as shown in Figure 4. In doing so, discrepancies and irregularities of one biometric modality can be verified by another one. Further, signal errors might be more reliable identified and corrected. T The methodology therefore can also be seen as a framework which provides an opportunity to posterior correct signal errors, elemimate background noises, enable a more reliable detection of attacks and perform a successful synchronization of information presented by two different media.

7.   Summary

In this article, a methodology is presented in order to analyze and evaluate digital technologies in a cross-cultural context as well as elaborating the impacts of cultural aspects on specific approaches applied in digital communication systems such as in particular biometric authentication systems.

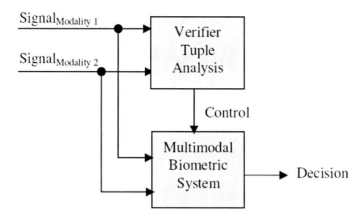

Figure 3.: Features regarding a fusion on functional and analytical semantic level

The methodology presented in this article classifies syntactic and semantic information levels regarding digital media and clusters specific information features depending on their belongings to a defined level. Thus, any kind of information can be consolidated not only on a syntactical level but also on a semantic level. The methodology generally differentiates between representation (syntax) and content (semantics) of information. In doing so, information changes can reliably be detected and localized, in particular changes or manipulations which otherwise would not have been noticed. Information changes in representation domain not necessarily result in changes on content domain.

The methodology as presented in this article can also be seen as a framework in which data can be analyzed in any kind of context such as the cultural societies, its individual values, legal aspects, specific skills as it is outlined in the motivation. Especially when designing and implementing applications for digital media and communication systems considering cultural aspects can be much of a benefit. The introduced twofold faced goals such as applying additional knowledge to approaches regarding the security aspects like integrity and authenticity on the on hand and deriving additional knowledge on the other hand could be achieved and demonstrated. The first goal is focussing approaches of authentication systems such as the field of biometrics provide while the second goal is concerning application fields where additional not directly contained information by the raw data needs to be derived. Those fields are e.g. forensics or digital rights management systems.

Summarizing this article and our research investigations targeting the goal to fulfill the aspects of IT-Security it can be said, that making semantic information available to digital applications has to be seen as the key in order to develop future trustworthy systems, which are trusted and accepted by different cultures at the same time.

8.   Acknowledgements

The information in this document is provided as is, and no guarantee or warranty is given or implied that the information is fit for any particular purpose. The user thereof uses the information at its sole risk and liability. The work described in this article has been supported in part by the EU-India cross cultural program (project CultureTech, see [1]) and partly by the Federal Office for Information Security (BSI), Germany. The views and conclusions contained herein are those of the authors and should not be interpreted as necessarily representing the official policies, either expressed or implied, of the Federal Office for Information Security (BSI), or the German Government, or the European Union.

Bibliography

[1] The Culture Tech Project, Cultural Dimensions in digital Multimedia Security Technology, a project funded under the EU-India Economic Cross Cultural Program, http://amsl-smb.cs.uni-magdeburg.de/culturetech/, last requested September 2005

[2] , W. Marotzki, J. Dittmann, F. Lesske: Virtual Communities: Trust, Identity, Participation and Technology. In: Computational Visualistics, Media Informatics, and Virtual Communities, Band 11 der Reihe Bildwissenschaft; Jochen Schneider, Thomas Strothotte, Winfried Marotzki (Eds.) Deutscher Universitäts-Verlag GWV Fachverlage Gmbh Wiesbaden, 2003, pp. 57-66.

[3] A. Oermann, J. Dittmann: Trust in E-Technologies. In: Encyclopedia of E-Commerce, E-Government and Mobile Commerce, Mehdi Khosrow-Pour (Ed.) Information Resources Management Association, USA, Idea Group Reference, Hershey London Melbourne Singapore, 2006, pp. 1101–1108

[4] A. Oermann, A. Lang, J. Dittmann: Verifyer-Tupel for Audio-Forensic to Determine Speaker Environment. City University of New York (Organizer): Multimedia and security, MM & Sec'05, Proceedings ACM, Workshop New York, NY, USA (2005) pp. 57 - 62

[5] J. Dittmann, Digitale Wasserzeichen, Xpert.press, Springer Berlin, ISBN 3-540-66661-3, 2000

[6] Simmel, G. (1978). The philosophy of money. Transl. by Tom Bottomore and David Frisby from a first draft by Kaethe Mengelberg. Boston: Routledge & Kegan Paul.

[7] H.R. Nielson, F. Nielson: Semantics with Applications: A Formal Introduction, revised edition, John Wiley & Sons, original 1992 (1999)

[8] A. Oermann, J. Dittmann, C. Vielhauer: Verifier-Tuple as a Classifier of Biometric Hand-writing Authentication - Combination of Syntax and Semantics. Dittmann, Jana

(Ed.), Katzenbeisser, Stefan (Ed.), Uhl, Andreas (Ed.): Communications and multimedia security, Berlin: Springer, Lecture notes in com, CMS 2005 9th IFIP TC-6 TC-11 international conference Salzburg, Austria, (September 2005) pp. 170 - 179

[9] A. Oermann, T. Scheidat, C. Vielhauer, J. Dittmann: Semantic Fusion for Biometric User Authentication as Multimodal Signal Processing. In: Proceedings of Int. Workshop on Multimedia Content Representation, Classification & Security IW MRCS, September 11-13, 2006, Istanbul, Turky, 2006, pp. 546–553

[10] K. Thibodeau: Overview of Technological Approaches to Digital Preservation and Challenges in Coming Years. Council on Library and Information Resources: The State of Digi-tal Preservation: An International Perspective, Conference Proceedings, July 2002 http://www.clir.org/pubs/reports/pub107/thibodeau.html , last requested on 24.06.2006 (2002)

[11] N. Chomsky: Syntactic Structures, Mouton and Co., Den Haag, 1957

[12] N. Chomsky: Aspects of the Theory of Syntax, MIT Press, Massachusetts Institute of Technology, Cambridge, MA, 1965

[13] S. Löbner: Semantik: eine Einführung, De Gruyter Studienbuch Berlin, 2003

[14] F. Wolf, T.K. Basu, P.K. Dutta, C. Vielhauer, A. Oermann, B. Yegnanarayana: A Cross-Cultural Evaluation Framework for Behavioral Biometric User Authentication.: From Data and Information Analysis to Knowledge Engineering. In: Proceedings of 29 Annual Conference of the Gesellschaft für Klassifikation e. V., GfKl 2005, University of Magdeburg, Germany. Springer-Verlag, 2006, pp. 654–661

[15] A. K. Jain, et al.: Soft Biometric Traits for Personal Recognition Systems. In: *Proceedings of International Conference on Biometric Authentication (ICBA)*. Hong Kong, LNCS 3072, 2004, pp. 731–738

[16] A. K. Jain, et al.: Can soft biometric traits assist user recognition?. In: *Proceedings of SPIE Biometric Technology for Human Identification*. Orlando, FL, U.S.A., 5404, 2004, pp. 561–572

[17] C. Vielhauer: Biometric User Authentication for IT Security, Advances in Information Security. Vol. 18, Springer, New York ISBN: 0-387-26194-X, 2005

[18] S. Schimke, C. Vielhauer, P.K. Dutta, T.K. Basu, A. De Rosa, J. Hansen, B. Yegnanarayana, J. Dittmann: Cross Cultural Aspects of Biometrics. In: *Proceedings of Biometrics: Challenges arising from Theory to Practice*, 2004, pp. 27–30

[19] A. Ross, A.K. Jain: Multimodal Biometrics: An Overview. Proceedings of the 12th Euro-pean Signal Processing Conference (EUSIPCO), Vienna, Austria, (2004) pp. 1221 - 1224

[20] A.K. Jain, A. Ross: Multibiometric Systems, Communications of the ACM, Vol. 47, No. 1, (2004) pp. 34 - 40

[21] T. Scheidat, C. Vielhauer: Fusion von biometrischen Verfahren zur Benutzerauthentifikation. In: P. Horster (Ed.), D-A-CH Security 2005 - Bestandsaufnahme, Konzepte, Anwendungen, Perspektiven, 2005, pp. 82–97

[22] C. Vielhauer, T. Scheidat: Multimodal Biometrics for Voice and Handwriting. In: Jana Dittmann, Stefan Katzenbeisser, Andreas Uhl (Eds.), Communications and Multimedia Se-curity: 9th IFIP TC-6 TC-11International Conference, CMS 2005, Proceedings, LNCS 3677, Salzburg, Austria, September 19 - 21, 2005, pp. 191 - 199

[23] A. Ross, R. Govindarajan: Feature Level Fusion Using Hand and Face Biometrics. In Proceedings of SPIE Conference on Biometric Technologie for Human Identification II, Vol. 5779, Orlando, USA (2005) pp. 196 - 204

[24] Y. Lee, K. Lee, H. Jee, Y. Gil, W. Choi, D. Ahn, S. Pan: Fusion for Multimodal Biometric Identification. In: Proceedings of Audio- and Video-Based Biometric Person Authentication: 5th International Conference, AVBPA 2005, Hilton Rye Town, NY, USA, July 20-22, 2005. Ed.: T. Kanade, A. Jain, N. K. Ratha, LNCS, Springer Heidelberg Berlin, Vol. 3546, (2005) p. 1071

9.   Definitions

Data Integrity: Preventing of forgeries, corruption, impairment or modification of resources like information, services or equipment. Data integrity is the quality or condition of being whole and unaltered, and it refers to the consistency, accuracy, and correctness of data.

Authenticity: Is divided in two sections: Data origin authenticity and entity authenticity. Data origin authenticity is the proof of the data's origin, genuineness, originality, truth and realness. Entity authenticity is the proof that a person or other agent has been correctly identified, or that a message is stored and received as transmitted.

Non-Repudiation: Service that provides proof of the integrity, origin of data, and the identity of a person, all in an unforgeable relationship, which can be verified by any third party at any time. Hence, it determines, wether or not a particular event occurred or a particular action happened.

Confidentiality: Non-occurrence of the unauthorized disclosure of information. The term confidentiality indicates aspects of secrecy and privacy. It implies the ensuring that information is accessible only to those authorized to have access.

Availability: Availability indicates the assurance that resources, like information, services, or equipment, are working adequately and available at a specified time to authorized entities. An available system has to be safe and secure from attacks.

Privacy: Right of the individual to be protected against intrusion into his personal life or affairs and the individual's right to decide what personal data of him or herself can be accessed and used publicly by others.

Trust: Trust as a form of knowledge. Trust is the hypothesis of future behavior, which is certain enough for establishing practical acting. Trust is the medium state between knowledge and ignorance [6].

Trustworthiness: Ability to create and develop trust. Trustworthiness is the assurance that a system deserves to be trusted.

Assurance: Statement, indication, or presumption that inspires confidence while excluding doubt. Assurance is an aspect of trust. Given the fact, that trust cannot be quantified precisely, assurance provides a basis for quantitatively or qualitatively specifying the level of trust towards a system.

Safety: Quality, state, or condition of being prevented of and/or protected against danger, risk, or injury, caused by accidental and unintentional effects or actions. Safety further includes the recovery from such accidental and unintentional effects or actions.

Security: Quality, state, or condition of being prevented of and/or protected against danger, risk, or injury, caused by intentional effects or actions such as access to information by unauthorized recipients and the intentional but unauthorized destruction or modification of that information. Security further includes the recovery from such unauthorized destructions or modifications.

Person Authentication Using Voice Biometrics

PATIL HEMANT A., DUTTA P. K., BASU T. K.

Contents

Abstract

In this report, we describe the contributions made by IIT Kharagpur team in the area of person authentication using voice biometrics for Culture Tech Project funded by European Union during 2004-2006. The fundamental goal of the project was to promote links, fusion of knowledge and the establishment of a durable open network between university media departments and non-profit associated partners from different cultural origin in Europe and India in respect to an interdisciplinary scientific area, bordered by technical, legal and cultural domains. Voice biometrics or Automatic Speaker Recognition (ASR) deals with person authentication based on his/her voice with the help of machines. ASR finds its applications in banking transactions, forensic science, access control and information retrieval. ASR can be classified as speaker verification, speaker identification and speaker classification. This report summarizes contributions made in the area of speaker identification (for monolingual, cross-lingual and multilingual mode), speaker classification (for open set and closed mode) and mimic recognition task.

1.   Introduction

Voice biometrics has been an active area of the research for several decades now, but it still remains active, as the problem is difficult. Moreover, speech remains the simplest method of input for personal biometrics, although its accuracy is lower than that of fingerprints or retinal scans. In addition to this, there is a growing interest for ASR in mobile domain [R N02]. ASR is a data driven field, i.e., the performance of ASR is dependent on the database. The factors affecting the performance are recording conditions, gender type used in population, speaker characteristics, monolingual or cross-lingual corpora, etc. Success rates obtained in an ASR system are meaningless if the recording or experimental conditions are not known [Hem05]. In this report, we describe the contributions made by IIT-K team in the area of person authentication using voice biometrics for Culture Tech Project funded by European Union during 2004-2006. The fundamental goal of the project was to promote links, fusion of knowledge and the establishment of a durable open network between university media departments and non-profit associated partners from different cultural origin in Europe and India in respect to an interdisciplinary scientific area, bordered by technical, legal and cultural domains. Following are the contributions for Indian and European languages (as shown in Fig. 1).

- Data collection and corpus design for Indian and European languages (later with support of partner from UNI-MD).

- Speaker identification in monolingual, cross-lingual and multilingual mode.

- Speaker identification in multilingual mode.

- Speaker identification of professional mimics in Indian languages.

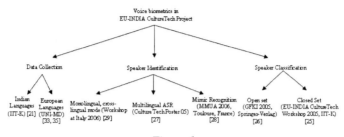

Figure 1

- Speaker classification for Indian and European languages in closed set and open set mode.

- Language detection experiment through confusion matrices.

2. Experimental Setup

In this section, a brief description of data collection and corpus design procedure, features employed for different ASR tasks and pattern classifier are presented.

2.1. Data Collection and Corpus Design

In this work, data is collected in Indian (Marathi, Hindi, Urdu, Bengali, Tamil, Telugu) and European (German and English) languages. European language data is collected from 4 subjects having German as their native language and English as a non-native language. Data is recorded in a laboratory environment (The data was collected by the partners of the EU-India Culture Tech Project, University of Magdeburg, Germany, under Prof. J. Dittmann and Dr. C. Vielhauer, [SCP+04], [CTJP]). For collecting Indian language data, a typical experimental setup consists of a close talking microphone, voice activated tape recorder and Pentium-III machine having speech processing software. The recording was done with the help of voice activated (VAS) tape recorders (Sanyo model no. M-1110C, Aiwa model no. JS299) with microphone input and close talking microphones (viz., Frontech and In-tex). The data is recorded on the Sony high fidelity voice and music recording cassettes (C-90HFB). A list consisting of five questions, isolated words, digits, combination-lock phrases, read sentences and a contextual speech of considerable duration was prepared in Marathi. The contextual speech consisted of description of nature or memorable events etc. of community or family life of the speaker. The topics were generally easy and simple for the speaker to think instantaneously and interact and the speech was usually conversational and quite varied. The interview was started with some questions to know about the personal information of the speaker such as his/her name, age, education, profession, etc. The data was recorded with 10 repetitions except for the contextual speech. Corpus is designed into single training segments of 30s, 60s, 90s and 120s durations and single testing segments of 1s, 3s, 5s, 7s, 10s, 12s and 15s in order to find the performance of the system for various training and testing durations [HT04]. Recent work in data collection and corpus design for forensic applications is reported in [JHC+04].

2.2.   Features Used

In this work, different state-of-the-art system features such as Linear Prediction Coefficients (LPC), Linear Prediction Cesptral Coefficients (LPCC), Mel Frequency Cepstral Coefficients (MFCC) are used for different ASR tasks [GMAD], [D A94]. In addition to this, several newly proposed feature sets such as Teager Energy Based MFCC (T-MFCC), Subband Based Cepstral Coefficients (SBCC), Wavelet Packet Cepstral Coefficients (WPCC) are also explored for ASR.

2.2.1.   SBCC and WPCC

Even though state-of-the-art feature set, viz., Mel Frequency Cepstral Coefficients (MFCC) is extensively used for speaker recognition, it has got following drawbacks and hence this motivates one to investigate other feature sets [EAY], [Hem05], [RBJ98]:

1. In MFCC, the filterbank is implemented with triangular filters whose frequency response is not smooth and hence may not be suitable for noisy speech data.

2. The implementation of triangular filterbank requires critical band windowing (in frequency domain) or critical band filter banks (in time domain) which are computationally expensive as it does not involve any multirate signal processing.

3. For computing the spectrum, Discrete Fourier Transform (DFT) whose resolution is constant in time and frequency is used in MFCC. The local changes in time-frequency plane will therefore not be highlighted very much in MFCC; this in turn will give less inter-zonal variability. Thus, speaker classification may not be satisfactory.

2.2.1a Wavelet Packet Transform
Wavelet packets (WP) were introduced by Coifmann, Meyer and Wickerhauser [RYM] by generalizing the link between multiresolution approximations and wavelet bases. The detailed wavelet analysis is discussed in [I D], [S M89], [S M99]. For implementing Wavelet Packet Cepstral Coefficients (WPCC), wavelet transform of log-filterbank energy is taken (rather than DCT as in case of SBCC) to decorrelate the sub-band energies. Fig. 2 shows block diagram for implementation of SBCC and WPCC.

2.2.2.   Teager Energy Based MFCC (T-MFCC)

Recently, Teager energy based MFCC has been proposed by Patil and Basu for twin identification problem [Hem05]. And it was felt desirable that it should be also employed for mimic recognition problem. Traditional methods of extraction of MFCC-based features involve Mel-spectrum of pre-processed speech, followed by log-compression of sub-band

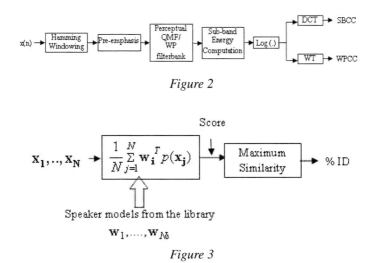

Figure 2

Figure 3

energies and finally DCT computation [SP80]. For the computation of T-MFCC, we employ Teager Energy Operator (TEO) for calculating the energy of speech signal. T-MFCC differs from the traditional MFCC in the definition of energy measure, i.e., MFCC employs energy in frequency domain (due to Parseval's equivalence) at each subband whereas T-MFCC employs Teager energy in time domain [FAE], [Hem05].

2.3.   Polynomial Classifier

In this report, polynomial classifier of 2nd and 3rd order approximation is used as the basis for all the experiments. Due to Weierstrass-Stone approximation theorem, polynomial classifiers are universal approximators to the optimal Bayes classifier [WKC02], [RPD]. The basic structure of the classifier is shown in Fig. 3. They are processed by the polynomial discriminant function. Every speaker i has as his/her model, and the output of a discriminant function is averaged over time resulting in a score for every [WKC02]. The score is then given by,

$$S_i = \frac{1}{N} \sum_{i=1}^{N} w^t p(x_i) \tag{1}$$

where $x_i = i^{th}$ input test feature vector
w = speaker model
p(x) = vector of polynomial basis terms of the input test feature vector.

Training polynomial classifier is accomplished by obtaining the optimum speaker model for each speaker using discriminatively trained classifier with mean-squared error (MSE) criterion, i.e., for speaker's feature vector, an output of one is desired, whereas for impostor data an output of zero is desired.

3.   Experimental Results

In this report, four different features, viz., LPC, LPCC [B S74], MFCC [SP80] and T-MFCC [Hem05] are employed in the experiments on the ASR system for various tasks and operating modes. For all the experiments, the dimension of the feature vector is kept as 12. Feature analysis was performed using a set of frames, each of 23.2 ms duration with an overlap of 50%. A Hamming window was applied to each frame and subsequently, each frame was pre-emphasized with the filter (1-0.97z-1). Pre-emphasis is a smooth high pass filtering process applied to each speech frame, which emphasizes high frequency components and de-emphasizes low frequency components, i.e., sharp/sudden changes in articulation are boosted up. This is also used to reduce the effect of the transfer function of the glottis and thereby track changes solely related to the vocal tract. Thus, pre-emphasis helps one to concentrate on articulator dynamics in speech frames and hence it is useful for tracking the manner in which the speaker pronounces a word. The experiments were performed for different durations of training such as 30 s, 60 s, 90 s and 120 s of approximately 2582, 5164, 7746, and 10328 frames. No data reduction technique or averaging was done. Majority of the experiments are performed over two major evaluation factors, viz., training (TR) speech durations (ranging from 30 s, 60 s, 90 s and 120 s) and testing (TE) speech durations (ranging from 1 s, 3 s, 5 s, 7 s, 10 s,12 s and 15 s). Average (Av.) success rates are computed over testing speech durations. Results for mono-lingual and cross-lingual ASR for Indian and European languages are reported in a companion paper [HPTa].

3.0.1.   Results for Multilingual Speaker Identification

In this experiment, database of 4 speakers from each of Marathi (M), Hindi(H), Urdu (U), Bengali (B), Tamil (TA), Telugu (TL) and German (GE), i.e., all together 28 speakers is considered [HPT06a]. Table 1 shows average success rates for different feature sets (FS), viz., LPC, LPCC and MFCC with 2nd order polynomial approximation whereas Tables 2 and 3 show confusion matrices (diagonal elements indicate % correct identification in a particular linguistic group and off-diagonal elements show the misidentification) for Marathi (M), Hindi (H), Urdu (U), Bengali (B), Tamil (TA), Telugu (TL) and German (GE) for the first set of population, i.e., 28 speakers. In Tables 2 and 3, ACT represents the actual language of the speaker and IDENT represents the identified language of an unknown speaker. Some of the observations from the results are:

1. Average success rates for all the three feature sets are almost equal.

2. Confusion matrices for MFCC are having all off-diagonal elements as zeros, meaning that all the speakers in a particular linguistic group are identified or misidentified in their respective language only. Confusion matrix for LPCC is slightly worse than MFCC.

TR/FS	30s	60s	90s
LPC	89.79	89.28	89.27
LPCC	88.77	85.71	86.21
MFCC	89.79	89.79	89.79

Table 1.: Average success rates for multilingual exp Marathi (m), Hindi (h), Urdu (u), Bengali (b), Tamil (ta), Telugu (tl) and German (ge).

IDENT/ACT	M	H	U	B	TA	TL	GE
M	100	0	0	0	0	0	0
H	25	75	0	0	0	0	0
U	25	0	75	0	0	0	0
B	0	0	0	100	0	0	0
TA	0	0	0	0	100	0	0
YL	0	0	0	0	0	100	0
GE	0	0	0	0	0	0	100

Table 2.: Confusion matrix for LPCC (tr=90s and te=15s)

IDENT/ACT	M	H	U	B	TA	TL	GE
M	100	0	0	0	0	0	0
H	0	100	0	0	0	0	0
U	0	0	100	0	0	0	0
B	0	0	0	100	0	0	0
TA	0	0	0	0	100	0	0
YL	0	0	0	0	0	100	0
GE	0	0	0	0	0	0	100

Table 3.: Confusion matrix for MFCC (tr=90s and te=15s)

3.1.   Results for Speaker Identification of Professional Mimics

In this section, results (i.e., average success rates) are reported on mimic recognition task for real and fictitious experiments [HPT06b]. Other studies in mimic recognition are reported in [G R74], [GT], [RA], [J E], [A E]. For real experiments, the training template contains the normal voice of professional mimic and 7 real target speakers whereas testing template contains the mimic's imitations for 7 real target speakers, his normal voice and normal testing voices of the 7 real target speakers. For this experiment, the success rates are found by counting the number of mimic's testing voices correctly identified as mimic's normal voice plus number of correctly identified target speakers' normal testing voices and mimic's normal testing voice, i.e., during recognition process, a total of 7+1+7=15 testing segments are compared with 1+7=8 training segments. Results are shown in table 4. It is

TR/FS	30s	60s
LPC	**98.09**	**99.04**
LPCC	**100**	**99.04**
MFCC	99.04	99.04
TMFCC	94.28	97.14

Table 4.: Average success rates (%) for real experiment with 2nd order approximation (Hindi mimic)

TR/FS	30s	60s	90s	120s
LPC	**57.14**	**58.43**	**59.08**	**61.03**
LPCC	**62.98**	**64.28**	**66.23**	**65.58**
MFCC	50.64	49.34	49.34	50.66
TMFCC	27.26	26.61	27.26	27.91

Table 5.: Average success rates (%) for fictitious experiment
with 2nd order approximation (marathi mimic)

clear from the results that the LP based features (i.e., LPC and LPCC) performed slightly better when compared with the filterbank based ones (i.e., MFCC and T-MFCC).

For fictitious experiments, the training template contains the normal voice of professional mimic and 22 imaginary target speakers whereas testing template contains the mimic's imitations for 22 imaginary target speakers only. For this experiment, the success rates are found by counting the number of mimic's testing voices correctly identified as mimic's normal voice, i.e., during recognition process, a total of 22 testing segments are compared with 1+22=23 training segments. The results are shown in Table 5.

Some of the observations from the results shown in table 5 are as follows:

1. LPC model gives 50-60% average success rates for almost all the cases of training durations.

2. The performance of MFCC is also very high but it proves to be less effective than LPC and LPCC model whereas T-MFCC does not perform so well. Its success rate is in the range of 30%.

3. It is evident from tables 4 and 5 that there is a significant difference between the results for real and fictitious experiments. This may be due to the fact that fictitious experiments have relatively larger number of comparisons between the testing and training segments. Moreover, the mimic employed in Hindi is an actor famous for his comic role in movies whereas for mimic Marathi is an extremely skillful one who has performed 2000 mimic experiments through one act play. So he is getting more success in acceptance by the system as compared to Hindi mimic.

4. On the whole, filterbank-based features such as MFCC and T-MFCC do not perform well as compared to LP-based features for this problem. This is contradictory to

the result in normal ASR where filterbank-based features perform better than LP-based features [D A94]. To validate this, we have performed a pilot experiment for speaker identification in which the testing and training template contains normal voice mimic and target speakers. It was observed that for 30s training duration, the average success rate for LPC was 96.42% whereas for MFCC it was 98.20%. Filterbank based features could not perform well for mimic recognition which may be due to the fact they are based on the human perception process and also the concept of energy (of the speech frame) involved in these models. So, when the mimic is performing, human perception process (in turn MFCC and T-MFCC features) will perceive these as the voice of a person whose voice the mimic is imitating. Hence the chances of misclassification will go up with these features.

5. LP-based features perform well in this problem, because LPC model represents the combined effect of vocal tract (formant frequencies and their bandwidths and thus in turn emphasizes the formant structure more dominantly), glottal pulse and radiation model and in turn the physiological characteristics of mimic's vocal tract. So even if mimic is imitating other person's voice to fool human perception process (so to the features based on it, viz., MFCC and T-MFCC), he cannot change his/her physiological characteristics of the vocal tract which are known to be nicely tracked by LP based features. So, in the testing phase, LP based features track these properties dominantly as compared to filterbank based features and hence outperform MFCC and T-MFCC feature sets in the identification process.

Results reported in table 4 and 5 are justified by finding Mean Square Error (MSE) between testing and training feature vectors for two cases, viz., case 1 represents MSE between mimic'c imitations for target speakers and his normal voice whereas case 2 represents MSE between mimic'c imitations for target speakers and normal voice of the target speakers and these results are reported in table 6 that for case 1 LP- based features show very less error between testing and training feature vectors compared to filterbank based features whereas LP-based features show relatively very large error (% jump of 91 % for LPC and 66.62% for LPCC) for case 2 as compared to filterbank-based features (18.16% for MFCC and 42.79% for T-MFCC). Thus, LP-based features show close match between mimic's imitations for target speaker and his normal voice and strong discrimination between his imitations and target speaker's voice. This may be due to the fact that LP-based features emphasize formant structure dominantly whereas in case of filterbank-based features formant peaks are blunted/distorted due to the averaging process in Mel frequency warping.

3.2.   Results for Speaker Classification

The problem of speaker classification (SC) can be defined in different ways [HFR]. We define SC as grouping of the speakers residing in a particular dialectal zone based on their similar acoustical characteristics of speech. Such problem may be useful in forensic science applications such as in identifying a criminal's place of origin or in anthropological study of social ethnic group. The feasibility of solution to the problem lies on the fundamental

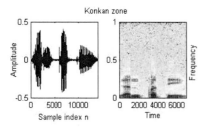

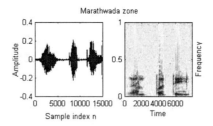

Figure 4a   Figure 4b

FS/AV.MSE	LPC	LPCC	MFCC	TMFCC
Case1	0.1433	0.1405	140.05	11.03
Case2	1.7161	0.4211	172.05	19.28
%jump	**91.65**	**66.62**	18.16	42.79

Table 6.: Analysis of results shown in tables 1-2 through overall (over 429 frames) MSE

fact that the parts which principally determine model (we refer model for describing similar acoustical characteristics of speech from a dialectal zone) are the vocal cavities and articulators. A still greater factor in determining the voice uniqueness is the manner in which the articulators are manipulated during speech. The articulators include the lips, teeth, tongue, soft palate, and jaw muscles, and the controlled dynamic interplay of these results in intelligible speech which is not spontaneously acquired by infants. It is a studied process of the imitation of those who are successfully communicating. The desire to communicate causes the infant to accomplish intelligible speech by successive steps of trial and error [L G]. So our claim is that in this process of imitation, speakers residing in a particular dialectal zone will have similar dynamic use-patterns for their articulators which will be reflected in their spectrograms. Thus, if we bring an infant from zone Z1 and bring him up in zone Z2, then at an adult stage he will have articulators use pattern similar to that of zone Z2 but not the zone Z1. Fig. 4 shows speech corresponding to the word, 'Ganpati', (chosen because it has nasal-to-vowel coarticulation and hence it is highly speaker and possibly zone specific) spoken by two rural males from each of Konkan, Marathwada and Vidharbh zones. It is a very commonly used word. Subjects were asked to read the word, 'Ganpati', with ten repetitions and third repetition was selected as the test sample. It is clear that there are distinct dialectal differences in speech spectrograms of males from different zones. SC task can be performed in closed set or open set mode depending upon whether training and testing classes are same or different. In this report, the problem of closed set and open set speaker classification is addressed in text-independent mode on the database prepared in realistic noisy environments from six distinct dialectal zones of Maharashtra, viz., Konkan, Kolhapur, Pune, Vidharbh, Marathwada and Khandesh in an Indian language, viz., Marathi. Following sub-section discusses this work.

3.2.1.   Results for closed set speaker classification

During training phase, 12 MFCC, 12 SBCC and 12 WPCC feature vectors were extracted per frame from the training speech as per the details discussed in section 2.2 and 3. SBCC and WPCC were extracted with Daubechies wavelets of 6 vanishing moments (db6). These 12 dimensional feature vectors are fed to the classifier for model training. The classifier builds up model for each dialectal zone for different training durations such 30s, 60s, and 90s by averaging polynomial coefficients of the feature vectors of 21 speakers for each zone. During testing phase, 12 MFCC, 12 SBCC and 12 WPCC feature vectors were extracted per frame from the testing speech of the same speakers (closed set) and score for each unknown speaker is computed against stored voiceprints of each dialectal zone. Finally, an unknown speaker is assigned to a zone whose score gives maximum value. The results are shown in Table 7 and 8 as average success rates for different training (TR) durations. Tables 9 and 10 show confusion matrices (diagonal elements indicate % correct identification in a particular dialectal zone and off-diagonal elements show the misclassifications) for Konkan (KN), Marathwada (MW) and Vidharbh (V) zone. In tables 9 and 10, ACT and IDENT represents actual dialectal zone and identified zone, respectively [HPT05]. Some of the observations from the results are as follows:

1. WPCC performed better than MFCC in majority of the cases of training speech durations.

2. As the number of dialectal zones increases, success rate decreases in all the type of feature sets.

3. WPCC showed better class discrimination power as compared to MFCC.

3.2.2.   Results for open set speaker classification

During training phase, 12 MFCC, 12 SBCC and 12 WPCC feature vectors were extracted per frame from the training speech as per the details discussed in previous section. SBCC were extracted with Daubechies wavelets of 6 vanishing moments (db6). Table 11 and 12 show average success rates for different training (TR) durations. Tables 13 and 14 show confusion matrices (diagonal elements indicate % correct identification in a particular dialectal zone and off-diagonal elements show the misclassifications) for Konkan (KN), Marathwada (MW), Vidharbh (V) and Khandesh (K). In Tables 13 and 14, ACT and IDENT represents actual dialectal zone and identified zone, respectively [HPTb].

Some of the observations from the results are as follows:

1. Average success rates improve slightly for 3rd order approximation as compared to 2nd order approximation (Tables 11 & 12).

TR/NZ	30s	60s	90s
2	66.19	66.19	69.04
3	42.54	40.63	41.27
4	43.09	43.33	44.76
5	42.47	44.00	46.28
6	39.36	45.55	48.41

Table 7.: Average success rates for MFCC with 2nd order approximation

TR/NZ	30s	60s	90s
2	**76.66**	**93.33**	**91.42**
3	**49.84**	**61.90**	**59.68**
4	51.66	55.00	40.00
5	32.57	33.90	33.90
6	26.82	27.93	27.93

Table 8.: Average success rates for WPCC (db6)with 2nd order approximation

IDENT/ACT	KN	MW	V
KN	**6.66**	0	93.33
MW	0	0	**100**
V	0	0	**100**

Table 9.: Confusion matrix for MFCC with 2nd order approximation for 3 zones

IDENT/ACT	KN	MW	V
KN	**80**	6.66	13.33
MW	0	**0**	**100**
V	0	**0**	**100**

Table 10.: Confusion matrix for WPCC (db6)with 2nd order approximation for 3 zones

TR/FS	30s	60s	90s	120s
MFCC	**64.28**	**63.09**	**63.94**	62.92
SBCC(db6)	62.07	62.75	59.35	58.67
WPCC(db6)	**65.98**	**65.47**	**66.66**	**66.66**

Table 11.: Average success rates (%) for 2nd order approximation (open set sc-marathi)

TR/FS	30s	60s	90s	120s
MFCC	61.22	57.99	61.90	63.09
SBCC(db6)	61.22	60.54	61.39	61.39
WPCC(db6)	**66.32**	**65.13**	**67.51**	**67.85**

Table 12.: Average success rates (%) for 3rd order approximation (open set sc-marathi)

ACT/IDENT	KN	MW	V	K
KN	0	0	9.5238	90.476
MW	0	61.905	38.095	0
V	0	9.5238	90.476	0
K	0	0	4.7619	95.238

Table 13.: Confusion matrix for MFCC With 2nd order approximation for 4 zones

ACT/IDENT	KN	MW	V	K
KN	0	0	0	100
MW	0	33.333	66.667	0
V	0	0	100	0
K	0	0	0	100

Table 14.: Confusion matrix for SBCC (db6)IV With 2nd order approximation for 4 zones

2. For 2nd order approximation, WPCC performs better than MFCC in majority of the cases of training speech durations whereas MFCC performs better than SBCC.

3. For 3rd order approximation, SBCC and WPCC both perform better than MFCC in majority of the cases of training and speech durations whereas MFCC performs better than SBCC.

4. SBCC showed better class discrimination power as compared to MFCC in majority of the cases of speaker classification.

5. The Konkan dialect has been misclassified as Khandesh by a large degree.

6. Low level of success rates are probably due to the use of different microphones for training and testing in realistic situations and loss of individual's identity in averaged characteristics of feature set.

4.   Summary and Conclusions

ASR is the use of machines to identify or verify a person's voice or classify his/her dialectal zone. In this report, an investigation on different case studies of ASR is reported for Indian and European languages during 2004-2006. The major contributions of the IIT-K team are as follows are as follows:

1. Specialties of ASR for the multilingual and cross-lingual mode as compared to their mono-lingual counterpart.

2. Investigation on effectiveness of LP-based features over filterbank-based features for identification of professional mimics in Indian languages.

3. Extension of conventional ASR problem to speaker classification in closed set and open set on rural subject in Indian language, viz., Marathi.

5.   Acknowledgements

The authors would like to thank the authorities of IIT Kharagpur, EU-India CultureTech Project and BCREC, Durgapur for their support to carry out this research work. They also thank Prof. Jana Dittmann, Dr. Claus Veilhauer, Dr. Bogert and Dr. Andrea Del Mastio for their kind help during manuscript preparation for various research publications during EU-INDIA CultureTech project.

Bibliography

[A E]   A E Rosenberg. Automatic speaker verification: A review. *Proc. IEEE, vol. 64, pp. 475-487.*

[B S74]   B S Atal. Effectiveness of linear prediction of the speech wave for automatic speaker identification and verification. *J. Acoust. Soc. Amer., vol. 55, no.6, pp.1304-1312,* 1 1974.

[CTJP]   C Vielhauer, T K Basu, J Dittmannn, and P K Dutta. Finding metadata in speech and handwriting biometrics. *Joint work with A.D. Rosa, S. Schimke, B. Yegnanarayana, J. Hansen, EU-India Culture Tech Poster.*

[D A94]   D A Reynolds. Experimental evaluation of features for robust speaker identification. *IEEE Trans. Speech Audio Processing, vol. 2, pp. 639-643,* 1 October 1994.

[EAY]   E Erzin, A E Cetin, and Y Yardimci. Sub-band analysis for robust speech recognition in the presence of car noise. *Proc. Int. Conf. Acoustics, Speech, and Signal Processing, ICASSP95, vol.1, pp. 417-420.*

[FAE]   F Jabloun, A E Cetin, and E Erzin. Teager energy based feature parameters for speech recognition in car noise. *IEEE Signal Processing Lett., vol. 6, pp. 259-261.*

[G R74]   G R Doddington. Speaker verification-final report. *Tech. Rep., Rome Air Development Center, Griffiss AFB, NY, RADC 74-179,* 1 1974.

[GMAD]   G R Doddington, M A Przybocki, A F Martin, and D A Reynolds. The nist speaker recognition evaluation-overview, methodology systems, results, perspective. *Speech Commun., vol. 31, pp. 225-254.*

[GT]   G D Hair and T W Rekieta. Mimic resistance of speaker verification using phoneme spectra. *J. Acoust. Soc. Amer., vol. 51, p. 131(A).*

[Hem05]   Hemant A Patil . Comparison of sub-band cepstrum and mel cepstrum for open set speaker classification. *Speaker recognition in Indian languages: A feature based approach, Ph.D. Thesis, Department of Electrical Engineering, IIT Kharagpur, India,* 1 2005.

[HFR]   H Jin, F Kubala, and R Schwartz. Automatic speaker clustering. *Automatic speaker clustering.*

[HPTa]   Hemant A Patil, P K Dutta, and T K Basu. Evaluation of non-technical meta data for speech, eu-india culture tech poster.

[HPTb]   Hemant A Patil, P K Dutta, and T K Basu. The wavelet packet based cepstral features for open set speaker classification in marathi, in studies in classification, data analysis, and knowledge organization. *Springer-Verlag, Berlin Heidelberg, Germany, pp. 134-141.*

[HPT05]   Hemant A Patil, P K Dutta, and T K Basu. Speaker classification using wavelet packet based features. *Presented in EU-India Culture Tech Workshop, IIT Kharagpur,* 1 November 2005.

[HPT06a] Hemant A Patil, P K Dutta, and T K Basu. Effectiveness of lp based features for identification of professional mimics in indian languages. *Int. Workshop on Multimodal User Authentication, MMUA06, Toulouse, France,* 1 May 2006.

[HPT06b] Hemant A Patil, P K Dutta, and T K Basu. On the mono-lingual and cross-lingual speaker identification in indian and european languages. *New Advances in Multimedia Security, Biometrics, Watermarking and Cultural Aspects, Florence, Italy, 23 ? 24,* 1 October 2006.

[HT04]   Hemant A Patil and T K Basu. Multilingual speech corpus design for speaker identification in indian languages. *Int. Workshop Standardization of Speech Database, Oriental COCOSDA 04, Noida, Delhi, India,* 1 November 2004.

[I D]   I Daubechies. Ten lectures on wavelets. *SIAM, Philadelphia, PA.*

[J E]   J E Luck. Automatic speaker verification using cepstral measurements. *J. Acoust. Soc. Amer., vol. 46, pp. 1026-1031.*

[JHC+04]   J P Campbell, H Nakasone, C Cieri, D Miller, K Walker, A F Martin, and M A Przybocki. Speaker recognition with polynomial classifiers. *The Speaker and Language Recognition Workshop, Odyssey 04, Toledo, Spain, pp. 29-32*, 1 May 2004.

[L G]   L G Kersta. Voiceprint identification. *Nature, vol. 196, no. 4861, pp.1253-1257, Dec. 29.*

[R N02]   R Norton. The evolving biometric marketplace to 2006. *Biometric Technology Today, pp. 7-8*, 1 October 2002.

[RA]   R. C. Lummis and A. E. Rosenberg. Test of an automatic speaker verification method with intensively trained mimics. *J. Acoust. Soc. Amer., vol. 51, p.131 (A).*

[RBJ98]   R Sarikaya, B L Pellon, and J H L Hansen. Wavelet packet transforms features with application to speaker identification. *IEEE Nordic Signal Processing Symp., pp. 81-84*, 1 1998.

[RPD]   R O Duda, P E Hart, and D G Stork. Pattern classification and scene analysis. 2nd edition. *Wiley-Interscience.*

[RYM]   R R Coifman, Y Meyer, and M V Wickerhauser. Speaker recognition with polynomial classifiers. *Wavelet analysis and signal processing, in Wavelets and Applications. Boston, Jones and Bartlett. B. Ruskai et al. editor, pp.153-178.*

[S M89]   S Mallat. A theory for multiresolution signal decomposition: The wavelet representation. *IEEE Tran. Patt. Anal. And Mach. Intell., vol. 11, no. 7, pp. 674-693,* 1 1989.

[S M99]   S Mallat. A wavelet tour of signal processing. *2nd Edition, Academic Press,* 1 1999.

[SCP+04]   S Schimke, C Vielhauer, P K Dutta, T K Basu, A De Rosa, J Hansen, J Dittmann, and B Yegnanarayana. Cross cultural aspects of biometrics icpr 04, cambridge, uk. biometrics: Challenges arising for theory to practice. *BCTP Workshop Cambridge,* 1 August 2004.

[SP80]   S B Davis and P Mermelstein. Comparison of parametric representations for monosyllabic word recognition in continuously spoken sentences. *IEEE Trans. Acoust., Speech, Signal Processing, vol. ASSP-28, no.4, pp. 357-366,* 1 August 1980.

[WKC02]   W M Campbell, K T Assaleh, and C C Broun. Speaker recognition with polynomial classifiers. *IEEE Trans. Speech Audio Processing, vol. 10, no.4, pp. 205-212,* 1 May 2002.

Legal Chances and Restrictions in International Research Projects

Jan Hansen, Katharina Selmeczi

Contents

Abstract

The workpackage "Legal Aspects of DRM and Biometrics" provides basic information about copyright, data protection and probative force of electronic documents.

1   Copyright

1.1   General Provisions

Copyright is a part of the big field of Intellectual Property. Intellectual Property protects two main types of intellectual creations.

One main type is Industrial Property with different kinds of special sections. Under Patent all kinds of new technical inventions are protected after a formalised registration procedure. Patents on compurter-programms are intensly discussed at the moment, for example; if business processes should be patentable and if there should be patents on trivial software solutions. Trademark means all kind of signs, word-combinations and symbols used for identification in commerce, so that the origin of goods or services can be distinguished. The second main type of intellectual property is Literary and Artistic Property, this covers novels, drama, film, and the Fine Arts. Here we find copyright law [Adr03].

Copyright law has to balance a fundamental conflict. We find a legal expression of this conflict in the Declaration of the Human Rights which was passed by the United Nations in 1948:

Art. 27 (1) Everyone has the right freely to participate in the cultural life of the community, to enjoy the arts and to share in scientific advancement and its benefits. (2) Everyone has the right to the protection of the moral and material interests resulting from any scientific, literary or artistic production of which he is the author.

These ideas have international acceptance, many countries agree to them. But how are these abstract ideas transported into daily life? They go through several steps of concretion. The first step to give life to these ideas was the conclusion of international multilateral treaties. One of the first and most important of these treaties is the Berne Convention. It was founded in 1886; in 1998 there were 157 member states. In order to this treaty, the members agree on basic standards for the protection of literary and artistic works. Each member state agreed to form their national law system in accordance to the convention. Participating countries give up a part of their identity to cope with the provisions of other nations. That can only work, if the convention describes at least a common denominator. Here we can find the General Provisions of copyright which guarantee a wide range of protection. Productions in the Scientific Domain are protected too, this covers also computer programs, printed and acoustic learning material and - as in our case - e-learning material. The protection of a work is granted, whatever may be the form of its expression.

The word expression is crucial to understand the concept of copyright: Only the concrete expression of the idea is protected, not the underlying ideas or concepts. Here is an example: If you were the first person to write a spelling check programm, you would have no rights in the concept of the program, that checks spelling; you would only have rights in the actual program that you had written. However, if you copy even a few lines of a program written by someone else, this could be copyright infringement. But in this field are a lot of dark zones. Where is the border between the underlying idea and the concrete form? The more a structure of work is determined by the subject matter, the nearer you are to the underlying ideas. It is difficult to know exactly where a court will draw the line. To be protected, the original work must have a certain individuality. If it is only an assembly of information which is created just out of the structure of the subject matter, there is no individuality and no copyright protection. If you have a list of participants in an e-learning course, the layout could be a standard MS word table. There is no individuality, so the list is not protected by copyright.

A work is protected in each member country according to national rules and according to the provisions of the Berne Convention Art. 5 (1). If countries have a different level of protection, it can happen that a work is protected in one country but not protected in another country. The reasons for this situation are different levels of originality to get protection. To avoid this, the Berne Convention contains the Country of Origin Rule, Art. 5 (4) as one of the most important attempts to secure at least a minimum level of protection. With this background, a work is protected, even if the work is published in a non-member state, if the author is a national of a member state.

There are two kinds of rights which are granted to the right-owners: Moral Rights and Economic Rights. Moral Rights are indefensible, they can not be transferred. They are connected to the author's personality. The main moral rights are the Claim of Authorship and the Objection to Modifications. These rights are applicable, if two conditions are met: A use of a work must have the character of a mutilation or a derogatory action, or the use infringes the authors honour or reputation. The Economic Rights grant the economic exploitation of a work. In contrast to the Moral Rights they are transferable, they can be bought or sold like objects and ownership can change. For example, the ownership of the object changes with the fulfillment of a purchase contract. In the beginning, the seller is the owner, in the end, the buyer becomes the owner. The same can be done with Economic Rights in copyright. Economic Rights are: Translation (Art. 8) Berne Convention, Reproduction (Art. 9) Berne Convention and Adaption or Arrangement (Art. 12) Berne Convention.

There is a special connection between Moral Rights and Economic Rights: In many countries in Europe the Moral Rights remain with the author, even after the transfer of Economic Rights. So owners of Moral Rights and Economic Rights can be different persons.

As a matter of principle, the author(s) of the work are protected (Art. 1 (6) Berne Convention). The basic rule is: authors are the first owners of copyright. The author must be a national of a member state (Art. 3 (1 a) Berne Convention), but in some cases even nationals of non-member states are protected. If they have published their work for the first time in a member state, or if they are publishing simultaneously in a member state and a non-member state they are protected. A work can be published in a legal way only with the consent of the author. If a work is published without the consent of the author, it is an infringement of the author´s copyright.

The author or owner of the right decides how a work may be used, this is guaranteed by Art. 27 (2) Declaration of Human Rights. This is a concentration of rights in a person or an institution. Such a concentration could be the death of free information flow, which we need in science. Every use would need the consent of a rightowner. Fortunately there are exceptions and privileged fields where no consent is necessary. In these fields protected works can be used without the consent of an owner of the rights. One of these fields is scientific research. We will find these provisions in the national law systems later on. The next main aspects that we have to consider, are connections between copyright and internet. In general, we can say that the rules apply in the same way to the internet. One feature of Internet seems to strengthen the idea of a world without rules: free access. Many websites have no access restrictions. The conclusion we could draw from this is: Free access means free use. But that is not necessarily so. You can compare this situation with bookshops in Germany where shelves of books are put out on display on the sidewalks. Every by-passer could get the impression that they can take a book home without paying for it. But that does not mean that each by-passer is entitled to do so. Of course they have to pay first. The same rules apply for the internet: free access does not automatically mean free use.

How can you know, whether a website component is protected or not? The well known copyright-sign © can help us. But the use of this symbol does not automatically create protection. The symbol means, a work is registered as a copyrighted work. Registration is granted only to such works, which have sufficient individuality and can be considered as an original work. In a court procedure there will be no conflict about this question and a quick decision can be achieved. A quick decision can be crucial in cases of intense ongoing infringement. But this is US law. In Germany and Italy there are no formalized registration procedures. Nevertheless, a © sign can be useful as a hint also in systems without registration procedure.

1.2   European Community

The law system of the European Community sets the framework for the law systems in Italy and Germany, so there is the need to have a look at this basic system. The European Community is based on several multilateral contracts, the first was closed in 1952. Today, 25 countries are member states; with their accession they gave up a part of their souvereignity and declared their consent to impliment the legal settings of the European Community into their national law systems [Han01] The central provisions for European Copyright are in the Directive of the Europen Community, Nr. 29 of the year 2001. Its title is Directive on the Harmonisation of certain Aspects of Copyright and Related Rights in the Information Society. The aim of this directive is the promotion of learning and culture by protecting works. In the recitals of the directive its aims are exemplified. For our purpose the following aim is important: The online service is a matter of authorisation (Nr.29). There is no total freedom. In our e-learning scenario this seems to erect borders. But there is an exception (exception means that protected works may be used without consent). This exception covers educational and scientific research purposes. There is a second exception we have to consider, because online material is a part of our subject matter. The exception includes issues of distance learning (Nr. 42). Now we are prepared to have a closer look at the directive. The directive obliges the member states of the Eurpoean Community to grant to their nationals an exclusive right to authorise or to prohibit the reproduction of their works in any form (copies in electronic form, on paper, temporary or permanent) by Art. 2. Also copying by communication to the public (by wire or wireless) is a right granted by the directive (Art. 3). This making available right is tailored to cover online access. Typical for online presentation is that members of the public get an access to works from a place and at a time chosen by them. Here are differences to the traditional right of communication to the public: The traditional right covers concrete events like broadcasting sessions or publication of books. The new making available right is not bound to a certain event any more. The next exclusive right is the distribution of a work (Art. 4). This right covers sale, rent or licensing of a work. The owners of these rights authors, performers (to this group also belong lecturers in respect to recordings of their lectures: They shall be entitled to control the exploitation of the recording), producers and broadcasting organisations; publishers also can be the owners of the rights. Some subject matters are out of scope. They are not covered by the copyright directive. These subject matters are computer programmes (Art. 1) - they are covered by the seperate directive 91/250/EEC- and data bases (Art. 1), which are also covered by the seperate directive 96/9/EC. We will discuss these directives later. Now we focus on the copyright directive which obliges the member states of the European Union to protect teaching material like text, tables, pictures, sketches and slides. As we already discussed, the concrete expression is protected, underlying ideas and principles are not protected. If we consider the situation so far, we see that there are exclusive rights which give a high amount of control to the rightholders. This control could severly block free information flow, which would be dangerous for research work. To prevent this danger, the directive provides exceptions to the excluse rights. The member states may provide exeptions (Art. 5), but they are not obliged to do it. An exception to the Reproduction Right, Art. 5, 2. (c) can be established for educational institutions and for educational purposes but not for commercial advantage, neither direct, nor indirect. Direct commercial advantage means to have commercial advantage out of the sale of the teaching material. Indirect commercial advantage is given, if a further-education department of a company does not sale their teaching material to employees, but uses it to qualify the employees. The qualifying takes place to increase the company´s profit. Therefore no exception is granted.

Here we see a main principle in copyright: If someone gets commercial advantage out of a work, the rightowncr shall share the profit. So commerial profit blocks the exception of use without consent. We should pay special attention to industry-founded projects. The applicability of the exception depends on the nature of the results. If the results can be used freely in research and teaching then they are within the exeptions scope. If the results belong to the industry, they are bought like a commodity. They are not open to teaching and research, there is no room for an exception. Exceptions to the rights of reproduction, communication to the public, making available, Art. 5, 3. (a) are granted in teaching or scientific research, if copyrighted works are used as illustrations for scientific discussions. If there is also a source indication with the name of the author or rightowner the use is justified by the exception. An additional interesting topic is the Digital Rights Management (DRM). The copyright directive provides also information about the handling of digital rights management systems.These provisions also have the structure of a rule with exceptions. The rule (Art. 6, Nr. 1) says, that the member states shall provide legal protection for technological measures, which prevent copying (e.g. copy protecion on a music CD). The target of copyright protection has changed here: Not the works are subject matter of the protection, now technological measures themselves are protected. Technology to cirumvent these protecting measures may not be used. Therefore any action connected to circumvention technology is forbidden: neither the import, nor the distribution is allowed, it is not allowed to sell or rent copies or to make advertisements. This protection of digital rights management systems could be again a block against free information flow in science. But there is again an exception (Art. 6, Nr. 4): Member states shall take appropriate measures to make the work available for the beneficiary of an exception. So scientists get the right to access protected material and the rightholder gets an obligation to grant access.

Databases are protected by the Directive 96/9/EC on Legal Protection of Databases. The scope is the protection of databases in a twofold way: As the author´s own intellectual creation by copyright protection and as an object of finacial investment by the Sui Generis Right protection. Sui Generis means 'right out of itself' and is independant from the traditional requirements of copyright. It has an own commercial character. Any financial investment in obtaining, verifying and presenting content is protected. Subject matter of data base protection is the organisation of content; the form in which it is presented, not protected is the content itself. Author of a database (Art. 4) is the person who created it, in most cases, there is a legal person as rightholder but national law describes cases, in which a legal person (company, university, research institute) can be rightholder as well. The rightholder has several exclusive rights out of copyright (Art. 5). These are: the display to the public, reproduction in any form - permanent or temporary - in whole or in part, alterations, translations and distributions of copies in any form. All which may be done, only with concent of the rightholder. But there is a limitation of these exclusive rights (Art. 6, 2 b) for teaching and scientific research, if the source is indicated and if there is no conflict with normal exploitation. There is a similar structure for rights connected to the Sui Generis Right. The owner of the right (PR Nr. 41) is the producer of the database, this could be a natural or legal person who takes the risk of investment. A special right (Art. 7/ PR Nr. 41) prevents unauthorised extraction and re-utilisation of the database. Exceptions (Art. 9) are made for the use for teaching and scientific research, if the source is indicated and there is no conflict with normal exploitation. The most important result for this project, is that there are exceptions for teaching and scientific research, which allow access within reasonable limits.

The next focus is on provisions for Computer Programmes and the Council Directive 91/250/EC on the Legal Protection of Computer Programmes. Art. 1 sets the same copyright protection as for literary works. Computer programs are protected as author´s own intellectual creation and again, there is no protection for underlying ideas. If a group of authors has developed the program, the exclusive rights are owned jointly (Art. 2, 2). What is covered by these exclusive rights? First, the permanent or temporary reproduction - that covers loading, displaying, running, transmission and storage -, the translation, adaption, arrangement - that covers any other alteration -, distribution and rental - that covers the original or any copy of the program. This utmost wide range of exclusive rights is a reaction in the fact, that computer programs can be copied so easily. In the first step an utmost amount of control is granted to the rightholders. On the other hand, the simple use of a program can be blocked by these provisions. Therefore exeptions exist also here. No authorization is necessary if a lawful acquirer (Art. 5, 1) in accordance with intended use makes a backup copy (Art. 5, 2). It is also possible to determine underlying principles and ideas of a program without consent of the rightholder (Art. 5, 3). Even a decompilation can be legally covered, if it is done for the purposes of obtaining information which are necessary to achieve interoperability with an indepently created computer program. The decompilation must be performed by the licensee or an authorised person. The results may not be used for other goals and may not be disseminated. Also the development of a competing product is forbidden.

1.3   National Law Systems Germany, Italy, India

The first countries to look at are Germany and Italy because the law systems of these countries are governed by the European Community provisions. Afterwards specific rules in India can be understood better. German Copyright Act (Urheberrechtsgesetz - UrhG) was passed in 2003. The European Copyright Directive had to be implemented in German law. Works with a certain individuality which are different from other works in the same field are protected (Sec.1UrhG). The making available right is set in Sec. 19a UrhG. There are special provision for works on internet servers: already the act of making available works by storing them on an internet server is a right which belongs to the author or rightowner. It doesn´t matter wether a work is percieved by someone else. The duration of copyright is set in Sec. 64 UrhG, it lasts for the authours lifetime plus 70 years after his death. There are exceptions for science and research in Sec. 52 a I Nr. 1 UrhG, which fall upon university lectures. It is allowed to make published works (part of long work or a complete short work) available for participants in a lecture or to use it for research (Sec. 52 a I Nr. 2 UrhG). But if an author does not wish to publish a work, this wish must be respected. Sec. 52 a IV UrhG anchors remuneration for the author, which are collected by collecting societies. Universitites negotiate periodically with collecting societies the remuneration in lump sums, to negotiate a concrete sum in every case would be too complicated.The way how to make quotations is set in Sec. 51 Nr. 1 UhrG, it is mandatory to obey quotation rules. There are also provisions for Digital Rights Management devices. The subject matter of protection is not the expression of an idea in a work (Sec. 95 a (1) UrhG) but the protection devices themselves like a copy blocker. Sec. 95 a (3) UrhG is ruling in connection to circumvention devices, that the use, advertising, import or sale of technical protected works under the UrhG is forbidden.

Exceptions for science and research are made in Sec. 95 b UrhG, but there are limits, which have to be respected. Even for science there is no right to hack, the user has the obligation to request the rightowner for an opening of the protection measures. Computer programs receive a special treatment in copyright, they are specially protected in Sec. 69

a UrhG because they can easily be copied and have a distributed technical nature. There is a peculiar exposure to illegal copying and illegal distribution. There is a wide range of rights for the rightowners, which are described in detail in the exclusive rights for authors and rightowners. In short they cover the reproduction, transient or durable ones in which form and for which purpose whatsoever. On the other hand there are explicit rights for lawful users to clear the border between legal and illegal activities. The connection between rightowners and users are mainly ruled by contracts. But there are also rights granted to the user by law, a rightowner can not revoke them, i.e. the making of a back-up copy and the study of basic ideas and principles. This belongs to the basic rule in copyright that the concrete expression is protected, but the underlying idea not, according to the agreement with the rightowner. Decompilation is allowed, if it is necessary to reach interoperability with other programms. Also in Germany a database is protected in two different ways. Copyright protected databases must be original works. The rightowner controls the use of the database and use is only permitted with the consent of the owner. The second way is, the way of investment protection. Here, the originality of the work does not matter, only the considerable effort for the creation of the work matters (like working time, money). But here are exceptions for science too. Within the limits of necessity, without commercial purpose, for own research, for lessons in universities and research institutes and if normal exploitation is not affected, the use of dababases is permitted.

Because of the European Community background, a lot of rules - even the structures of the law - in Italy are rather simular to the german law. The European Copyright Directive was implemented in Italy into the law about protection of author rights and other rights in connection, which was executed in 2004. The protected works are i.a. literary works, texts, computer programs, pictures, grafics, animations etc. (Art. 2). The right to make a protected work available to the public (Art. 16) covers the storage of a work on an internet server. The duration of protection is defined by the lifetime of the author plus 70 years, which is the same duration like in Germany. Also in Italy, there are exceptions for the use of a copyrighted work. For purposes of science and research Art. 70 (1) permits to use parts of a work in scientific discussions within justified limits as far as the regular exploitation is not affected and there is no commercial purpose behind. As an example of the affection of regular exploitation, the LAN on a university campus can be taken. One textbook can be bought, scanned and used exclusively on wireless LAN, but if this is done systematically by a central body of the university, this would be an affection of regular exploitation. Art. 70 (3) states that the information must be in quotations.

In Italy the rules for technical protection measures for digital rights management (DRM) may be used by rightowners, Art. 102/4. Access rights for science and research are settled in Art. 71/5 (2). A written application must be negociated with the Permanent Copyright Consulting Committee. There are disputes from the whole nation about this committee, because of bureaucratic delays. There are no users representatives in the committee because a conflict of interest may arise. There are permanent discussions about the role of the committee.

Art. 71/5 (2) settles a reimbursement for the rightholders. Technical protection measures may be used by rightowners (Art. 102/4), scientists can get access under certain conditions.

The conditions for access for science and research are a bit harder in Italy than in Germany.

For computer programs, there are the same considerations as in Germany: The technical nature of computer programs - special dangers by copying and distribution - ask for a wide range of control of reproduction, transient or durable in which form, for which purpose whatsoever. On the other hand, there are the usage rights. They are fixed mainly by an agreement between rightowner and user. A written contract helps to avoid misunderstandings. Some rights have to be granted to the user in every case, like the back-up copy and the study of basic ideas and principles. This is limited by the rule, that only the using of the program in a way according to the agreement with the rightowner is permitted. Decompilation to reach an interoperability with other programs is allowed, but results of the decompilation can not be use for other purposes or transfered to others, and it is not allowed to develop competitive products. Also in Italy there are two ways of data base protection: the copyright protection in Art. 1 (protection as an original work) and the investment protection in Art. 102/2 (where originality does not matter, only the amount of work and time for the creation of the database must be considerable). A wide range of control is set in Art. 64/5. Because of the technical nature of data base the situation is similar to the protection of computer programs. The exceptions for science (Art. 64/6, para 1a) are mainly the same as in Germany.

In India, the Copyright Act was passed in 1957 and amended by act No. 49 of 1999 [T. 02]. With regard to protected works, there is no difference to the provisions in Italy and Germany (Sec. 13). The rightowner controls the publication, be it by issuance of copies (books) or by communicating a work to the public (internet server) (Sec.3). The duration of protection is shorter than the 70 years in Europe; it lasts only 60 years after the death of the author (Sec. 22). There are also provisions for science and research, which are settled in Sec. 52 (1) (a) (i). Copyrighted works may be used without consent of the rightowner, but in the interest of fair dealing, the limits of use we already know from the European Community are applicable also here: Copyrighted works may be used only within justified limits; without the affection of regular exploitation and without any commercial purpose. But this exception does not cover computer programs. In India, special dangers arise out of the technical nature of computer programs. India is a multilingual country where translations get a special importance. Therefore, there are special provisions for computer programs in Sec. 32 (1A) (4) (ii) (2). There are no exeptions for science and research, Sec. Sec. 52 (1) (a) (i). Usage rights which are independant of a consent exist in a structure similar to Europe: Back-up copies may be created, Sec. 52 (1) (a) (aa) (ii), the study of underlying ideas and principles is granted in Sec. 52 (1) (a) (ac) and decompilation for limited purposes is allowed in Sec. 52 (1) (a) (ab). It is also set as a rule, that the export of computer programs, without consent of the rightowner is prohibited. But there is an exception for exports with a science and research background. For scientists outside of India, who use one of the Indian languages, computer programs may be exported. The provision Sec. 52 (1) (p) is applicable for reproductions of unpublished works. Reproduction is allowed in institutions to which the public has access, if the purpose is research and it happens 60 years after the author's death. This long period has been set up to respect the author's wish not to publish the work. Regarding to the DRM, there are currently no legal provisions in India. Provisions corresponding with the rules in Europe are planned. In India, databases are protected, if they have the quality of an orignal work with enough individuality. If a data base does not reach a certain level of individuality, it is not protected by copyright. There is no investment-bound database protection besides copyright protection like the Sui Generis Right in Europe, so the threshold for data base protection is higher in India than in Europe.

2   Data Protection

2.1   General Provisions

Data protection law has to balance interests which are mutually exclusive. On the one hand, there are the interests of scientists who need access to information, this is crucial for their work. On the other hand, individuals want to controll their personal information to protect themselves. Consequently, both position can not be judged as completely wrong, there is no optimum which suits both sides perfectly. So a compromise which realizes as much of both positions as possible has to be found [Pet04]. Only personal data is protected by data protection law. Personal data is information related to a natural person, like data about health (psychic deseases), economic (income, real estade details), culture (membership in a certain ethnic group) and social dates (membership in trade unions). Data is personal data, if it identifies an individual. That can happen directly or indirectly. If several parts of information form a chain which leads to the idenficiation of a person, the parts of the chain can be personal data. A certain information can be non-personal data, if it is isolated and does not lead to an indiviual. If it becomes part of an idenfifcation chain, the information changes its nature and can become personal data.

To non-personal data data protection rules are not applicable, they are not in the scope of data protection and can be used in greater freedom. One kind of non-personal data are anonymize data. Data are anonymized, if there is no connection between an information and an individual person, e.g if no name, address or telephone number is mentioned. In this case the reader of a publication would not know which indivduals were involved in a data collecting process. Direct or indirect identification would be impossible. There are two levels of anonymization: utterly anonymization and factual anonymization. In the first case, identification of individuals is not possible, in the second case, identification would be possible, but it would be extremly complex or disproportionally time-consuming. In consequence, data protection law is not applicable in both cases.

But even if the result of the anonymization process is out of the scope of data protection, the process itself is within the scope. So there is a need to look on the anonymization process. Data protection rules are applicable as far as personal data are processed. If they are separated from processing, data protection rules are no more applicable. The next general rule tells us that personal data which are not longer needed must be extinguished completely as early as possible. One of the main problems of data protection is the file-keeping for the verification of research results. Here, the private interest of extinguishing data affects the scientific interest of conservation. To find a well-balanced solution, a consideration of values has to be conducted. Such a consideration of values is a typical approach to solve legal problems: To sort out a conflict of mutual diverging interests, the private and scientific interests must be weight against each other. The first step consists in finding arguments for both parties. Aspects weighing for private interest are a high exactitude of collected personal data, a small number of steps to identify the individual and a large scale of collected data. Apects weighing in favour for scientific interest are a necessity of personal data for research result. A high intensity of public interest and a code of conduct in the scientific community that research results must be checkable. In a second step the arguments must be balanced: Which arguments are stronger? If personal data should be kept for verification it will depend on the circumstances of the special case, even for the Culture Tech Project no general statement is possible. Each single processing of personal data was scrutinised. The result was a specific consent form, which is used within the project. Another way to bypass the data protection rules is the pseudonymization of personal data. Personal data are displaced by other data after a rule of displacement. A name could be displaced by a number code or by fantasy names like Donald Duck or Peter Pan. The connection of pseudonymized data to individual person is cognisable by applying the rule of displacement.

2.2   European Community

The European Conmmunity sets a legal framework for Italy and Germany. It is fixed in the Directive 95/46/EC of the European Parliament and of the Council on the Protection of Individuals with Regard to the Processing of Personal Data and on the Free Movement of such Data. A wide range is defined. What we do within the Culture Tech Project is within the scope of the directive. So the directive must be checked closer. Art. 7 tells us in which cases processing of personal data is in compliance with the law: Unambiguous consent, contract, legal obligation, vital interest, task in public interest, and other legitimate interererests. This list does not contain what applies to this project. We are looking for a privilege for science which allows us to process data without any restriction.

The most rigid provision of the directive concerns the processing of sensitive data. Art. 8 says that the member states shall prohibit processing in the cases of racial and ethnic origins, political opinions, religious or philosophical beliefs, trade-union membership and information about health and sexuality. For this project, health and sexuality could be a barrier, because facial and speech recognition is concerned. The directive demands a set of information to be given to the individual, this can be found in Art. 10. The individual must be informed about the purpose of processing, the recipients of his data and about details of access to his data. A controler of personal data can be sued to provide information to the individual.

Art. 11 concerns information that is not obtained from the individual. The consequences are similar, it does not matter whether personal data was obtained from the individual or from another source, e.g. database of a health insurance company. The individual has the right to object under certain circumstances at anytime. This right to object is only given on compelling legitimate grounds, e.g.: data is not correct or the processing of data is not any more legitimate. The data individual must be informed about this right and about the restrictions of the right.

The member states are authorized by the Data Protection Directive - when justified by grounds of important public interest - to derogate from the prohibition of processing sensitive categories of data where important reasons of public interest so justify in areas such as scientific research - recital Nr. 33. This sentence contains important information for the considerations of values applied to this problem. Scientific research is an important reason of public interest, which can justify an exeption from the prohibition of processing personal data. The Preliminary Consideration Nr. 39 gives us an additional assistance: It is not necessary to impose this obligation if the provision of information proves impossible or involves disproportionate efforts, which could be the case where processing is for scientific purposes. Now, the way out of the trap has to be checked closer. The most dangerous kind of data is sensitive data and as we already know, sensitive data is involved in our project. In the directive are set expemtions even for this data, there are some cases in which the processing of this data is permitted. There is no help in Art. 8 (2) which permitts processing in the cases of explicit consent by individual, employment law, vital interests of the individual and legitimate activities, but there is an additional hole in the protection for sensitive data in Art. 8 (2) in form of a blanket clause. This blanket clause permits the member states to lay down additional exceptions for reasons of important public interest to those laid down in Art. 8 (2) either by national law or by decision of the supervisory authority. If this can help us, it has to be checked later on during the examination of national law. The directive itself states not more than that. The reasons of important public interest will be a topic in national law. Art. 11 (2) covers personal data, which are not sensitive data. An exemption restricts the right of the data individual to be informed about the data processing. According to Art. 11 (2) no information to the individual is required in the case when scientific research is concerned and the provision of information proves impossible or the information of the indivudual involves a disproportionate effort or the recording or disclosure is laid down by law and appropriate safeguards are implemented to ensure the enforcement of the provisions. Member states must ensure that the information-right of the individual is restricted only in the cases written in the provision and not also in other cases. That means, the provions in the national law systems may not create any doubt about the scope of the exemptions. We will see how that works, if we come to provisions in national law. The next exemption concerns the individuals right to access his/her personal data. The access right can be restricted, if - following Art. 13 (2) - the processing takes place solely for the purposes of scientific research and the data is not used for taking measures or decisions regarding any particular individual, for example social insurance contributions may not be increased, because the participation is in a medical research project and shows a higher risk of a certain desease in the future. But an exemption of consent is not given in this provision.

2.3   Germany

The structure of the German national law system has to be explained closer. Germany is a Federal Republic, which is a compound of 16 federal states. Two of these federal states are Sachsen Anhalt (Magdeburg) and Hessen (Darmstadt). The legal framework is set at federal level, the details at state level. The legal framework is the Bundesdatenschutzgesetz (BDSG), this is the data protection law at federal level. Details are set in the Landesdatenschutzgesetz, this is the data protection law at state level. In German national law we find again the system of rule and exeption. The general rule is: Processing of personal data is forbidden. The exeption is: In specific cases processing is legitimate [Her05].

§ 4 Bundesdatenschutzgesetz (BDSG) provides us with the rule, that creation, processing and exploration of personal data is only allowed if this law or another statutory instrument permits it. That is not what we need for our project. The exeption which could help is laid down in § 40 BDSG concerning the processing of personal data by research institutes. Creation and internal use of personal data is legitimate if the purpose is scientific research. Personal data must be anonymized and pseudonymised as early as possible. These provisions are similar to the European Community Data Protection Directive. The publication of personal data is only legitimate, if there is a written consent of the individual. The legislation in Germany can not go beyond the European Community framework, so there is no exemption in case of publication. The reason is that publication is the most intensive danger for privacy, so the requirements are high [PR05]. These are the facts. In legal theory there are arguments in favour of our wish: The law provides an exemption of consent for scientific publications about events of historical impact. This excemption is granted because it would be impossible to do research on historical events without using personal data of the protagonists. It is wrong to convey an exemption only to this research area, because there are other research areas, which have the same nature like medical research or research concerning biometric data. But this is only legal theory. There is no judgement of a court in Germany which grants such an additional exemption. So we have to consider the consent a bit closer. The Bundesdatenschutzgesetz tells us more about the consent. The consent must be unsolicited and unambigouous, the rule is again, that there must be a written consent of the individual (§ 4a I BDSG). But there is an exeption: The consent must not be written, if it is for the intention of research and this purpose is gravely affected by the requirement of written permission (§ 4a II BDSG). In our project we would not need a consent if our work would be gravely affected by obtaining a consent. This would be the case if objective time constraints in our work would make it impossible to get a consent in time. In our project we evaluate personal data of people in interviews. This situation allows us to get the consent before an interview starts. So the exeption is not applicable in our project. The personal data created in the project do not affect important secrets of the involved states. So this additional way to the exception is also blocked. We must get the consent otherwise the individual could block the use of his or her data. § 27 Data Protection Law Sachsen-Anhalt says that the processing of personal data is legitimate if the purpose is for scientific research. Anonymisation and seperation has to take place as early and far as possible. The transfer is allowed among research for scientific purposes and also publication is legitimate if there is a consent or an event of actual historical impact is the research topic. But transfer does not cover publication [Jür]. There are special rules for publication we already know. The Federal State Law of Sachsen Anhalt may not grant more freedom than the Federal Law. There are different solutions in other German Federal States, but we can not use these solutions because the rules are only applicable in the involved federal states.

2.4   Italy

The Italian Personal Data Protection Code (passed by June 30. 2003) contains interesting provisions. Sec. 100 affects Data Concerning Studies and Researches. This Provision sets a rule for Universities and Research Institutions. They may create and process personal data by autonomous decision. Personal data may be communicated and disseminated to Graduates, Post-Graduates, Technicians, Engineers, Researchers, Professors, Experts, Scholars without consent of the individual.

This freedom is granted for the use of experts and scholars for personal data. But there is also sensitive data, which is excluded from this freedom. So we have to look further for regualtions concerning sensitive data. Sensitive data is also defined in the Italian Personal Data Protection Code. Sec. 4)1.d) defines race, ethnic origin, faith, political opinions, membership of parties, trade unions, etc. and information about bealth and sexuality as sensitive data. Processing these data is allowed under some restrictive circumstances. They are applicable for public bodies like universities. In cases expressly authorised by law they may process defined categories of sensitive data in defined categories of operation. There must also be a substantial public interest. High requirements have to be fulfilled. A first hint can be found in Sec. 98 (1.c), which permits the processing of sensiteve data for scientific pupuses, if they are considered to be in substancial public interest. The first requirement (scientific purpose) is already fulfilled in our project, but there are other requirements still open. We need a law, which authorizes processing of sensitive data. One possibility is Sec. 20 (2): The law specifies scientific research as a substancial public interest. So the second requirement is fulfilled for our project. But the law does not specify categories of data and operations. Categories of data and operations meet this requirement, if they are published by a university in form of a code of conduct. This code of conduct must be approved by the Italian Data Protection Authority. The Italian project partner did not negotiate such a code of conduct. So we need a consent in Italy for processing sensitive data.

But this consent is not the only requirement. Sec. 26 (1) Italian Personal Data Protection Code requires the Garante´s prior authorisation (Garante is the short name for the Italian Data Protection Authority). So the requirements are hard: we need both - consent and authorisation. The result is more restrictive than in Germany. As usual, we look for further exeptions. We have to consider Sec. 26 (3) Italian Personal Data Protection Code. There is a list of exemptions - e.g. the processing is necessary to protect a third party´s life or the processing is necessary to comply with obligations laid down by law in the employment context. But the listed exemptions do not apply for Science/Research [Rob06].

2.5   India

Now we come to regulations in India. Currently (Spring 2006), there is no data protection law in India, but there is an ongoing legislation process [Pro06]. A draft version is currently discussed in the Ministry of Communications and Information Technology. Although India did not sign the TRIPSs (Trade Related Intellectual Property Rights) Agreement, planned regulations are designed to be in line with European and US Legislation. One of the reasons for this orientation is the so called "Save Harbour Principle". Any transfer of personal data of EU / USA nationals to third countries is only allowed if the target country meets the EU / USA standards. The background of this legislative develpoment is the fact that European and US companies still hesitate to outsource business processes to India. If the Indian data protection law becomes effective, employees in EU and USA will be globalisation losers and employees in India are globalisation winners. India has a better position in the global low wages competition.

There are other applicable provisions. We find them in the IT Act of 2000. Sec. 72 concerns confidentiality and privacy. It protects electronic records, books, registers, correspondence, information, documents or other material and disclosure. Prior consent is necessary. This section also contains severe punishment rules: Imprisonment up to two years, fine up to Rs. 100.000 - approx. 1.770 Euros - or both.

Now we are at the end of our general view to Data Protection Basics in India, Italy and Germany. The following conclusions can be drawn: We are not as free as we would like to be concerning the processing of Personal/Sensitive Data. The processing of personal data is possible in many cases; the use of sensitive data is bound to prior consent in every case. In the internal field we have more freedom than in the public area. Publication of personal data without consent may not be based on purposes of science and teaching. We need a consent for publication. All that leads us towards a pragmatic approach: Personal and sensitive data should be used as little as possible and in an anonymised form.

3   Probative Force of Electronic Documents

The focus of this part is the role an electronic document can play in an international legal procedure.

3.1   General Provisions

We start with a survey of the functions of evidence. Evidence is every type of statement which helps to prove a fact in trial. Judges or juries have to be convinced. This can be done by oral testimony, objects, pictures or documents. Some types of information are excluded from court procedures, they are non-admissible. Unreliable information like hearsay evidence or an experts opinion based on unaccepted facts are non-admissable. There are other reasons which transform reliable information into non-admissible information. If it is too complex or too costly to present a testimony compared to its value, the testimony becomes non-admissible. This could be for example a witness of an accident who lives far away and did not see the critical phase of the accident. Non-admissible are facts that are gathered by illegal methods, like torture. This 'Fruit of the Forbidden Tree' doctrine is one of the pillars of a constitutional state.

If we consider admissible evidence, we find that there are several kinds of admissible evidence. The circumstancial evidence creates belief by showing surrounding cirumstances which logically lead to a conclusion of fact. The direct evidence creates belief by the presentation of a fact itself. Here we see that the central idea of all kinds of evidence is to create belief and trust. Court procedure takes place after the event which is subject to trial; judges did not see the event themselves. All they have is what they get in the case files and during the trial by presentation of evidence. The result of a court procedure depends not primarily on what has happened, it depends primarily on what can be proved. Therefore trust is a central aspect of evidence. A classical method to create trust is the paper document evidence. It has a traditional form, where content is written or drawn on paper. The content can be fixed thoughts, ideas, obligations, entitlements, etc., which are signed by the responsible person to clarify who is obliged or entitled by a document. Paper documents have two traditional functions: The first function is the fixation of thoughts, ideas, obligations, entitlements, which are expressed in the document. The second function is warning. The person who signs shall become aware of the obligation which comes into existance by signature. The signed paper serves as an identification of the person who is responsible for the fixed content.

How can these principles be assigned to electronic documents? We know that the central aspect of evidence is trust [AZ05]. It is also known that trust is created by two main aspects: integrity (content was not changed) and authenticity (signature by responsible person). Electronic documents must compensate two main disadvantages: There is no original tangible object for a fixation and there is no physical act of signature. The technical measurement for compensation is the electronic signature. Not all kinds of electronic signature are acceptable as a full compensation of a signed paper document.

3.2   European Community

To create an adequate amount of trust, we need an advanced electronic signature, which must be based on a qualified cerificate. The signature must be created by a secure signature creation device.What does this mean for the legal point of view? To answer this question, some rules about legal requirements on trust creating electronic signatures must be checked. Some general requirements can be found in certain European Union directives. The most important is the "Directive 99/93/EC of The European Parliament and of The Council of December 13, 1999 on a Community Framework for Electronic Signatures". The aim of the directive picks up the idea of trust. It shall strengthen the confidence in new technologies (recital 4). This generic goal becomes more strengthen, if you read recital 21: The directive shall contribute to the general acceptance of electronic authentification method and shall ensure that electronic signatures are valid in all member states of the European Union. Electronic signatures shall be used as evidence in legal proceedings.

The scope of this directive does not cover rules about the conclusion of contracts. Rules about contracts can be found in the E-Commerce Dircetive 2000/31/EC. This directive obliges the member states to ensure that contracts by electronic means (Art. 9 / 1) can have the same binding powers as a contract traditionally fixed on paper. Electronic format may not be an obstacle for binding power. To conclude a contract, you need nevertheless binding declarations of the contract partners. This is a basic contract rule in all European countries [Alt05].

Art. 5 I of the Electronic Signature Directive determines that an electronic signature has the same legal effect like a handwritten signature and that it is admissible as evidence. Three requirements must be fulfilled. The first one is the Advanced Electronic Signature. Art. 2 Nr. 2 rules, that it must be uniquely linked to the signatory and it must be capable of identifying the signatory. It must be created by means under the control of the signatory and must be linked to the document that subsequent change of data is detectable. The second requirement for an equation of a digital signature with a written signature is the qualified certification. Features of a qualified certification out of the legal point of view can be found in the Annex I of Electronic Signature Directive. The certificate must contain the indication as qualified certificate, the identification of certification-service-provider, the name of the signatory, specific attributes of the signatory (legal roles a signatory can have like lawyer or custodian), signature verification data corresponding to signature creation data, beginning and end of validity of certificate, the identity code of certificate, the advanced electronic signature itself, limitations to scope of certificate and the limits of financial value of transactions. The third requirement states, that the signature must be created by a secure signature creation device. Annex III of the Electronic Signature Directive determines that there must be appropriate technical and procedural means. These means it must ensure the following features: Signature creation data can occur only once, secrecy is reasonably assured, signature-creation data can not be derived, the signature is protected against forgery, signature-creation data can be protected by the legitimate signatory against others, data to be signed must not be altered, and data to be signed must be prevent from being disseminated prior to the signature process.

The words *reasonable assured* tell us that creation devices must meet the state of the art, but the state of the art is changing permanent, so the requirements for the qualified electronic signature are changing dynamically. The signature must be protected against forgery, so there is a need to use the current available technology [Mau06]

Besides the qualified electronic signature there exist other kinds of electronic signatures, which do not meet the three requirements. Art. 5 II of the Electronic Signature Directive is engaged with these kinds. The most imortant information is that such a signature is still an admissible evidence and that it keeps a certain legal of effectiveness. But the probative force is weaker because it rises higher chances for objections.

The directive defines several additional principles, which all member states have to implement. Some of them are the supervision of certification-service- providers (Art. 3 Nr. 3), the supervision of secure signature creation devices (Art. 3 Nr. 4), the liability of certification-service-providers (Art. 6) and the acknowledgement of foreign certificates (Art. 7).

What has been shown till now is that there is a set of rules which has only one goal: To create trust. There is a system of requirements and control which contains explicit requirements for Signatures, Certificates, and Certification Authorities. There are also defined procedures of control, which are exercised by defined institutions with defined powers. All that has been set up to ensure that electronic documents have the quality of integrity (content has not been changed) and the quality of authenticity (the person which appears as signer is also in reality responsible for the document).

3.3   Germany

In Germany two laws contain the main rules of producing trust. The first one is the Civil Procedure Code (Zivilprozessordnung - ZPO), which concerns is the probative force of electronic documents, the second is the Digital Signature Act (Signaturgesetz - SignG), which settles the rules for certificates, certification authorities and the control of certification authorities. We will start with the Civil Procedure Code (Zivilprozessordnung - ZPO). The main principle is the free evaluation of evidence (Sec. 286 I ZPO). The probative force of an electronic document depends on its power as evidence. Any evidence is as strong as a judge can be convinced. We can see this function of evidence in a well known German proverb saying "On sea and in front of court you are in the hands of god". But a judge can not decide really arbitrarily, he has to establish the reasons for his decision in the judgement, and a judgement can be an attacked in front of a court of a higher instance. An incorrect judgement would be repealed, so a judge must be careful.

But as so often in law there are rules and exceptions. In German evidence law, the rule states the freedom of evidence evaluation (Sec. 286 I ZPO). The exceptions cut this freedom by setting evidence rules (Sec. 286 II ZPO). Here judges are bound to a certain evaluation, they are not free in their decision anymore. Evidence rules are a great help, if you are trying to predict the outcome of a trial. For documents an evidence rule is set in Sec. 416 ZPO. Probative force of private documents is given, if they are written or drawn on paper and are signed by hand. They have full probative force, that the statement was willingly disseminated by the signer. If a plaintiff presents a contract signed by himself and the defendant, this contract binds the judge in one way: The judge must assume that the defendant gave the contract willingly after signature. The judge is not free to assume otherwise. Now let us assume that the defendant was not quite sure whether he really wanted to be bound by the contract, he deposited the contract on his desk to think it over and an employee found the contract, wanted to do his boss a favour and faxed it to the claimant. What is now the legal situation of the defendant? The judge is bound to assume that the defendant gave the contract out of his hands willingly. Only if the defendant can formally prove, that the contract was not given away willingly, he can escape the duties fixed in the contract. This is in short the function of this evidence rule [GP02]. There is a second kind of evidence, we have to consider if we are checking the probative force of documents: the circumstancial evidence. The principles of circumstancial evidences are based on case law, not on statutory law. Case law consists of principles, which are derived out of a lot of judgements. The principle of circumstancial evidence assumes that the text of a document is correct and complete. If an opponent on trial wants to attack this circumstancial evidence he must prove concrete facts, which show that the text of the document is incorrect or incomplete. This rule is only applicable for paper documents.

Given the spreading of electronic documents, it is important to see, how electronic documents are treated within the traditional legal framework. Sec. 371 a ZPO is the central rule for the legal treatment of electronic documents in Germany. For engineers it is of value to know this provision. Is says, that an electronic document with a qualified electronic signature has to be treated like private paper documents. This means, that the evidence rule about giving away a document is applicable. Whoever has an electronic document with an electronic signature of the opponent at hand, is in a good position as far as the question of giving away the document is at stake. Also the case law principle of circumstancial evidence, which says, that the content of a document is unchanged and complete, is applicable. There are two more functions of electronic documents in court procedures. Sec. 126a ZPO requires written form, electronic form is only admissible if it is signed by a qualified electronic signature. An electronic contract in this form concerning the purchase of land would have full evidential power. Sec. 130 a ZPO concerns procedural documents like applications, pleadings, submissions, and expertises. An electronic document is admissible, but its probative force is small. A qualified electronic siganture would increase the probative force to full evidental power.

The Digital Signature Act (Signaturgesetz - SignG) defines requirements on qualified electronic signatures and on the whole procedure of producing, usage and controlling of electronic signatures.

We find a definition of electronic signature in Sec. 2 Nr.1. Electronic signature consists of data in electronic form which are attached or logically linked to other electronic data (document) and which are used for authentication. The advanced electronic signature (Sec. 2 Nr. 2) is exculsively assigned for the owner of the signature code and enables the owner to be identified. It is produced with means under the control of the owner. If it is linked to the document, any subsequent alteration can be detected. The qualified electronic signature (Sec. 2 Nr. 3) is the safest form of electronic signature. It is based on a valid qualified certificate which is produced with a secure signature-creation device. These terms describe the core elements of a qualified electronic signature, they should be explained in detail. Relevant legal requirements to a qualified certificate are defined in Sec. 7 of the Signaturgesetz (SignG). These requirements have more a formal than a technical character: A qualified certificate must include the name or unmistakeable pseudonym of the owner of the signature, the current number of the certificate, start and end of validity, name and state of certification-service provider, limitations to certain applications, declaration as qualified certificate and attributes of the signature-code owner. It must be assigned to the signature-test code. Algorithms for use in signature-test codes must be in control of the signature code owner and certification-service provider. There are also some requirements which aim to the technical features, they are defined in connection with Secure Signature Creation Devices. Secure Signature Creation Devices (Sec. 17) demand, that forged signatures or false signed data could be identified reliably and that there is protection against the unauthorised use of the signature codes. The signature codes must be unique and secret. The storage outside the device must be impossible. The possibility of falsification of time stamps must be excluded.

The requirement of "Identifying forged signatures reliably" must be checked more in detail, because here we have to face one of the big problems in dealing with law: the interpretation of a rule. "Reliable" describes a feeling. The feeling, that something is reliable, comes into existance, if one has the impression that everything which can be done, definitely has been done. This leads us to the next question: Is there a point within the process of designing and manufacturing an electronic product, at which we can say, that everything possible has been done? Such a point may exist theoretically, but not in reality. Therefore the legal requirement of reliability means that all has been done which is within the range of the state of the art. This is enough to fulfill the legal requirement [GPI04]. For a definite assignment of a signature to a document the Secure Signature-Application Components must show (Sec. 17) to which data (document) the signature refers, whether the signed data are unchanged, the signature-code owner, the contents of qualified certificate and attributes, and the result of subsequent check of certificate. These are a lot of requirements. All of them aim to the creation of trust. But how can someone be sure, that these requirements are really fulfilled? By establishing liablitiy of the certification-service providers (Sec. 11). The certification providers are the key players. If the key players can be forced to obey the rules, any user can trust the signatures. So the law states, that the infringement of requirements leads to a reimbursement of third parties damages which were suffered from relying on the certificate or time stamp. The liability is connected to users relying on digital signatures, here we find again the element of trust. And the law provides an additional element of reliablity, the Compulsory Cover (Sec. 12). It imposes appropriate financial penalties, the minimum of damages is set to 250,000.00 EUROS. To get permission to offer qualified signatures, the staff members must show a specialised knowledge (Sec. 4, para 2), this means, they must have sufficient knowledge, experience, and skills. The last point of this survey is about international acceptance of foreign electronic signatures and products for electronic signatures (Sec. 23). All members of the European Union have the same legal requirements concerning hand written signatures, so electronic signature is admissible as evidence in legal proceedings within the European Union. If other countries have legal requirements in the same manner concerning written signatures, they are admissible as evidence in legal proceedings, but the minimum is the advanced electronic signature. All these regulations lead to an enormous infrastructure, which has only one intention: to creat trust [AZ05]. On the other hand: The infrastructure is too big and too complicated for a lot of people. As a result, the advanced electronic signature is not popular in Germany [DMK+06].

3.4   Italy

In Italy, the applicable rules are also spread over a multitude of acts. The most important rules for us are the Italian Codice Civile (CC), where evidence rules can be found, and the decrees implementing the EC Signature Directive. A main principle of this rules is, that the probative value of the electornic signature depends on the kind of signature. Italian law knows the electronic signature as data in electronic form, which is attached to a document as a method of authentication. This is the lowest level, there are no specific requirements for signatures, devices or certificates. The features of the advanced electronic signature are the features described in the EC Signature Directive. The Digital Signature unites the advanced electronic signature with a public key infrastructure [LR04]. We will recognise the core principle of a connection between the quality of a signature and the evidential value in the following evidence rules: An electronic document without a signature does prove facts (free evaluation) but it does not prove the connection between the document and a certain person (Art. 2712 CC). Electronic documents with electronic signatures allow free evaluation of quality and security (Sec. 116 Civil Process Code). The evidential value can be strong or weak; this depends on the circumstances and whether the originality of the document is attacked. An electronic document with advanced or digital signature has the same probative value as a private deed with a handwritten signature (Art. 2702 CC). To assure the security level of the advanced and digital signature, there are several special rules. We start with a decree from the year 2002, when the implementation of the EC Electronic Signature Directive was established. The definitions of electronic signatures, certificates, secure signature creation devices and the accreditation of certifications service providers are set in Sec. 2, all these definitions are according to EC directive and we know them by now. In this decree, further regulations on quality standards for Certification Authorities (Sec. 5), liability of Certification Authority (Sec. 7) and compliance of secure signature creation devices with EC Directive (Sec. 10) can be found. Now we turn to another decree, to the Decree of April 7, 2003 No. 137. It is about the adaption of other rules with connection to the probative force of electronic documents. The following enumeration shows that a national law system is networked to a high degree and that an alteration of rules at one point leads to consequences in other fields: documents in public administration (Sec. 3), payments by telecommunication (Sec. 5) and replacement of seals, punches, stamps, tokens, marks (Sec. 9). All these regulations deal with the validity of electronic documents with advanced digital signatures. This decree covers also the Quality Assurence for Certification Authorities regarding the organisation, the technical equipment, the financial background and the staff. The detailed rules for accreditation are also similar to the rules in Germany. Now we turn to a decree of January 13, 2004. It gives us a set of technical rules concerning the key characteristics (Sec. 4), the generation and storage of keys (Sec. 6,7), information in certificates (Sec. 15), revocation of certificates (Sec. 17), security plans for certification authorities (Sec. 30) and a public list of certification authorities (Sec. 41). All these provisions are similar to rules in the German Digital Signature Act; both laws are compliant with the EC directive on Electronic Signatures. Now we have an idea of the system in Europe and we can turn to India.

3.5 India

Again the most important rules are spread over the legal system, due to its netlike complexion. We find rules, inter alia, in the Information Technology Act and in the Indian Evidence Act. We start with the Indian Information Technology Act, which was passed in the year 2000. It sets the rules for Authentication of Electronic Records (Sec. 3) by affixing the digital signature with a symmetric crypto system and a public key infrastructure. It regulates the Legal Recognition of Electronic Records (Sec. 4) too, which means, that the written form on paper can be substituted by electronic form. This definition of digital signature is similar to the definition of the advanced electronic signature in Europe. But that does not say anything about authenticity. Nothing is fixed, which concerns a signature as a measure to link a certain person to a certain document. This link is decribed in Sec. 5 (Legal Recognition of Digital Signatures) which says, that any electronic document with a digital signature shall be presumed to be of the originator. The legal framework for Certifying Authorities is set in the IT Act too. The requirements on qualification, expertise, manpower, finances and infrastructure can be found in Sec. 21, they are similar to the requirements in Europe. The background is the wish to participate in the international e-commerce. The controller of Certifying Authorities is appointed by the Central Government (Sec. 17), his duty is to supervise the standards of technology, organisation, staff and finances (Sec. 18). Details of the Digital Signature like identitiy of signatory, name of certifying authority, qualification of staff members, etc. are set in Sec. 35-38. We know these details from the rules in Europe.

The Indian Evidence Act was amended in a lot of details. Some examples are electronic records and how they are admissible in court procedures (Sec. 65 B), the secure digital signature, where a connection between an electronic document and the subscriber must not be proved (Sec. 67 A), and the non-secure digital signature, where the court may summon a member of the certification authority or controller as witness (Sec. 73 A). The secure digital signature is defined in Sec. 15 IT Act as a unique fixation, which is capable of identifying the subscriber, who controlls the device. These regulations are similar in Europe. Now we see two examples of legally covered presumptions. In these cases a court has to take a fact as given without further scrutiny. Against the assumption that the contrary can be proved but this would be a duty of the party, not the duty of the court. These presumptions are instruments to reduce the duration and complexity of a court procedure. They are like evidence rules in Europe. For us, the following presumptions are interesting: For the secure digital signature (as defined in Sec. 15) the court assumes, that the electronic record has not been altered (Sec. 85 B) and regarding the Digital Signature Certificate the court assumes, that the information in the certificate has not been changed (Sec. 85 C).

Now you have a survey of regulations on electronic documents in court procedures. The system in India requires the same enormous infrastructure as in Europe. It remains to be seen, whether the further development in India will face the same difficulties as in Germany and Italy. As a result we can see that rules for electronic documents are harmonised to a high degree. We have a comparable legal framework in India and Europe.

4   Virtual Presence in International University Examinations

4.1   General Provisions

In this chapter a concept for replacing the traditional physical presence in university examinations by a virtual presence will be discussed. Due to the highly formal character of university exminations the virtual presence shall be secured and documentated in a way which
leads to legally effective electronic documents. The main aspects that will be elucidated are
the function of physical presence, the legal framework in universities, the document features
oral examinations, and document features written examinations.

The physical presence in oral examinations has several functions. Of course it shall prove the identity of the candidate and the integrity of direct communication. It shall be possible for the examiners to evaluate immediate answers to questions and contributions to a discussion. Examinators shall have the possibility to test the technical and social skills of the candidate. Interaction with the candidate is the basis for evaluation. So a virtual presence in oral examinations is possible, if there is an electronic document, which provides equivalent information to a face to face encounter. The document must provide the impression of the candidate with regard to physical appearence, voice, tempo of activity, clearness, coherence of reasoning and record of the discussion as a process.

Now we should throw a glance at the functions of physical presence in written examinations. The physical presence shall ensure the identity of the candidate and his activity. He/she shall prove that he/she is able to give the defined output within a defined timeframe. The physical presence shall grant equivalent circumstances for all candidates, no one shall enjoy a more helpful environment than the others. The most critical element here is the exclusion of forbidden recources. The electronic document must prove that the candidate had no possibility to get additional information about the subject matter for the written examination. This was the discussion of the functions of physical presence in examinations and a first step to the features which an equivalent electronic document shall provide to cope with these functions.

The next element to be checked is the legal framework in universities, to find out whether an electronic document should provide additional features to comply also with the legal framework.

4.2 Germany

In Germany, there are regulations in several levels, because Germany is a federal state like the US. In the federal level is stated, that examinations have to be formally organised in examination regulations. The states are responsible for setting up the rules. In the state Sachsen Anhalt, of which Magdeburg is the capital, examination regulations are set by the universities in cooperation with the state. These are exam regulations of the Computer Sciences Department of the Magdeburg University: There are two forms of exams (Sec. 4 / 4), a written examination and an oral examination. It is set, that the examiner must be independent and there must be an evaluation of the candidates contributions. So far there are no additional features required for electronic documents. The regulations of the Computer Science Department in Magdeburg concerning written examinations also give us some hints in Sec. 9: The candidate shall prove that he is able to find solutions for problems within limited time and with limited resources. So our electronic document must record start and end of the time slot and it must record and prove that the candidate did use only admissible ressources. There are also some rules for oral exminations in Sec. 9: The candidate shall prove knowledge of the coherence of a subject matter. This should take place in front of an examiner with one or more candidates at a time. The results must be kept in minutes. Out of this rule we can draw the additonal requirement, that also actions of more than one candidate must be recorded and that a protocol must be created. The electronic protocol must provide the same kind and amount of information which is recorded by a traditional paper protocol. There is also a rule concerning international cooperations. (Sec. 7 / 2) requires, that syllabus examination requirements and substance as well as amount of subject matters must be equivalent to German standards. The candidate has a right to read his examination files (Sec. 36) up to one year after the examination.

4.3   Italy

In Italy, a lot of leeway is given to the professors at the University of Florence. The exam regulations leave the details of the procedure to the discretion of the professor. The aim of the examination is the demonstration of knowledge of the coherence of a subject matter. The student has to keep a report book containing the subject, date, mark, signature of lecturer. The examination minutes must include the registration number of the student, the subject, date, mark, questions, arguments and the signatures of examiners. The conservation of documents is again in the discretion of the examiners. It is only stated, that the conservation should last at least up to the discussion with students.

4.4   India

Now we turn to regulations in India, especially to the Indian Institutes of Technology (IIT) Chennai and Kharagpur. The IITs have a more independant status than universities and a more independant status of professors. There are more individual decisions of course instructors concerning the acceptance of exam results and the acceptance of foreign students. First we consider the Exam Regulations in IIT Chennai. As a legal framework there are ordinances, which require (R. 16.0) lecture / tutorial based subject quiz tests, lecture based subject, end semester examination (three hours duration) and project evaluations as a project report and an oral examination. The course instructor is supreme in dealing with the evaluation, there is no fixed procedure. The custody period has a duration of approximatly 6 months, it depends on the decision of the instuctor. These details show us, that the amount of freedom for a professor in IIT Chennai is much higher than in Magdeburg/Germany. In IIT Kharagpur the exam regulations also grant a lot of freedom to professors. There are different densities of formal requirements. The most formal events are the final exams. The regulations are the following: A written examination with physical presence in examination center is required. The candidates have to answer identical questions within a fixed time. The requirements for the mid semester exam are identical, but the teacher chooses the form of attendance, assignment and decides if it is a class test or individual test. There is no duty of custody, exam results must not be kept longer than until the final discussion.

Some general conclusions can be drawn of these facts: Despite of the different density of regulation in India, Italy and Germany, some features can be found, which are common in all project universities. Document features for oral exminations shall provide equivalent information about the impression of the candidate in terms of physical appearence, oral, the tempo of activity and the clearness and coherence of reasoning. Equivalent information about the actions of the examiners and candidates must be granted also. It must be assured, that no additional resources can be used, so there is the need of a prepared room for candidates and a confirmation of correct conditions by staff members of the involved universities. To make the documentation safe, there is a need for audio-video equipment, digital watermarks and an electronic signature of examiner. There is no need of a longterm storage, only short custody periods are required. Now the document features for written examinations have to be checked. The application features for written examination shall provide equivalent information about the impression of the candidate (audio, video), give a reliable identification of the person, the time frame and the exclusion of additional resources. There must be a prepared room for the candidates, and a confirmation of correct conditions by the staff members of the foreign university. While the exam takes place, there must be periodical video and audio checks.

A final conclusion can be drawn: It is theoretically possible to create documents, which preserve those elements for an examination, being necessary to evaluate the candidates contributions and to prove the candidate´s identity. There is no law, which expressly prohibits the substitution of a physical presence by a virtual presence. But the trust-creating power of our electronic documents has to be strong to provide a sufficiant level of reliability.

5   Acknowledgement

The authors would like to thank all project partners for contributing information which made it possible to adapt the presentation of legal aspects close to the projetc partner's needs. The work described in this article has been supported by the EU-India cross cultural program. The views and conclusions contained herein are those of the authors and should not be interpreted as necessarily representing the official policies.

Bibliography

[Adr03]   Adrian Sterling. *A World Copyright Law*. Sweet and Maxwell Publishers, 100 Avenue Road Swiss Cottage, 2003.

[Alt05]   Alty van Luijt. *Beyond DRM: Balancing of Interest, in: Distribution und Schutz digitaler Medien durch Digital Rights Management, Pages 61 - 74.* Number ISBN 3-540-23844-1. Springer, Tiergartenstrasse 17, D-69121 Heidelberg, 2005.

[AZ05]   Andreas U. Schmidt and Zbynek Loebl. *Legal Security for Transformations of Signed Documents: Fundamental Concepts in: Lecture Notes in Computer Science vol. 3545/2005, pp. 255-270.* Number 978-3-540-28062-0. Springer, Tiergartenstrasse 17, D-69121 Heidelberg, 14November 2005.

[DMK+06] Dragana Damjanovic, Michael Holoubek, Klaus Kassai, Hans Peter Lehofer, and Wolfgang Urbantschitsch. *Handbuch des Telekommunikationsrechts.* Number ISBN 3211838953. Springer, Tiergartenstrasse 17, D-69121 Heidelberg, 1 August 2006.

[GP02]   Gerhard Lüke and Peter Wax. *Münchener Kommentar zur Zivilprozeßordnung. Aktualisierungsband ZPO-Reform.* Number 3406484174. C.H. Beck, Wilhelmstraße 9, D-80801 München, 31October 2002.

[GPI04]   Gerald Spindler, Peter Schmitz, and Ivo Geis. *TDG : Teledienstegesetz, Teledienstdatenschutzgesetz, Signaturgesetz ; Kommentar.* Number ISBN 3-406-49548-6. C. H. Beck, Wilhelmstraße 9, 80801 München, 2004.

[Han01]   Hans Georg Fischer. *Europarecht, 3. Auflage.* Number ISBN 3-406-48370-4. C. H. Beck, Wilhelmstraße 9, D-80801 München, November 2001.

[Her05]   Hermann Christoph Kühn. *The Implementation of the Data Protection Directive 95/46/EC in Germany in: Implementation of the Data Protection Directive in Relation to Medical Research in Europe,pages 121 - 140.* Number 0754623696. Ashgate Publishing, Gower House, Croft Road, Aldershot, Hants GU11 3HR, 30January 2005.

[Jür]   Jürgen Ancot. *Sächsisches Datenschutzgesetz, Kommentar.* Number ISBN 3415032000. Boorberg Verlag, Scharrstraße 2, D-70563 Stuttgart.

[LR04]   Luigi Martin and Roberto Pascarelli. Electronic signature: value in law and probative effectiveness in the italian legal system. *e-Signature Law Journal, vol. one, pp. 17-23,* 31January 2004.

[Mau06]   Maurice H. M. Schellekens. *Electronic Signatures: Authenticaton Technology from a Legal Perspective.* Number 9067041742 in IT and Law. Asser Press, P.O. Box 16163, 2500 BD The Hague, The Netherlands, 3 February 2006.

[Pet04]   Peter Carey. *Data Protection: A Practical Guide to UK and EU Law.* Number 0199265682. Oxford University Press, Great Clarendon Street, Oxford ox2 6dp, 6 May 2004.

[PR05]   Peter Gola and Rudolf Schomerus. *Bundesdatenschutzgesetz: BDSG, Kommentar 8. Aufl.* Number ISBN 3-406-49548-6. C. H. Beck, Wilhelmstraße 9, D-80801 München, 2005.

[Pro06]   Probir Roy Chowdhury. Update: India - service tax, data protection and customs rules, pages61 - 62. *Computer Law Review International,* 30 April 2006.

[Rob06]   Roberto Lattanzi. *Processing of Personal Data and Medical/Scientific Research within the Framework of Italy's Legal System in: Implementation of the Data Protection Directive in Relation to Medical Research in Europe, ; pages 193 - 208.* Number 0754623696. Ashgate Publishing, Gower House, Croft Road, Aldershot, Hants GU11 3HR, 30January 2006.

[T. 02]   T. Ramappa. *Intellectual Property Rights Under WTO: Tasks before India.* Number 817544214X. A H Wheeler Publishing, Lal Bahandur Shastri Marg, Allahabad, Uttar Pradesh 21 1001, India, 1 January 2002.

Summary of Research in order to Evaluate Biometrics in Metadata Context

Andrea Oermann, Tobias Scheidat, Claus Vielhauer

Contents

Abstract

In this article the impact of the cultural background of users of multimedial (different types media) and multimodal (different channels) applications such as biometrics is elaborated by summarizing different research studies. Keeping the task in mind that we want to find out if the cultural background of users plays a significant role and has a direct impact on technology, we established differently focussed tests and evaluations. Our evaluations are facing in two directions: On the one hand the impact of metadata on the performance of biometric authentication systems is analyzed while on the other hand deriving metadata from the available biometric data is focussed. Thus, multimedial as well as multimodal applications in a cross-cultural context are benchmarked considering three dimensions: 1. Examining the adaptability of speech- and handwriting based biometric recognition systems towards multiple languages and scripts as well as cultural aspects of end user perception common in the territories of project partners. 2. Combining handwriting and voice technologies in order to improve recognition results. 3. Evaluating in the application domains biometric user authentication and text recognition. These dimensions have to be seen as criteria for the characterization of technologies in respect to their applicability in inter-cultural domains as our target has been in this the EU-India CultureTech Programme [1].

1.   Motivation

Today, a variety of biometric approaches in order to recognize human speech and handwriting by computer systems exists. Applications for these technologies include user authentication and semantic recognition of the written or spoken text. Systems presented in related scientific work are typically designed in context of a specific cultural area, as they are evaluated for a specific language and script type. Research investigations in respect to the supported language and the combinations of both handwriting and speech modalities can rarely be found. This summary gives an overview about published contributions targeting our research investigations and results regarding this the EU-India CultureTech Programme [1]. In order to fill this gap of the inter-cultural domain of India and the European countries such as Italy and Germany involved in the project our work focusses on the following three dimensions:

- Adaptability of speech- and handwriting based biometric recognition systems towards multiple languages and scripts as well as cultural aspects of end user perception similarities in the territories of project partners.

- Combination of handwriting and voice technologies to improve recognition results.

- Evaluation in the application domains biometric user authentication and text recognition.

Furthermore, by focussing on these three dimensions we want to determine criteria for the characterization of technologies in respect to their applicability in inter-cultural domains.

These criteria will be applied to select particularly qualified techniques for the two modalities of handwriting and voice and perform a field evaluation of these techniques. Besides the evaluation of recognition rates, our work also focusses on the problem of language/script recognition, allowing conclusions on cultural origin of the speaker or writer. Furthermore, performing a fusion of handwriting and speech modalities is subject of our research.

We are concentrating on the following goal: We want to elaborate the impact of the cultural background of users of multimedial (different types media) and multimodal (different channels) applications such as biometrics. Here, we want to find out if the cultural background of users plays a significant role and has a direct impact on the technology. One example for this dependency is the area of automated handwriting recognition as a biometric user authentication system.

This article is structured as follows. In section 2, biometric systems and the methodology for evaluating its performance are briefly introduced. In section 3, the classification of metadata and its impacts on biometric authentication systems will be described. A summary of our research results is presented in section 4. The article closes in section 5 with a summary.

2.   Biometrics

This section introduces the research field of biometrics. Biometric authentication systems and their application fields will be outlined as well as a methodology for evaluating their performance will be presented.

2.1.   Biometric Systems

Biometric Authentication Systems are developed in order to provide a rather secure way of accessing certain resources, equipment or facilities, users need to be identified or verified. Basically there are three authentication methods: secret knowledge, personal possession and individual characteristics of a human being (biometrics) [2]. The secret knowledge approach refers to the users knowledge, such as passwords or PINs while personal possession implies the user owning something like a physical key, smartcard or special token. Biometrics provide an authentication method based on the user's individual biometrical characteristics. Biometric techniques are either concerning passive characteristics (fingerprint, face, iris, retina, or hand geometry as physiological modalities), also called traits, or active traits (speech and handwriting as behavioral-based modalities). Active traits referring a characteristic that is learned and acquired over time while passive traits imply rather static characteristic of an individual.

By applying biometric systems, a person can be uniquely identified based on his or her given characteristics instead of needing external information, which can be lost, stolen or handed over. In doing so, biometrics provide a higher level of security especially in digital communication systems.

In a biometric system users get either identified or verified. Basically, unimodal biometric systems, which consider only one source of information to authenticate an individual, are established in common applications. But those systems are often associated with certain problems such as background noise, attacks, overlapping of similarities, and non-universality of biometric characteristics [3]. Hence, the development of multimodal biometric systems, which consider multiple sources of information, is subject of recent research. A biometric

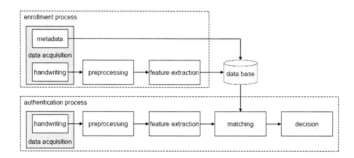

Figure 1.: Biometric user enrollment and authentication (see also [9])

system consists of two steps: the enrollment and the authentication, as presented in Figure 2. At enrollment the biometric parameters of an user's particular attribute are captured and stored in a database, whereby one or more reference signals are captured at time of registration. At authentication a particular user wants to be authenticated by again taking one ore more samples and comparing these data with the stored reference data. The user gets accepted and is allowed to access if the instances of the biometric data match, otherwise the user gets rejected.

The authentication operates in two different modes, the verification and the identification. Verification implies the biometric system confirming or rejecting a particular prior known identity and indicates a comparison of n signal samplings to 1 particular reference storage sampling (1:1 comparison). Identification is a biometric system automatically determining the identity of a particular not known user and indicates a comparison of 1 signal sampling to n reference storage samplings (1:n comparison).

Several approaches for user authentication have been published, but it is just starting to evaluate it regarding cultural aspects such as language, script and personal background of users.

2.2.   Evaluating the Performance of Biometric Authentication Systems

For evaluating biometric user authentication systems regarding verifications and forgeries, the methodology suggested in [4] will be followed. Enrollments, verifications and forgeries are captured in order to estimate the authentication performance of an biometric system. During the enrollment process, the data of users are registered in the system as reference data which can be accessed at any time. Verification samples are taken to simulate an authentication of users by the system. Further, so called attacks are simulated in order to create forgeries and test the performance of the system.

Depending on the strength of the attack, the attacker's knowledge about the the original biometric data and their owners, forgeries are differentiated into four groups.

1. Random attack

2. Blind attack

3. Blind Meta attack

4. Low force attack

5. Brute force attack

The *random attack* is based on all verification data except the data of the examined user him- or herself. In the *blind attack*, the forger only knows the semantics (e.g. signature or name) he or she shall falsify. The low force attack implies the forger's allowance to trace an offline representation of the shape of e.g. a handwriting sample before attacking it. If the forger can rely on the complete available information about the original sample (e.g. the temporal characteristics of position or pressure), the attack is called brute force attack. In addition to the described attacks, a new attack type based on the metadata has been developed by us, which we call blind meta attack. Based on the level of given information, it is ranked between blind attack and low force attack. The forger is provided additional background information about the persons such as for example gender or grade of education before attacking.

The verification data as well as the forgery data is then compared with the reference data in order to determine the error rates of the system and hence, estimate the systems performance. Therefor test groups are usually created based on the metadata. In order to evaluate the performance of an biometric authentication system and being able to compare the results of different tests the equal error rate (EER) is used. EER denotes the point in the error characteristics, where FNMR and FMR yield identical values. The false non match rate (FNMR) indicates the frequency in which authentic persons are rejected from the system and its calculation is based on the comparison of the enrollment and verification data. The false match rate (FMR) represents the acceptance rate of non-authentic subjects. The determination of the FMR is based on the relation of enrollment and forgery data of the different levels. To read more about error rates we refer to [2], [5], or [6]. It needs to be stated however, that the EER does not represent the optimal operating point of a biometric system. The optimal operating point depends on the desired level of the security and/or comfort of the planned biometric system. The indicated test data might not necessarily have a sufficient statistical significance, but it can be used to demonstrate our fundamental procedure, motivate further extensive tests and point out first ideas.

3.   Cultural Context and Metadata

In order to get access to the cultural context of the user of a biometric user authentication system metadata need to be collected. A taxonomy for meta data is presented in [7], where it is divided in two main classes, the technical and the non-technical one. While the technical meta data implies hardware and software parameters, the non-technical meta data addresses the cultural and personal background of a person. An enhanced classification of meta data, as presented in Figure 2, is introduced in [8] and further applied in [9].

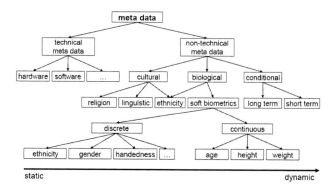

Figure 2.: Classification of metadata (see also [9])

Technical metadata include aspects of the used device or sensor and tool such as hardware and software specifications. Exemplarily, for handwriting sampling technical metadata specify the digitizer tablet and the used pen as well as the used framework, while for speech sampling the used microphone as well as the used framework is indicated. Three classes of non-technical metadata have to be differentiated: One class includes biological aspects of a person such as for example gender, handedness, or age. Those metadata is also described as soft biometric traits in [10] and [11], and refer to continuous or discrete parameters to describe the biological background of a person. Ethnicity can be part of it, but it also refers to the second class of non-technical metadata - the cultural class, which joins religious, linguistic and ethnic aspects together as almost static parameters. The third class of non-technical metadata is determined though dynamic, conditional parameters of a person. This class is divided in the long term metadata (experiences of the past) and the more dynamic short term conditional metadata (emotions, environment of situation, e.g. being nervous, happy, ill, excited, or in a hurry). Our research investigations base upon the goal, to which extend the metadata influences the biometric data during collection.

The reason for meta data being a major focus of recent research in the field of biometric user authentication is their impact to improve the performance of traditional biometric systems. In our investigations we established a double tracked procedure. In order to improve the accuracy and reliability of algorithms for biometric handwriting user authentication systems, we analyze static, as well as dynamic parameters of meta data. Static meta data of the cultural background of a person is collected at the beginning of a sample enrollment, and it is stored as a profile in a data base. Once being collected, this meta data is valid for all upcoming tests, concerning the specified subject. Dynamic meta data of the conditional background of a person is collected through a questionnaire before and after the enrollment.

This meta data includes the experiences of a person, which have been gained during his or her biographic past. These dynamic parameters can significantly change over time. New experiences can be made, old experiences can be forgotten. Short term conditional parameters have a very dynamic characteristic. They can be applied exclusively while data enrollment, since they describe the persons actual condition during recording.

Two goals are aimed to achieve by applying metadata to the biometric authentication: Given the fact, that personal information like age and gender can be statistically estimated by analyzing human handwriting [12], deriving cultural characteristics of a person such as ethnicity, education, and language by statistical or analytical means can also be much of a benefit. The second goal is to evaluate the impact, which certain metadata can have on biometric user authentication systems. Especially the impact of the personal background like culture, spoken and written languages as well as ethnicity on a biometric authentication process wants to be analyzed in order to estimate its accuracy. Further, effects regarding a person's condition during the process of experimental testing can influence the behavioral biometric data such as voice or handwriting. Evaluating these effects is also subject of our research due to their influence as a special class of meta data on biometric handwriting data.

Conditional metadata refer to cross-cultural experiences a person explored in the far or near past, i.e. the persons sojourns abroad, familiarity with given tasks like the person's familiarity with the hardware such as the digitizer tablet and pen and the attitude towards digital biometric systems in general. Also, emotions belong to the class of conditional metadata such as if a person is nervous while capturing the biometric data.

Hence, not only technical metadata but also and especially non-technical metadata seem to be an important aspect which needs to be taken into account when evaluating and developing biometric user authentication systems. Especially in an interconnected world where trustworthy identities need to be provided and biometric authentication systems are gaining more and more importance.

4. Summary of Different Studies

This section is summarizing our different research studies regarding the evaluation of cultural impacts on biometric user authentication systems, which have been developed within the EU-India CultureTech programme [1].

4.1. Finding Meta Data in Speech and Handwriting Biometrics

The goal of this paper [7] was to present results of our research investigations on the analysis of speech and handwriting biometrics related to metadata. A first classification of metadata has been presented, which differentiate technical meta data (system hardware specifications) and non-technical meta data (personal attributes). System related metadata represent physical characteristics of biometric sensors and are essential for ensuring comparable quality of the biometric raw signals. This approach has been developed based on previous work in personal related metadata which has shown that metadata such as script language, dialect, origin, gender and age can be estimated by statistically analyzing human handwriting and voice data.

Making metadata available for the authentication system seem to improve the recognition or authentication algorithm's accuracy. Further, sensor dependency of biometric algorithms in relation to hardware properties such as sampling resolution might be analyzed. Also, cultural background information (such as native language, or ethnicity) might be derived by statistical or analytical means from voice or handwriting dynamics. It needs to be evaluated to which degree grouping of users by persons with identical or similar metadata results in better biometric recognition accuracy. All these aspects have been widely neglected by research until today.

The presented discussion of approaches is focussing on exploring the impact metadata can have on authentication systems. Thus, we might be able to develop strategies in order to find features by introducing a new metadata taxonomy. Further, this paper has been focussed on developing a test methodology used for our experimental evaluation in different cultural regions of India and Europe. First results for sensor hardware related metadata in handwriting biometrics as well as language related metadata in speaker recognition will demonstrate the methodology's applicability.

4.2.   A Cross-Cultural Evaluation Framework for Behavioral Biometric User Authentication

The goal of this work [8] was to analyze cross-cultural aspects of biometric handwriting data. We could rely on our earlier designed and developed a biometric evaluation framework within the CultureTech project which focuses on cultural impacts to technology in an Euro-pean-Indian cross-cultural context. This framework, and in particular its methodology as well as a short outline of evaluation aspects have already been presented in [13]. In this paper evaluation aspects have been enhanced and first three hypotheses of the correctness and usability of biometric user authentication systems for different cultures could be derived.

The first hypothesis implies a person's conditional metadata influence on his or her writing style, especially numbers. A varying typeface of written numbers "1", "7" and "9" could be observed. We found out, that staying abroad not only influences the habit of writing numbers, it also impacts the choices of individual samples and the orthography: English phrases are preferably used. The second hypothesis indicates gender belongings influences. Hence, it could be observed that men have a remarkable higher writing pressure than women while women show a higher pressure variability than men. The third hypothesis also refers to the gender belongings influences. In particular, male subjects showed a much higher writing variability than the female subjects.

4.3. Analyzing Handwriting Biometrics in Metadata Context

In this paper [9] methods for user recognition based on online handwriting have been ex-perimentally analyzed using a combination of demographic data of users in relation to their handwriting habits. The advantage of online handwriting as a biometric user authentication method is its characteristic of being rather relyable and secure due to its ability of capturing a high variation of biometric attributes. Not all of this attributes and its variations have been subject of research investigations. Especially when considering cross-cultural applications, the impact of personal background information of users in relation to security aspects such as integrity and authenticity needs top be elaborated. The personal background is repre-sented by metadata which, as explained into detail before, refer to cultural, biological and conditional (changing) aspects like first language, country of origin, gender, handedness, experiences the influence handwriting and language skills.

Therefore, the goal of this paper has been evaluating the intercultural impacts on handwrit-ing in order to achieve higher security in biometrical systems. Hence, experiments with a relatively high coverage have been developed. 48 different handwriting tasks have been accomplished by 47 users from three countries (Germany, India and Italy). Aligned hy-potheses have been evaluated using the measurement of the well-known recognition error rates from biometrics (FMR, FNMR and EER). Considering differently skilled forgeries, the evaluation has been testing the system reliance as well as security threads. In doing so, we have been able to set up recommendations for specific user groups and handwriting samples.

4.4. Verifier-Tuple as a Classifier for Biometric Handwriting Authentication - Combination of Syntax and Semantics

This paper [14] introduced a new concept for classifying handwriting data whose evaluation is presented in the context of a biometric user authentication system. In general the concept bases on a combination of syntax and semantics. Its applicability has been demonstrated for online handwritings and the user verification. Hence, the benefit of applying information of higher levels of semantics within the authentication process could be shown. In par-ticular, we demonstrated our concept on the Biometric hash algorithm [2] and test results have shown that by integrating additional knowledge as an additional parameter into the authentication algorithm, its performance could be improved.

5. Summary

Summarizing all of our research investigations it can be stated that we have been able to contribute promising approaches and evaluations. This has shown, that not only metadata and its integration into authentication systems such as biometrics seem to be promising.

But also it is possible to derive metadata as additional information which is not directly included in the captured signals such as biometric data of a certain modality. This can also be much of benefit in other research areas such as e.g. forensics [15], E-Technologies [16] or archiving where aspects of IT-Security (integrity, authenticity).

In particular, behavioral biometrics are major subjects in this research field due to its advantage of providing an additional factor of time which can be analyzed. Therefore, the focus of present and future work lies for example in analyzing the synchronization of two different biometric modalities such as for example handwriting, speech and face. Here, we have been able to develop a methodology (*Semantic Fusion for Biometric User Authentication as Multimodal Signal Processing* [17]) in order to demonstrate that knowing additional semantic information may help the synchronization or fusion of different modalities of biometric authentication system. The presented theoretic methodology now needs to be translated into practice and tests need to be set up in order to evaluate it.

Our present research investigations are further focussing on not only deriving non-technical but also technical metadata from the captured biometric data, such as automatically determining the used device (tablet and pen regarding handwriting, or microphone regarding speech) ([18]).

In general, it can be said that with our research we have been able to detect and evaluate tendencies as well as to specify directions in analyzing multimedial and multimodal applications in a cross-cultural context as the three dimensions have outlined our goals in the motivation:

- Adaptability of speech- and handwriting based biometric recognition systems towards multiple languages and scripts as well as cultural aspects of end user perception common in the territories of project partners.

- Combination of handwriting and voice technologies to improve recognition results.

- Evaluation in the application domains biometric user authentication and text recognition.

Closing this summary, it can be outlined that we have been able to determine criteria for the characterization of technologies in respect to their applicability in inter-cultural domains as our target has been in this the EU-India CultureTech Programme [1].

6.   Acknowledgements

The information in this document is provided as is, and no guarantee or warranty is given or implied that the information is fit for any particular purpose. The user thereof uses the information at its sole risk and liability. The work described in this article has been supported in part by the EU-India cross cultural program (project CultureTech, see [1]) and partly by the Federal Office for Information Security (BSI), Germany. The work on developing test methodologies and handwriting algorithms has been supported in part by the European Commission through the IST Programme under Contract IST-2002-507634 BIOSECURE. The views and conclusions contained herein are those of the authors and should not be interpreted as necessarily representing the official policies, either expressed or implied, of the Federal Office for Information Security (BSI), or the German Government, or the European Union.

Bibliography

[1] The Culture Tech Project, Cultural Dimensions in digital Multimedia Security Technology, a project funded under the EU-India Economic Cross Cultural Program, http://amsl-smb.cs.uni-magdeburg.de/culturetech/, last requested September 2005

[2] C. Vielhauer: Biometric User Authentication for IT Security, Advances in Information Security. Vol. 18, Springer, New York ISBN: 0-387-26194-X, 2005

[3] A. Ross, A.K. Jain: Multimodal Biometrics: An Overview. Proceedings of the 12th Euro-pean Signal Processing Conference (EUSIPCO), Vienna, Austria, 2004, pp. 1221–1224

[4] F. Zoebisch, C. Vielhauer, A Test Tool to support Brut-Force Online and Offline Signature Forgery Tests on Mobile Devices. In: Proc. of IEEE International Conference on Multimedia and Expo 2003 (ICME), Baltimore, U.S.A., Vol. 3, 2003, pp. 225–228

[5] C. Vielhauer, T. Scheidat: Multimodal Biometrics for Voice and Handwriting. In: Jana Dittmann, Stefan Katzenbeisser, Andreas Uhl (Eds.), Communications and Multimedia Se-curity: 9th IFIP TC-6 TC-11International Conference, CMS 2005, Proceedings, LNCS 3677, Salzburg, Austria, September 19 - 21, 2005, pp. 191–199

[6] T. Scheidat, C. Vielhauer: Fusion von biometrischen Verfahren zur Benutzerauthentifikation. In: P. Horster (Ed.), D-A-CH Security 2005 - Bestandsaufnahme, Konzepte, Anwendungen, Perspektiven, 2005, pp. 82–97

[7] C. Vielhauer, T. Basu, J. Dittmann, P.K. Dutta: Finding Meta Data in Speech and Handwriting Biometrics. In: Proceedings of SPIE-IS&T. 5681, 2005, pp. 504–515

[8] F. Wolf, T.K. Basu, P.K. Dutta, C. Vielhauer, A. Oermann, B. Yegnanarayana: A Cross-Cultural Evaluation Framework for Behavioral Biometric User Authentication.: From Data and Information Analysis to Knowledge Engineering. In: Proceedings of 29 Annual Conference of the Gesellschaft für Klassifikation e. V., GfKl 2005, University of Magdeburg, Germany. Springer-Verlag, 2006, pp. 654–661

[9] T. Scheidat, F. Wolf, C. Vielhauer: Analyzing Handwriting Biometrics in Metadata Context. To appear in: SPIE Proceedings - Electronic Imaging, Security and Watermarking of Multimedia Contents VIII, 2006

[10] A. K. Jain, et al.: Soft Biometric Traits for Personal Recognition Systems. In: *Proceedings of International Conference on Biometric Authentication (ICBA)*. Hong Kong, LNCS 3072, 2004, pp. 731–738

[11] A. K. Jain, et al.: Can soft biometric traits assist user recognition?. In: *Proceedings of SPIE Biometric Technology for Human Identification*. Orlando, FL, U.S.A., 5404, 2004, pp. 561–572

[12] C. I. Tomai, D. M. Kshirsagar, S. N. Srihari: Group Discriminatory Power of Handwritten Characters. In: Proceedings of SPIE-IS&T Electronic Imaging, 2004, pp. 116-123

[13] S. Schimke, C. Vielhauer, P.K. Dutta, T.K. Basu, A. De Rosa, J. Hansen, B. Yegnanarayana, J. Dittmann: Cross Cultural Aspects of Biometrics. In: *Proceedings of Biometrics: Challenges arising from Theory to Practice*, 2004, pp. 27–30

[14] A. Oermann, J. Dittmann, C. Vielhauer: Verifier-Tuple as a Classifier of Biometric Hand-writing Authentication - Combination of Syntax and Semantics. Dittmann, Jana (Ed.), Katzenbeisser, Stefan (Ed.), Uhl, Andreas (Ed.): Communications and multimedia security, Berlin: Springer, Lecture notes in com, CMS 2005 9th IFIP TC-6 TC-11 international conference Salzburg, Austria, September 2005, pp. 170–179

[15] A. Oermann, A. Lang, J. Dittmann: Verifyer-Tupel for Audio-Forensic to Determine Speaker Environment. City University of New York (Organizer): Multimedia and security, MM & Sec'05, Proceedings ACM, Workshop New York, NY, USA, 2005, pp. 57–62

[16] A. Oermann, J. Dittmann: Trust in E-Technologies. In: Encyclopedia of E-Commerce, E-Government and Mobile Commerce, Mehdi Khosrow-Pour (Ed.) Information Resources Management Association, USA, Idea Group Reference, Hershey London Melbourne Singapore, 2006, pp. 1101–1108

[17] A. Oermann, T. Scheidat, C. Vielhauer, J. Dittmann: Semantic Fusion for Biometric User Authentication as Multimodal Signal Processing. In: Proceedings of Int. Workshop on Multimedia Content Representation, Classification & Security IW MRCS, September 11-13, 2006, Istanbul, Turky, 2006, pp. 546–553

[18] A. Oermann, C. Vielhauer: Sensometrics: Identifying Pen Digitizers by Statistical Multimedia Signal Processing. Submitted at SPIE Electronic Imaging 2007, Multimedia Processing and Applications, Multimedia on Mobile Devices, 2007

Retrieval of 3D Objects by Structural Similarity

G. ANTINI, S. BERRETTI, A. DEL BIMBO, P. PALA

Contents

Abstract

Along with images and videos, 3D models have raised a certain interest for
a number of reasons, including advancements in 3D hardware and software
technologies, their ever decreasing prices and increasing availability, affordable
3D authoring tools, and the establishment of open standards for 3D data interchange. The resulting proliferation of 3D models demands for tools supporting
their effective and efficient management, including archival and retrieval.

In order to support effective retrieval by content of 3D objects and enable retrieval by object parts, information about local object structure should be combined with spatial information on object surface. In this paper, as a solution
to this requirement, we present a method relying on curvature correlograms to
perform description and retrieval by content of 3D objects.

Experimental results are presented both to show results of sample queries by
content and to compare the proposed solution to alternative techniques.

1   Introduction

In recent years the use of 3D models has been progressively spreading throughout many application domains: in manufacturing industries, 3D models are used in the design of many
different objects and components, and are archived to enable reuse and rapid prototyping of
new products; in medicine, many tests that are fundamental for disease study and diagnosis
provide output data in the form of 3D models; in the entertainment industry, reuse of available models may speed up the development of new videogames; in video production, where
high quality 3D models are used for special effects, considerable resources, in terms of time
and effort, can be saved by reusing or adapting existing models; in cultural heritage, regular acquisition of the 3D structure of statues, bas-reliefs and art-pieces supports monitoring
potential deformations of object structure caused by inappropriate preservation conditions.

Moreover, it should be pointed out that a growing number of techniques enabling generation of 3D models is increasing their availability. These techniques differ in terms of costs,
resolution and type of acquired information (the un-textured external surface of the object, the textured external surface, or even the internal structure of the object), and include
CAD, tomography, magnetic resonance, 3D laser scanners, structured light systems and
photogrammetry.

In this framework the development of techniques to enable retrieval by content of 3D models assumes an ever increasing relevance. This is particularly the case in the fields of cultural
heritage and historical relics, where there is a growing interest in solutions enabling preservation of relevant artworks (e.g. vases, sculptures, and handicrafts) as well as cataloguing
and retrieval by content. In these fields, retrieval by content can be employed to detect com-
monalities between 3D objects (e.g. the "signature" of the artist) or to monitor the temporal
evolution of a defect (e.g. the amount of bending for wooden tables).

1.1   Retrieval of 3D models

Methods addressing retrieval of 3D models can be distinguished based on different aspects, such as the type of representation used for geometry, the use of information about models' appearance (i.e. colour and/or texture), the need for manual annotation. Generally, two broad classes of approaches can be distinguished: *view-based* and *structure-based*. In the former, salient features of an object are extracted from a set of 2D views of the object itself. In the latter, object features are computed directly in the three-dimensional space in order to capture prominent characteristics of the object structure.

Description and retrieval of 3D objects based on description and retrieval of 2D views has been addressed in [1] and [2]. However, the effectiveness of these solutions is limited to description and retrieval of simple objects. In fact, as complex objects are considered, occlusions prevent to capture distinguishing 3D features using 2D views.

Recently, a hybrid approach—that is not entirely view-based or structure-based—has been proposed in [9] relying on the use of spin images for content description and matching. Description of 3D structure for the purpose of recognition or retrieval has been addressed for some time. A few authors have investigated analytical 3D models, but this is not always a viable solution, as there are many limitations in providing parameterizations of arbitrary models. In [3] retrieval of 3D objects based on similarity of surface segments is addressed. Surface segments model potential docking sites of molecular structures.

Much attention has been recently devoted to free-form (i.e. polygonal) meshes. The system developed within the Nefertiti project supports retrieval of 3D models based on both geometry and appearance (i.e. colour and texture) [4]. Also Kolonias et al. have used dimensions of the bounding box (i.e. its aspect ratios) and a binary voxel-based representation of geometry [5]. They further relied on a third feature, namely a set of paths, outlining the shape (*model routes*). In [6] a method is proposed to select feature points which relies on the evaluation of Gaussian and median curvature maxima, as well as of torsion maxima on the surface. In [7], Elad et al. use moments (up to the 4-7th order) of surface points as basic features to support retrieval of 3D models. Differently from the case of 2D images, evaluation of moments is not affected by (self-)occlusions.

In order to capture geometric features as well as their arrangement on the object surface, in [8] description and retrieval of 3D objects is accomplished through a combination of warping and projection. However, this method can be applied only to objects whose surface defines the boundary of a simply connected 3D region. Moreover, warping may introduce irregular deformation of the object surface before its projection on a 2D map.

Correlograms have been previously used with success for retrieval of images based on color content[14]. In particular, with respect to description based on histograms of local features, correlograms enable also encoding of information about the relative localization of local features. In [15], histograms of surface curvature have been used to support description and retrieval of 3D objects. However, since histograms do not include any spatial information, the system is liable to false positives.

In this paper, we present a model for representation and retrieval of 3D objects based on curvature correlograms. Correlograms are used to encode information about curvature values and their localization on the object surface. For this peculiarity, description of 3D objects based on correlograms of curvature is expected to capture distinguishing features of 3D objects and thus enable effective retrieval by similarity. To investigate and assess the ability of curvature correlograms to capture prominent features of 3D objects, we compare the proposed solution with alternative models for 3D retrieval by content proposed in the literature.

This paper is organized as follows: in Sect.2 representation of object structure through curvature correlograms is presented; in Sect.3 some distance measures are defined to be used for computing the similarity between two curvature correlograms; in Sect.4 alternative models for 3D retrieval by content used in the comparative analysis are briefly described; finally, in Sect.5 experimental results are presented and in Sect.6 conclusions are drawn.

2   Computation of Curvature Correlograms

High resolution 3D models obtained through scanning of real world objects are often affected by high frequency noise, due to either the scanning device or the subsequent registration process. Hence, smoothing is required to cope with such models for the purpose of extracting their salient features. This is especially true if salient features are related to differential properties of mesh surface (e.g. surface curvature).

Selection of a smoothing filter is a critical step, as application of some filters entails changes in the shape of the models. In the proposed solution, we adopted the filter first proposed by Taubin [10]. This filter, also known as $\lambda|\mu$ filter, operates iteratively, and interleaves a Laplacian smoothing weighed by λ with a second smoothing weighed with a negative factor μ ($\lambda > 0$, $\mu < -\lambda < 0$). This second step is introduced to preserve the model's original shape.

Let $\mathcal{M}$ be a mesh. We denote with E, V e F, the sets of all *edges*, *vertices* and *faces* of the mesh. With N_V, N_E and N_F, we denote the cardinality of sets V, E and F.

Given a vertex $v \in \mathcal{M}$, the principal curvature of $\mathcal{M}$ at vertex v is indicated as $k_1(v)$ and $k_2(v)$. The mean curvature $\bar{k}_v$ is related to the principal curvature $k_1(v)$ and $k_2(v)$ by the equation:

$$\bar{k}_v = \frac{k_1(v) + k_2(v)}{2}$$

Details about computation of the principal and mean curvature for a mesh can be found in [11].

Values of the mean curvature are quantized into $2N + 1$ classes of discrete values. For this purpose, a quantization module processes the mean curvature value through a stair-step function so that many neighboring values are mapped to one output value:

$$
\mathcal{Q}(\bar{k}) \;=\; \begin{cases} N\Delta & \text{if} \quad \bar{k} > N\Delta \\ i\Delta & \text{if} \quad \bar{k} \in [i\Delta, (i+1)\Delta) \\ -i\Delta & \text{if} \quad \bar{k} \in [-i\Delta, -(i+1)\Delta) \\ -N\Delta & \text{if} \quad \bar{k} < -N\Delta \end{cases} \tag{1}
$$

with $i \in \{0, \ldots, N-1\}$ and Δ a suitable quantization parameter (in the experiments reported in Sect.5 $N = 100$ and $\Delta = 0.15$). Function $\mathcal{Q}(\cdot)$ quantize values of $\bar{k}$ into $2N+1$ distinct classes $\{c_i\}_{i=-N}^{N}$.

To simplify notation, $v \in \mathcal{M}_i$ is synonymous with $v \in \mathcal{M}$ and $\mathcal{Q}(\bar{k}_v) = c_i$.

Definition 2.1 (Histogram of Curvature) *Given a quantization of curvature values into $2N+1$ classes $\{c_i\}_{i=-N}^{N}$, the histogram of curvature $h_{c_i}(\mathcal{M})$ of the mesh $\mathcal{M}$ is defined as:*

$$
h_{c_i}(\mathcal{M}) = N_V \cdot \Pr_{v_i \in \mathcal{M}}[v_i \in \mathcal{M}_i]
$$

being N_V the number of mesh vertices.

In doing so, $h_{c_i}(\mathcal{M})/N_V$ is the probability that the quantized curvature of a generic vertex of the mesh belongs to class c_i.

The correlogram of curvature is defined with respect to a predefined distance value δ. In particular, the curvature correlogram $\gamma_{c_i c_j}^{(\delta)}$ of a mesh $\mathcal{M}$ is defined as:

$$
\gamma_{c_i,c_j}^{(\delta)}(\mathcal{M}) = \Pr_{v_1,v_2 \in \mathcal{M}}[(v_1 \in \mathcal{M}_{c_i}, v_2 \in \mathcal{M}_{c_j}) \,|\, ||v_1 - v_2|| = \delta]
$$

In this way, $\gamma_{c_i,c_j}^{(\delta)}(\mathcal{M})$ is the probability that two vertices that are δ far away from each other have curvature belonging to class c_i and c_j, respectively.

Ideally, $||v_1 - v_2||$ should be the geodesic distance between vertices v_1 and v_2. However, this can be approximated with the $k-$ring distance if the mesh $\mathcal{M}$ is regular and triangulated[12].

Definition 2.2 (1-ring) *Given a generic vertex $v_i \in M$, the* neighborhood *or* 1-ring *of v_i is the set:*

$$
V^{v_i} = \{v_j \in \mathcal{M} : \exists e_{ij} \in E\}
$$

being E the set of all mesh edges (if $e_{ij} \in E$ there is an edge that links vertices v_i and v_j).

The set V^{v_i} can be easily computed using the morphological operator *dilate* [13]:

$$
V^{v_i} = dilate(v_i)
$$

Through the dilate operator, the concept of *1-ring* can be used to define, recursively, generic k^{th} order neighborhood:

$$ring_k = dilate^k \cap dilate^{k-1}$$

Definition of kth order neighborhood enables definition of a true metric between vertices of a mesh. This metric can be used for the purpose of computing curvature correlograms as an approximation of the usual geodesic distance (that is computationally much more demanding). According to this, we define the $k-$ring distance between two mesh vertices as $d_{ring}(v_1, v_2) = k$ if $v_2 \in ring_k(v_1)$.

Function $d_{ring}(v_1, v_2) = k$ is a true metric, in fact:

1. $d_{ring}(u, v) \geq 0$, and $d_{ring}(u, v) = 0$ if and only if $u = v$.

2. $d_{ring}(u, v) = d_{ring}(v, u)$

3. $\forall w \in \mathcal{M} \ \ d(u, v) \leq d(u, w) + d(w, v)$

Based on the $d_{ring}(\cdot)$ distance, the correlogram of curvature can be redefined as follows:

$$\gamma_{c_i,c_j}^{(k)}(\mathcal{M}) = \Pr_{v_1,v_2 \in \mathcal{M}}[(v_1 \in \mathcal{M}_{c_i}, v_2 \in \mathcal{M}_{c_j}) \,|\, d_{ring}(v_1, v_2) = k]$$

3   Matching Curvature Correlograms

Several distance measures have been proposed to compute the dissimilarity of distribution functions. In order to compute the similarity between curvature correlograms of two distinct meshes $\gamma_{c_i,c_j}^{(k)}(\mathcal{M}_1)$ and $\gamma_{c_i,c_j}^{(k)}(\mathcal{M}_2)$ we experimented the following distance measures:

Minkowsky-form distance

$$d_{\mathcal{L}_p} = \left[\sum_{i,j=-N}^{N} \left| \gamma_{c_i,c_j}^{(k)}(\mathcal{M}_1) - \gamma_{c_i,c_j}^{(k)}(\mathcal{M}_2) \right|^p \right]^{1/p}$$

Histogram intersection

$$d_{HI} = 1 - \frac{\sum_{i,j=-N}^{N} \min\left(\gamma_{c_i,c_j}^{(k)}(\mathcal{M}_1), \gamma_{c_i,c_j}^{(k)}(\mathcal{M}_2)\right)}{\sum_{i,j=-N}^{N} \gamma_{c_i,c_j}^{(k)}(\mathcal{M}_2)}$$

χ^2-*statistics*

$$d_{\chi^2} = \sum_{i,j=-N}^{N} \frac{\left(\gamma_{c_i,c_j}^{(k)}(\mathcal{M}_1) - \gamma_{c_i,c_j}^{(k)}(\mathcal{M}_2)\right)^2}{2\left(\gamma_{c_i,c_j}^{(k)}(\mathcal{M}_1) + \gamma_{c_i,c_j}^{(k)}(\mathcal{M}_2)\right)}$$

Kullback-Leibler divergence

$$d_{KL} = \sum_{i,j=-N}^{N} \gamma_{c_i,c_j}^{(k)}(\mathcal{M}_1) log \frac{\gamma_{c_i,c_j}^{(k)}(\mathcal{M}_1)}{\gamma_{c_i,c_j}^{(k)}(\mathcal{M}_2)}$$

Using a groundtruth database, the above distance measures have been compared in terms of precision and recall figures. Results of this analysis (not reported in this paper for lack of space) suggest that the best performance is achieved by using χ^2-statistics to measure the distance between curvature correlograms.

4   Implementation of Alternative Approaches

For the purpose of comparison, we have taken into consideration solutions for global 3D shape content based retrieval. Among the methods presented in the literature, we have selected five methods as representative of the major categories of approaches of 3D shape description. In detail:

Statistics-based approaches:

- Curvature histograms ([16]);
- Shape functions ([17])

Geometric approaches:

- Geometric moments ([7]);

View-based approaches:

- Spin images ([18]);

Principles of operation, characterizing elements and details of their implementation are shortly resumed in the rest of the section.

4.1   Curvature histograms

Surface curvatures are estimated at a generic vertex v_i of the 3D object mesh by considering the variations of the surface normal over the *platelet* V^{v_i} of vertex v_i, i.e. the set of all 1-connected mesh vertices around v_i. Given a generic vertex of the platelet $v_j \in V^{v_i}$, $v_j^{\perp}$ is defined as the normal to $\mathcal{M}$ at point v_j. The curvature γ_{v_i} at vertex v_i is then estimated as:

$$\gamma_{v_i} = \frac{1}{2} \frac{\sum_{v_j \in V^{v_i}} |v_i^{\perp} - v_j^{\perp}|}{|V^{v_i}|} \quad (2)$$

According to this definition, the value of γ_{v_i} is always in $[0, 1]$.

Curvature values are quantized into $2N + 1$ classes of discrete values according to Eq(1).

The histogram of curvature $h_{c_i}(\mathcal{M})$ of the mesh $\mathcal{M}$ is defined as:

$$h_{c_i}(\mathcal{M}) = N_V \cdot \Pr_{v_i \in \mathcal{M}}[v_i \in \mathcal{M}_i]$$

being N_V the number of mesh vertices.

To evaluate the dissimilarity between two objects we have used the Kullback-Leibler divergence:

$$\text{Kullback} - \text{Leibler divergence}: \quad d_{KL} \quad = \sum_{k=0}^{N} h_k(\mathcal{M}_1) log \frac{h_k(\mathcal{M}_1)}{h_k(\mathcal{M}_2)} \tag{3}$$

4.2   Shape functions

Object shapes are described by the probability distribution of a shape function that measures the geometric properties of the 3D object. In our implementation, the shape function measures the Euclidean distance between pairs of vertices of the 3D object mesh $\mathcal{M}$. The probability distribution is approximated through the 128 bin histogram that quantizes values of the shape function.

$H(\mathcal{M}) = (h_0(\mathcal{M}), \dots, h_{127}(\mathcal{M}))$,

where:

$$h_k(\mathcal{M}) = \Pr_{v_i, v_j \in \mathcal{M}} (\delta(v_i, v_j) = k)$$

being $\delta(v_1, v_2)$ the normalized and quantized value of the distance between two vertices $v_1 = (x_1, y_1, z_1)$ and $v_2 = (x_2, y_2, z_2)$ of the object mesh:

$$\delta(v_1, v_2) = 128 \left\lfloor \frac{\sqrt{(x_1 - x_2)^2 + (y_1 - y_2)^2 + (z_1 - z_2)^2}}{L} \right\rfloor$$

All objects must be uniformly scaled so as to fit within a 3D box of predefined size so that values of the shape function are normalized with respect to the box diagonal.

To evaluate the dissimilarity between two objects we have used the Kullback-Leibler divergence (Eq.3).

4.3   Geometric approaches: Moments

For any 3D object polygonal mesh of N vertices $\{P_i = (x_i, y_i, z_i)\}_{i=1}^{N}$, the (prq)-th moment is defined according to the following expression:

$$m_{pqr} = \frac{1}{N} \sum_{i=1}^{N} w_i x_i^p y_i^q z_i^r$$

where w_i is a weight proportional to the area of the polygonal faces adjacent to vertex P_i. Weights w_i make the moment-based representation invariant with the number of vertices of the mesh. Scale invariance is obtained by taking the coordinate system centered in the center of mass m_{100}, m_{010}, m_{001} of the model and scaling all the models uniformly so as to fit within a regular 3D box of predefined size.

For our experiments, moments up to the 6-th order have been used. A generic object is therefore represented through a feature vector $\mathbf{f}_{mom} \in \mathbb{R}^6$. The dissimilarity between two objects is measured by computing the Euclidean distance of the corresponding feature vectors.

4.4   Spin Image signatures

For each mesh vertex O, a *spin image* is built mapping any other mesh vertices $\boldsymbol{x}$ onto a two-dimensional space according to(see also Fig. 1 for notation):

$$S_O(\boldsymbol{x}) \to [\alpha, \beta] = [\sqrt{\|\boldsymbol{x} - \boldsymbol{p}\|^2 - (\boldsymbol{n} \cdot (\boldsymbol{x} - \boldsymbol{p}))^2}, \boldsymbol{n} \cdot (\boldsymbol{x} - \boldsymbol{p})]$$

Grey-level spin images are derived that encode the density of mesh vertices that map on the same point of the spin image, taking into account the extent to which each vertex contributes to the neighborhood of its projection. A bilinear interpolation scheme can be used to spread vertex influence over several spin image points.

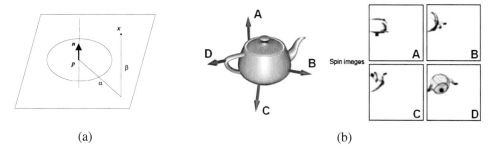

(a)   (b)

Fig. 1: Given an oriented point $\langle \boldsymbol{p}, \boldsymbol{n} \rangle$ on the object surface, a generic point $\boldsymbol{x}$ is mapped on point $[\alpha, \beta]$ on the spin map, being $[\alpha, \beta]$ the radial distance and the elevation of $\boldsymbol{x}$ w.r.t. to $\langle \boldsymbol{p}, \boldsymbol{n} \rangle$. (a) The object centred 3D coordinates system. (b) A 3D object, along with 2D point images and spin images computed from 4 distinct points on the object surface.

In Fig.1(b) a sample model of a teapot is shown with spin images computed from four different vertices of the model.

Although spin images are effective for the description of three-dimensional objects, one critical problem is that complex objects usually need a huge number of spin images as many as the number of mesh vertices) to obtain a complete representation of their appearance. Besides, each image requires considerable storage space. This makes the representation impractical for retrieval purposes. Spin image signatures ([18]), make this representation suitable for content based retrieval. Spin images are partitioned into regions following an approach similar to that expounded in [19]. Three types of regions are considered: sectors of circular crowns for the upper ($\beta > 0$) and lower ($\beta < 0$) half-planes and circular sectors centered in the origin. For each of them, a signature is defined ($C^p = \langle cp_1, \ldots, cp_{np} \rangle$, $C^n = \langle cn_1, \ldots, cn_{nn} \rangle$, and $S = \langle s_1, \ldots, s_{ns} \rangle$, respectively), where the elements represent the number of surface vertices projections in the region.

Experimentally $np = nn = ns = 6$ has been found to be a satisfactory trade-off between representation compactness and selectivity. This leads to compress the spin image informative content into a 18-dimensional vector $D = \langle C^p, C^n, S \rangle$.

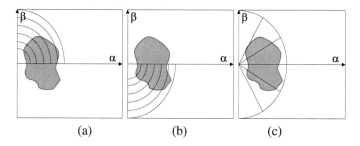

$$(a) \qquad\qquad (b) \qquad\qquad (c)$$

Fig. 2: Compound object descriptors comprise descriptors for a) np crowns in the half-plane $\beta > 0$, b) nn crowns in the half-plane $\beta < 0$, c) ns sectors. In our experiments $np = nn = ns = 6$.

To reduce the number of spin image descriptors, description vectors are clustered using fuzzy clustering [20]. The centers of the clusters are taken as signatures of the spin image representation. The optimal number of clusters c is derived according to the method proposed in [21]: given two functions that express a measure of under- and over-partitioning, respectively, the optimum number of clusters is defined as that number that minimizes the sum of the two functions— representing the trade-off between under- and over-partitioning.

Similarity between 3D objects represented with spin image signatures is evaluated by computing the distance Δ between the two descriptors. This requires to find the best cluster-center correspondence function, through the permutation $p : \{1, \ldots, l\} \rightarrow \{1, \ldots, k\}$ that minimizes the sum of distances between the corresponding cluster centers.

5   Experimental Results

In this section we present results of an experimentation aiming at the evaluation of the effectiveness of 3D object retrieval based on curvature correlograms. Examples of retrieval and comparison with alternative approaches are carried out using a test database composed of approximately 300 models. These comprise four classes of models: taken from the web, manually authored (with a 3D CAD software), high quality 3D scans from the De Espona 3D Models Encyclopedia[1], and variations of the previous three classes (obtained through deformation or application of noise, which caused points surface to be moved from their original locations). All database models represent objects with smooth surface with a resolution ranging from 3180 to 5150 mesh vertices. Content descriptors according to the curvature correlograms approach as well as to all the approaches described in Sect.4 were

---

[1]http://www.deespona.com

extracted from database objects and stored to enable retrieval by similarity.

In the following, retrieval results are presented for some representative sample queries. For each query, 7 distinct result sets are provided. These correspond to retrieval based on Curvature Correlograms with Minkowski distance, Curvature Histograms with Minkowski distance, Shape Functions with Minkowski distance, Geometric Moments with Minkowski distance and Spin Images.

(a)

(b)Curvature correlograms, Minkowski distance

(c) Curvature histograms, Minkowski distance

(d) Shape functions, Minkowski distance

(e)Geometric moments, Minkowski distance

(f) Spin Images

Fig. 3: *Retrieval by similarity using as query the model of the crucified Christ. (a) The query model. (b-f) top retrieved models according to different approaches. The first retrieved model is never shown as it is always the query model.*

Figs.3,4,6 show retrieval results for three sample queries. Each figure shows the query model (on top) and the top ranked retrieved models according to the considered approaches.

For each approach, retrieved models are ordered by decreasing similarity score, from left to right. For all the queries and all the approaches, the top ranked model was always the query model. To improve readability this is never shown in the result set.

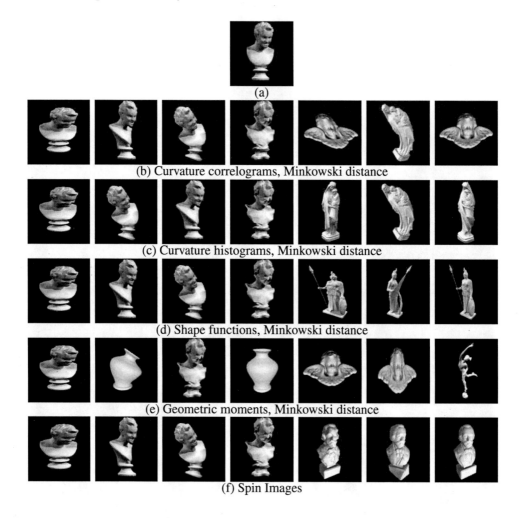

Fig. 4: Retrieval by similarity using as query the model of a bust. (a) The query model. (b-f) top retrieved models according to different approaches. The first retrieved model is never shown as it is always the query model.

Fig.3(a-f) shows retrieval results for a high resolution query model (3164 vertices) characterized by the presence of several protruding elements (the arms and the legs). The approach based on Spin Images is the only one that is able to retrieve perceptually consistent models in all the first eight positions. In particular, all models of the same category of the query model are ranked in the top four positions. Retrieval by Curvature Correlograms feature an improved performance with respect to Curvature Histograms, confirming that combination of spatial and curvature information enable more effective retrieval with respect to the use of the sole curvature information.

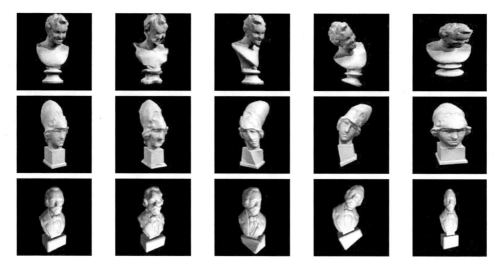

Fig. 5: Models of busts included in the archive.

In Fig.4(a-f) retrieval results are shown for a query representing a model of a bust (5144 vertices). The query model is shown in Fig.4(a). Models of busts included in the archive are shown in Fig.5. All approaches but the one based on Geometric Moments, retrieve in the top seven position all the four models originated through a deformation of the query model. Also in this case, the approach based on Spin Images is the only one that retrieves all relevant models in the top positions.

In Fig.6(a-f) retrieval results are shown for a query representing a low resolution model of a vase (1004 vertices). Use of a low resolution model is expected to penalize the performance of approaches based on curvature information, as estimation of curvature becomes unreliable for low resolution models. Furthermore, retrieval results for this sample query highlight robustness of each approach with respect to differences among models of the same object type. The archive includes 21 models of vases with some distinguishing features that characterize their visual appearance (as shown in Fig.7). Also in this case, the approach based on Spin Images retrieves relevant elements in all the top eight positions.

6 Conclusions

In this paper we have presented an approach to retrieval by content of 3D objects based on curvature correlograms. The main advantage of correlograms relates to their ability to encode not only distribution of features but also their arrangement on the object surface. Experimental results have shown that the proposed solution improves retrieval based on curvature histograms and proves to be effective for retrieval of medium and high resolution

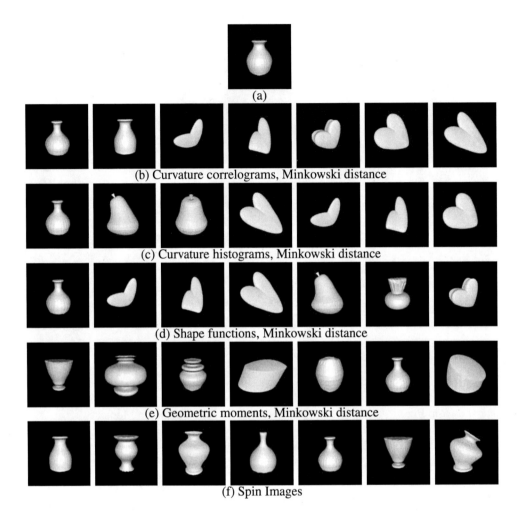

Fig. 6: Retrieval by similarity using as query the model of a vase. (a) The query model. (b-f) top retrieved models according to different approaches. The first retrieved model is never shown as it is always the query model.

models. In contrast, the effectiveness of retrieval based on curvature correlograms decreases on low resolution models. In fact, for these models, accurate and reliable estimation of curvature values is often prevented. Future work will address extension of correlograms to deal with multiresolution descriptors as well as the definition of suitable distance measures to cope with retrieval by object parts.

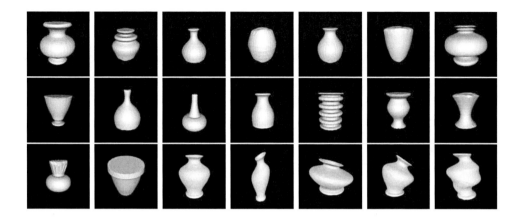

Fig. 7: Models of vases included in the archive.

7   Acknowledgements

The work described in this article has been supported in part by the EU-India cross cultural program. The views and conclusions contained herein are those of the authors and should not be interpreted as necessarily representing the official policies.

Bibliography

[1] S. Mahmoudi, M. Daoudi, "3D models retrieval by using characteristic views", in *Proc. of 16th Int'l Conf. on Pattern Recognition*, Vol.2, pp.457-460, 11-15 Aug, 2002.

[2] R. Ohbuchi, M. Nakazawa, T. Takei, "Retrieving 3D Shapes based on Their Appearance", in *Proc. of MIR'03*, Berkeley, CA, USA, Nov. 2003, pp.39-46.

[3] H.P. Kriegel, T. Seidl, "Approximation-Based Similarity Search for 3D Surface Segments", *GeoInformatica Journal*, 2(2):113-147, Kluwer Academic Publisher, 1998.

[4] E. Paquet, M. Rioux, "Nefertiti: a query by content system for three-dimensional model and image database management", *Image Vision and Computing*, 17(2):157-166, 1999.

[5] I. Kolonias, D. Tzovaras, S. Malassiotis, M. G. Strintzis, "Content-Based Similarity Search of VRML Models Using Shape Descriptors", in *Proc. of International Workshop on Content-Based Multimedia Indexing*, Brescia (I), September 19-21, 2001.

[6] F. Mokhtarian, N. Khalili, P. Yeun, "Multi-scale free-form 3D object recognition using 3D models", *Image and Vision Computing*, 19(5):271-281, 2001.

[7] M. Elad, A. Tal, S. Ar, "Content Based Retrieval of VRML Objects - An Iterative and Interactive Approach", *EG Multimedia*, September 2001, 97-108.

[8] J. Assfalg, A. Del Bimbo, P. Pala, "Curvature Maps for 3D CBR", in *Proc. of Int'l Conf. on Multimedia and Expo (ICME'03)*, Baltimore (MD), July 2003.

[9] J. Assfalg, G. D'Amico, A. Del Bimbo, P. Pala, "3D content-based retrieval with spin images", in *Proc. of Int'l Conf. on Multimedia and Expo (ICME'04)*, Taipei, Taiwan, June 2004.

[10] G. Taubin, "A Signal Processing Approach to Fair Surface Design", *Computer Graphics (Annual Conference Series)*, 29:351–358, 1995.

[11] G. Taubin. "Estimating the Tensor of Curvature of a Surface from a Polyhedral Approximation". In Proc. of Fifth International Conference on Computer Vision (ICCV'95), pp.902-907.

[12] Mathieu Desbrun, Mark Meyer, Peter Schroder and Alan H. Barr, "Discrete Differential-Geometry Operators in nD", Caltech, 2000.

[13] Christian Rössl, Leif Kobbelt, Hans-Peter Seidel, "Extraction of Feature Lines on Triangulated Surfaces using Morphological Operators" In *Smart Graphics*, Proceedings of the 2000 AAAI Symposium

[14] J. Huang, R. Kumar, M. Mitra, W.-J. Zhu, R. Zabih, "Statial Color Indexing and Application" In *Internation Journal of Computer Vision*, Vol. 35, pp. 245-268, 1999

[15] G. Hetzel, B. Leibe, P. Levi, B. Schiele. "3D Object Recognition from Range Images using Local Feature Histograms". In Proc. of Int. Conf. on Computer Vision and Pattern Recognition (CVPR'01), Kauai Marriott, Hawaii, Dec. 9-14, 2001.

[16] J.-Ph. Vandeborre, V. Couillet, M. Daoudi, "A Practical Approach for 3D Model Indexing by combining Local and Global Invariants", in *Proc. of the 1st Int'l Symp. on 3D Data Processing, Visualization, and Transmission (3DPVT'02)*, 2002.

[17] R. Osada, T. Funkhouser, B. Chazelle, D. Dobkin. Shape Distributions. *ACM Transactions on Graphics*, Vol. 21, No. 4, October 2002, pp.807-832.

[18] J. Assfalg, A. Del Bimbo, P. Pala. Spin images for retrieval of 3D objects by local and global similarity. In *Proc. of 17th Int. Conf. on Pattern Recognition (ICPR-04)*, Cambridge, UK, August 23-26, 2004.

[19] A. Goshtasby, "Description and descrimination of planar shapes using shape matrices", *IEEE Transactions on PAMI*, 7:738-743, 1985.

[20] J.C.Bezdek, J.Keller, R.Krishnapuram, N.R.Pal, *Fuzzy Models and Algorithms for Pattern Recognition and Image Processing*, Kluwer Academic Publisher, Boston, 1999.

[21] D.-J. Kim, Y.-W. Park, D.-J. Park. "A Novel Validity Index for Determination of the Optimal Number of Clusters", *IEICE Transactions on Information and Systems*, Vol.E84-D, N. 2, Feb.2001, pp.281-285.

E-Learning in University Teaching

IRINA REUTER, JAN HANSEN

Contents

Abstract

The dissemination strategy and the dissemination activities of the project are presented in this chapter. All strategies and activities can be seen in line with the worldwide progression of E-Learning as a column of a universiy's teaching strategy. Within the project recording tools were used and evaluated. An online dissemination platform serves to spread project results among the academic community, the media, and enterprises.

1.   Introduction

This workpackage is part of the project´s dissemination strategy. It describes the projects dissemination goals and their realisation in special parts of the project web site, which were implemented for educational access. Here, all the educational offers are delivered in the dissemination phase, are multiplexed and made accessible for students participating in the educational axis of the project, such as M.Sc. programmes. This part of the project website is not only a platform for the partners, it is also a platform for professionals, for the media, for enterprise dimensions and post-graduates as well as teaching staff for the university dimension. Course material created during the project is accessible in a lot of formats like .pdf, .ppt., .doc etc. This dissemination part of the project is connected to general developments in the university teaching community.

We have to consider not only the chances that learning at universities gains with distance and net-based learning but also factors that oppose changes. And finally, we have to weigh up these different factors. Only in a long-term perspective the change of learning at universities will be drastic, in a medium-term perspective static factors will be too strong [Rol06].

One of the learning goals of universities all over the world is independent thinking, learning and working. In a virtual environment, learners could have all chances to develop these competences. Therefore E-Learning can change the work of students drastically [Det06].

- All of the functions of a university are likely to be available online: teaching and learning, administration, research, library, information about activities of the university, informal student life, assignments, etc.. This will facilitate learning at universities

- The learner will be independent of place and time. So that learners all over the world can become students, more independent of social circumstances.

- Learning will be more convenient than in traditional environments, because all information is only a few mouse clicks away.

- Learning can come closer to the research activities at universities. It will be easier to make ongoing research projects and results transparent to learners who are not directly involved.

- Multimedia applications will outstrip one-dimensional learning materials and teaching arrangements.

But despite these chances [Mau01] there are strong opposing factors that will restrain drastic changes of the learning at universities for a long time: the learners themselves, the organisational structure of the universities and the teaching staff [Rol06].

- Distance and net-based learning require a new learning behaviour. The students have to be independent of the judgment of others. This is very difficult in the life situation of students who need judgement of a peer group and of elder persons to locate themselves in society. Virtual universities will hardly be able to replace this important function for the socialisation process during the first higher education.

- The virtual university also requires a change of the - partly - several hundred years old organisational structures, which are quite resistant to fundamental changes. Hierarchies, system of finance, division of work, demands for scientific work, learning architecture, etc. build a complex system with redundancies. Changes in one subsystem cause resistance.

- A change of learning requires a change of the teaching staff. But the thinking structures of the teaching staff are adapted to the organisational structure of universities and the traditional way of teaching. A new learning culture has to be anchored in the every day life both of learners and teachers.

For these opposing factors there will not be a drastic change in learning at universities in a medium-term perspective. But there will be a lot of little changes that provoke a conversion of the traditional structures:

- Learning at universities will have many different forms. There will be a lot of combinations of distance/net-based learning and traditional classroom learning. This way learners, teachers and universities try to integrate some of the new opportunities in the old learning system.

- Learning in virtual environments will bring new opportunities for lifelong learning very fast. Learners in the field of further higher education will be offered more distance and net-based learning.

In a long-term perspective, these tendencies will more and more rebuild learning at universities and all the chances mentioned at the beginning will be developed. Learning at universities will become a lifelong opportunity. Universities will continue being the place for the first higher education but additional there will grow big departments of further education which use the opportunities of distance and net-based learning even more extensive. This evolution to a drastic change of learning at universities already started, and in different countries at different universities, you can see different stages of these developments [Jam06].

Places of higher education are currently enjoying greater autonomy and are clearly emphasising national and international competition in the fields of science and research. In recent years, this process of change has been supported by applying state-of-the-art information and communication technologies. Today E-Learning has emerged as essential feature of the modern university teaching landscape and is considered to be a profile-relevant performance criterion for universities.

To support an E-Learning process with the project partners, a twofold advancement was implemented. To record teaching events, a recording software was bought and spread to all project partners. To disseminate the recordings and additional teaching material, the Lecturnity Dissemination Center was implemented as part of the project web site.

2.   Lecturnity Recording Software

The process of restructuring traditional models of teaching in favour of an integration of E-Learning has long since begun at all universities. Teaching events will be made available online in future increasingly, so that they can be accessed from anywhere and at any time. Lecturnity is a tool to record talks, lectures, seminars, etc. The speaker and his or her voice are recorded by a camera and a microphone. The speaker needs to use slides. Slides changes and annotations on the slides are recorded. For the student user the screen is divided into a slides section, where the changes of subseeding slides is shown, a video section, were a video of the author is synchronised with the slides and an overview section, were the slide titels are organised in the structure of a table of contents. A voice recording is also synchronised with the slides and the video. Questions in the audience can be recorded, if there is a second microphone synchronised and given as one audio stream to the Lecturnity system. For the production of a Lecturnity recording a video recording equipment and a sound recording equipment are necessary.

The Lecturnity recording tool is based on the approach of producing learning content by Lecture Recording. You can make use of the potential for knowledge transfer of material which is already available without making any changes: slides, hand-written annotations, animations and videos can all go into the production along with the spoken text and the didactic scenario of a genuine teaching event. Lecturnity was developed by IMC AG Germany [1] out of basic university research and is an example of the transfer of technology from academia to product-based research and development. The following posibilities are provided:

- Recording of all data streams with only one tool
- Intuitive user interface
- Lecturer can keep his classic way of lecture
- Flexible output formats of recordings
- Flexible electronic distribution of E-Lectures via CD-ROM, DVD, FTP, Streaming
- Editing (cut, copy and paste) of Lecturnity-Recordings possible
- Wide range of imaginable asynchronous learning-scenarios

For the preparation of a recording MS Powerpoint slides have to be converted by the lecturnity tool. A life recording catched the lesson. During a post-processing procedure the adequate output formats are created. The complete effort for the production of a high quality recording of a 90 minutes lecture with three different output formats (with video, without

---

[1]   http://www.im-c.de/

video, streaming format) sums up to 1,5 man-days. The complete effort for the production of a low quality non-video version in a proprietary Lecturnity output format sums up to 0,5 man days.

2.1. Lecturnity Usability Questionnaire

To discover, wether there are differences due to culture in the perception of the recording technology in comparable settings, a questionnaire was developped and evaluated. Questions concerning settings, advantages and disadvantages of the tool lecturnity were compilated. The Questionnaire was distributed to Lecturnity users of all partners. It is an instrument designed for exploring information about preferences and dislikes of the student users and the authors. All partners were requested to answer the same questions. Completed questionnaires were checked for connections between preferences and dislikes on the one hand and national cultures on the other hand. If there should occur certain preferences or dislikes in one country, this can be a hint to a cultural influence on the perception of the lecturnity tool. Further scrutiny of such a difference would be focussed to the reasons of the the differences.

Questionnaires of similar design were distributed to student users and authors as seperated groups. This will show, whether the actual design of the tool is perceived in different ways by the different groups. If there are different perceptions in comparable teaching scenarios, the next step would be to compare the nationalities within each group. This can lead to information about cultural bound differences within the groups of student users and authors.

The first distribution was sent to the seniors of the project partners. The Lecturnity Software was new for all teaching senior project partners. They were prepared by httc staff in the same way and had a comparable background of information and training.

Everybody used the software within the local teaching scenario for about two months. During this phase an e-mail discussion of weak and strong features of the tool Lecturnity took place. After a phase of experience-gaining of two months, the questionnaire was sent to the authors. The comments in the questionnaires showed some perseption features which were shared by all authors. Other perseption features differed between the authors.

Two features of the tool were valued as obstacles for enhanced E-Learning by all partners:

- Recordings covering a term longer than 15 minutes showed an increasing missynchronisation of text and video-streams. Discrepancies became notable after appr. 10 minutes and reached an unaceptable dimension after appr. 15 minutes.

- Animations like flash films within a powerpoint slides could not be preserved as animations within the slides. The video stream had to be substituted by the animation. It was not possible to show both - video and animation - on the students screens.

The perception of usability was mainly influenced by the personal teaching style of the teachers. Lectures by IIT-C are characterised by a teacher walking up and down in front of a big blackboard with lively gestures and writing on the board with chalk to illustrate the the lecture. There were also many elements of dialogue between teacher and students. The dialogue elements could not be preserved by the Lecturnity software. IIT-C used Lecturnity mainly for the recording of phd talks, not within the setting of lectures or dialogue dominated exercises. Lectures were recorded by a video camera, which was permanently operated by a person following the movements of the teacher. Video tapes can be borrowed by students.

The perception of usability in IIT-K was also strongly influenced by the pre-existing infrastructure in the institute: Lectures were recorded in three prepared studios. The lecturer is recorded by four cameras. They capture the lecturer, slides conveyed by a beamer, or writing on paper sheets conveyed by a ceiling camera and a beamer. The four streams are edited on the fly. They can be broadcasted or stored. This estabilshed system was not changed by the use of Lecturnity. Lecturnity was applied for recordings of phd talks. Within this scenario the obstacle concerning powerpoint animations was estimated as main constraint for extended use. In comparison to the established recording system at IIT-K, Lecturnity showed one feature which was regarded as a main strength: Video and slides both can be seen constantly. The IIT-K system offered either the video or the slides.

UNI-MD stated also limited editing features concerning slides animations and critisized synchronisation problems in long time recording (more than 15 minutes without break). Like by IIT-C, a limitation in presentation stile (gestures, walking) was mentioned as a main obstacle for long time recordings. Positive impacts of the tool were discovered in scenarios of software demonstrations using the screengrabber mode for recording webserver activities. No additional hardware had to be transported, which was a clear improvement for the organisational point of view. Lecturnity was also useful for enriching a lecture with short time recordings of limited scope.

httc did not use Lecturnity for recordings of complete lectures, but for recordings of relatively short presentations of single topics. A set of short recordings covered more extensive subject matters. Animations were not used in powerpoint slides. The chosen stile of minimalistic slide design caused no perfomance problems. A minimalistic design of the slides was a didactical decision due to the intention of utmost clarity in presentation.

As main results, the seniors of the project partners stated similar fortes and weaknesses of the tool. Constraints for free movement of the lecturer and contraints of recording duration were predominant in the perception of the tool. Within the group of authors/teachers no national or cultural bound differences could be detected concerning the weaknesses of Lecturnity. Concerning the fortes of the tool also no differences due to the cultural background could be detected. The use of lecturnity was dominated by objective circumstances in the different institutes and the features of the tool. There was no hint, that comparable features were percepted in different ways within comparable teaching scenarios. All seniors tended to use Lecturnity for short time recordings of limited scope.

2.2.   First Questionnaire: Point of View of Students

The students completed a form with the following questions:

In which way did you profit from using the recording?

Which features of the recording were helpful for a better understanding of the recording´s subject matter?

Which features of the recording had a negative effect on the understanding of the recording´s subject matter?

Which features of the recording were more helpful than in comparison to a traditional study support?

Which features of the recording were less helpful in comparison to a traditional study support?

What did you miss in comparison to a traditional study report?

Which features of the recording were helpful to enhance your learning?

2.3.   Second Questionnaire: Point of View of Authors and Teachers

The authors and teachers completed a form with the following questions:

In which way did you profit from using the tool?

Which features of the tool were helpful for a better understanding of the recording´s subject matter?

Which features of the tool had a negative effect on the study support?

Which features of the tool were more helpful in comparison to a traditional study support?

Which features of the tool were less helpful in comparison to a traditional study support?

What did you miss in comparison to a traditional study report?

Which features of the tool were helpful to enhance your teaching?

Which constraints of the recording led to obstacles for your teaching?

3.   From CLIX to Lecturnity Dissemination Center

One of the central requirements placed on a learning management system is the organisation of learning processes. It is possible to publish events like lectures, practicals and seminars in event catalogues, thus providing access to those events and the relevant learning materials (e.g. exercise sheets). Individual teaching contents, such as lecture notes, interactive learning modules, animations, simulations, tests and feedback questionnaires are brought together in events. Within events, curricula can be freely defined. Explorative learning scenarios are possible, as well as adaptive, tutorially mentored learning paths. Communication and collaboration between learning groups are supported by an extensive range of tools (mail, chats, forums, virtual classrooms, whiteboards, etc.). All platform activities remain system-controlled and can be assessed via a wide selection of reports. These goals can be realised by the following funcionalities:

Training measure management: Combines a range of different courses and teaching events to training programmes.

Course management: Generates individual teaching plans and defines learning logics.

Workflow and messaging management: Develops appropriate workflow and messaging processes adapted to your organisational needs.

Tutor centre: Administers trainers, teachers, courses, participants and learning processes.

Communication and collaboration: Uses communities to enable online communication between participants in learning events and integrates functions such as chats, forums, libraries and mail-based communication into curricula-driven learning processes.

Adequate training and teaching is not possible without learning contents. The Learning Management System CLIX provides an all-round autonomous learning content management system supporting all kinds of training contents, ranging from MS PowerPoint slides, training scripts and E-Learning modules to interactive tests. The dedicated system database facilitates the administration, adaptation and publication of a wide range of learning objects. Compliance to internationally recognised standards, such as Dublin Core, LOM, AICC or SCORM ensures smooth integration of externally provided learning contents. Wizards support the production of tests, feedback questionnaires or glossaries. Programmes aimed at further training or internal communication measures can be published and acquired in the system via portals. Within courses, learning components can be defined and structured via learning logics.

The ability to model individual organisational structures is a key strength in any learning management system. CLIX domain, group and user management gives the option of grouping the addressees of learning contents by organisational groups and to assign them to appropriate users. High-performance access rights management allow to channel knowledge and information to the appropriate addressees and provide protection where confidentiality is an issue. User-friendly system functions, such as component and licence management, enable maintenance and administration to be kept within the organisation, thus avoiding extra costs. Such a number of functionalities locates the CLIX System in a transitional position from a Learning Management System to a Content Management System, because it provides functionalities for course creation as well as functionalities for storage and administration of learning material [Pet04].

This multitude of functionalities turned out to be a technical overkill in comparison with the project partners goals. Discussion with the project partners led to a simplified version of CLIX. The simplified version is called the "Lecturnity Dissemination Center". httc set up a version, which is designed for the specific needs of the project partners. The version for the project is based on the CLIX lerning management system.

The workflow for users of the Lecturnity Dissemination Center has been tailored to be as intuitiv and simple as possible. Goal of the design was to attract as less attention to the handling of the systeme as possible.

A login system grants access only to registered project members (see fig.1: Login Page). Project members are entitled to disseminate the material within the Lecturnity Dissemination Center for their purposes.

After the login procedure the project members will find their access to the Lecturnity Dis-

Figure 1.: Login Page

semination Center. In a news section they can get information about the latest uploaded recordings (see fig. 2: Personal Desktop).

After entering the Lecturnity Dissemination Center, the available recordings can be reached in the document archive. All documents are organised according to the project´s workpackages (see fig. 3: Document Archive).

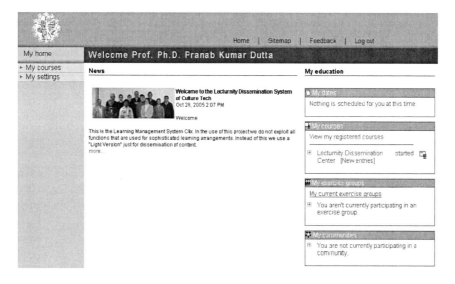

Figure 2.: Personal Desktop

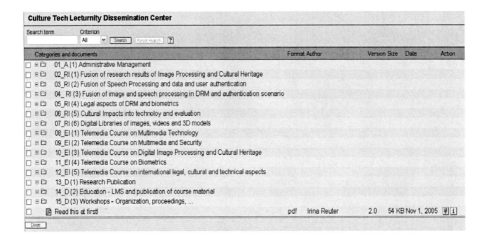

Figure 3.: Document Archive

Uploading a new recording is simply done by pressing a button "new document" on the top of the document archive page .

Then a small number of metadata has to be inserted in an electronic form. The new recording must be named, a short decription and a short comment should be added for a quick overview in the document list. Information about the author and keywords describing the content complete the set of metadata, which allows a clear organisation and search within the document archive.

4.   Course Material on the Project Web Site

Organised course material is available on the project web site. Papers, lecture slides, scripts, recordings of lectures and recordings of talks can be found on the projects website.

Course material is available in the following categories

- Image Processing and Cultural Heritage

- Speech Processing and Data and User Authentication

- Image and Speech processing in DRM and Authentication Scenarios

- Legal Aspects of DRM and Biometrics

- Cultural Impacts into Technology and Evaluation

- Digital Libraries of Images, Videos and 3D Models

The course material can be found here: https://amsl-smb.cs.uni-magdeburg.de/culturetech/

5. Acknowledgement

The authors would like to thank all project partners for contributing information which made it possible to keep the dissemination system services close to the projetc's needs. The work described in this article has been supported in part by the EU-India cross cultural program and in part by the Innovation Initiative of the State Hessen. The views and conclusions contained herein are those of the authors and should not be interpreted as necessarily representing the official policies.

Bibliography

[Det06] Detlev Nothnagel. *Wissensmedien und die Vermittlung zwischen externer und interner Repräsentation, in: Knowledge and Media Design.* Number ISBN 3-486-58014-0. Oldenbourg Verlag, Rosenheimer str. 145, D-81671 München, January 2006.

[Jam06] James J. Forest. *The Scholarship of Teaching and Learning in Higher Education: Contributions of Research Universities (review),* volume 77 of *The Journal of Higher Education.* The Ohio State University Press, 1070 Carmack Road Columbus, OH 43210-1002, April 2006.

[Mau01] Maureen E. Kenny. *Promoting Civil Society through Service Learning: A Review of the Issues.* Outreach Scholarship Series. Kluwer Academic Publishers, 233 Spring St Fl7, New York, NY 10013-1522, 31 December 2001.

[Pet04] Peter Baumgartner, Hartmut Häfele, Kornelia Maier-Häfele. *Content Management Systeme in e-Education.* Number ISBN 3-7065-1968-2. Studien Verlag, Amraser Str. 118, A-6020 Innsbruck, 31May 2004.

[Rol06] Rolf Schulmeister. *eLearning: Einsichten und Aussichten.* Number ISBN 978-3-486-58003-7. Oldenbourg Verlag, Rosenheimer str. 145, D-81671 München, March 2006.

Overview to workpackages EI (1) to EI (5)

ALL PROJECT PARTNERS

Contents

Abstract

This chapter provides an overview and background information to courses implemented by the project partners. The material for these courses was created or enriched by using project results of the workpackages RI (1) to RI (6).

1   Otto-von-Guericke-Universität Magdeburg

1.1   EI(1) - Course on Multimedia Technology

Name of the Course: Multimedia Technology

Didactical concept: The aim is to learn about Multimedia Technology.

Topic Overview:

- Discussion of the requirements demanded by multimedia systems towards computer systems and the approaches to handle these requirements
- Introduction of production and management of content
- Illustration of the characteristics of and the possibilities provided by multimedia systems
- Study of aspects of distributed multimedia systems which cover important research and application areas

Number of slides: 400.

Number of Lecturnity recordings: 3 recordings of demonstrating MPEG structure and interlacing effects (total lenght of all: ca. 30 minutes).

Number of course participants: winter semester 2005 about 34 in the exercise, more in the lecture itself (maybe double).

Evaluation concept of the course: written, evaluation questionnaires were given to the students.

Evaluation feedback: in gereral overall positive feedback of course structure and use of material.

Information about the use of material from other project partners: legal aspects highlighted in the courses on copyright, digital documents, virtual presence and data protection from httc.

1.2   EI(2) - Course on Multimedia and Security

Didactical concept: The students learn to identify and solve Security problems in Multimedia Applications. To reach this aim, the students engage in the implementation of multimedia specific security protocols for image, video and audio.

Topic Overview:

- Motivation, Introduction and Basics
- Intellectual Property Rights (IPR), Digital Rights Management (DRM)
- Access Protection
- Hidden Communication: Steganography
- Authenticity and Integrity of digital Media
- User Authentication: Multimodal Biometrics

Number of slides: 500.

Number of Lecturnity recordings: 1 recording of a whole lecture.

Number of course participants: sommer semester 2005/sommer semster 2006 about 23 in the exercise, more in the lecture itself (maybe double).

Evaluation concept of the course: written, evaluation questionnaires were given to the students.

Evaluation feedback: in gereral overall positive feedback of course structure and use of material.

Information about the use of material from other project partners: legal aspects highlighted in the courses on copyright, digital documents, virtual presence and data protection form httc.

1.3   EI(4) - Course on Biometrics

Didactical concept: The aim is to understand and utilise general and specific biometric systems. To reach this aim the students learn about mathematical, statistical and technical fundamentals of the different systems.

Topic Overview:

- Opening
- Mathematical and Statistical Fundamentals
- Technical Fundamentals and Sensor Technology
- Handwritten Biometrics
- Fingerprint Biometrics
- Voice, Keystroke and Gait
- Face and Iris Recognition
- Technical Integration Aspects
- Evaluation of Biometric Systems
- Standardization

Number of slides: 400.

Number of Lecturnity recordings: 4 recordings of parts of lecture on topic gait and keystroke.

Number of course participants: sommer semester 2005/sommer semster 2006 about 44 in the exercise, more in the lecture itself (maybe double).

Evaluation concept of the course: written, evaluation questionnaires were given to the students.

Evaluation feedback: in gereral overall positive feedback of course structure and use of material.

Information about the use of material from other project partners: Information about the use of material from other project partners: legal aspects highlighted in the courses on copyright, digital documents, virtual presence and data protection from httc.

2   Media Integration and Communication Center - Università di Firenze

2.1   EI(3) - Course on Digital Image Processing and Cultural Heritage

Name of the course: Image Processing; Internal course on Edge Detection for Cultural Heritage

Didactical concept: Image Processing: The aim of this course is to supply the students with the basic knowledge concerning image processing technologies, from the theoretical and practical point of view. Furthermore during the course seminars relating image processing are possible. Internal course on Edge Detection for Cultural Heritage: the aim of this course is to bring up-to-date all the people involved in the laboratory, about the latest development in the research concerning the Edge Detection for the Cultural Heritage field. The course has been devoted only to an internal use, i.e. it has been restricted to only people afferring in any way to the laboratory.

Topic Overview:

Image Processing

- Basic and Human Visual System
- Image acquisition and representation
- Point operators
- Spatial operators
- Image enhancement and restoration
- Edge detection and extraction
- Image segmentation
- Digital transforms

- Image sequence processing

Internal course on Edge Detection for Cultural Heritage

- Use of Edge Detection techniques

- First order derivative methods

- Second order derivative methods

- The problem of colors

- Pre and post-processing filters

Number of slides: 488 slides for the basic course 89 slides for the seminar about Computer Graphics and 3D processing 71 slides for the course about Edge Detection for Cultural Heritage

Number of Lecturnity recordings: 1 Lecturnity recording for the course about Edge Detection for Cultural Heritage

Number of course participants: 40; 10 for the internal course

Evaluation concept of the course: None

Evaluation feedback: in gereral overall positive feedback of course structure and use of material.

2.2   EI(2) - Course on Multimedia and Security

Name of the course: Multimedia terminals

Didactical concept: The aim of this course is to supply the students with the basic knowledge concerning some of the most recent applications for the distribution of multimedia content, and the issues related to the distribution itself through open networks.

Topic Overview:

- Security problems in the distribution of multimedia content
  - Cryptography techniques
  - Digital watermarking techniques
- Applications for the distribution of multimedia content
  - Technologies for Streaming Media
  - Technologies for creation and transmission of contents through wireless devices (WAP)
- Digital Terrestrial Television (DTT)

Number of slides: 309 slides for the basic course 29 slides for the seminar about Standard of Video Compression

Number of Lecturnity recordings: 1 Lecturnity recording for the seminar about Standard of Video Compression

Number of course participants: 10

Evaluation concept of the course: oral

Evaluation feedback: in greral overall positive feedback of course structure and use of material.

3   Indian Institute of Technology Madras (Chennai)

3.1   EI(4) - Course on Speech Technology

Name of the Course: Multimedia Technology

Didactical concept: Lecture with chalkboard writing and intense dailogue elements. All movements of the lecturer were catched by a video camera.

Topic Overview: Reference mostly "Speech Recognition" by L.R.Rabiner and B.H.Juang, Prentice-Hall USA, 1993

Number of slides: 50 hours vidoe tape.

Number of Lecturnity recordings: No Lecturnity Recordings

Number of course participants: About 40.

Evaluation concept of the course: Assignments, midsemester exams, and final exams. The final exams are oral exams with 30 minutes with each student. The Speech Technology course has also a lab component. The weightage: Assignment/lab (20 percent), two midsemester exams (2x15 percent), and the final exam (50 percent).

Evaluation feedback: in greral overall positive feedback of course structure and use of material.

3.2   EI(4) - Course on Artificial Neural Networks

Didactical concept: Lecture with chalkboard writing and intense dailogue elements. All movements of the lecturer were catched by a video camera.

Topic Overview: Reference is the book Artificial Neural Networks, by B.Yegnanarayana, Prentice-Hall India, New Delhi, 1999

Number of slides: 50 hours video tape.

Number of Lecturnity recordings: No lecturnity recordings

Number of course participants: About 50

Evaluation concept of the course: Assignments, midsemester exams, and final exams. The final exams are oral exams with 30 minutes with each student. The Speech Technology course has also a lab component. The weightage: Assignment/lab (20 percent), two midsemester exams (2x15 percent), and the final exam (50 percent).

Evaluation feedback: in gereral overall positive feedback of course structure and use of material.

4 Indian Institute of Technology Kharagpur

At IIT Kharagpur, Lecturnity was used to record the following seminars. Furthermore, part of the course material on Digital Multimedia Technology by Prof. Jana Dittmann of university of Magdeburg was used by the students involved with the project works and related to Data Communication and multimedia technology. Culture-tech workshop at IIT Kharagpur was fully recorded containing eleven presentations of the workshop.

4.1 EI (1) - Course on Face Biometrics for Person Authentication

Topic Overview:
Biometric is a physical or behavioral person characteristic which is unique, universal, permanent and collectable. Most commonly used biometric is speech. Speech signal has proven to be a valuable source of speaker dependent information but its performance is poor under noisy environments and channel mismatch conditions. The problem of such impact on speech has led to the technology for person authentication based upon lip movements. It has been shown in different reports that lip information not only presents speech information but also characteristic information about a person's identity. Fusing this information with speech information will produce robust person identification under adverse condition. The present work aims to build a bimodal person identification system which uses speech and lip information. Person identification system generally involves four steps. The first step is the data (image/speech) acquisition, the second step is feature extraction, the third step involves the speaker modeling using the feature vectors. Decision making through pattern matching is the last step. The performance of person identification system has been investigated using three different sets of visual features, one set of speech feature and the improvement in the recognition rate of the system when the decisions made by the systems using visual and speech features are fused using a adaptive weighing technique.

- Name of the Speaker: B.KARTIKEYAN
- Number of slides: 63
- Time duration: 30 minutes
- Number of participants: 20

4.2 EI (1): Course of Digital Watermarking of Still Images Using Wavelet Transform

Topic Overview:
In this work the implementation of various robust watermarking schemes has been presented. Various aspects of the embedding watermarks in digital images, their extraction and

subsequent detection have been dealt with. All schemes involved embedding of watermarks in frequency domain being based almost entirely on wavelet transforms. Wavelet transforms have been used to separate the image into different frequency zones and watermark embedded in suitable zones. As is usual for robust watermarks the most important criteria for the schemes was robustness against attacks. In one of the schemes the watermark was used to replace a certain block of wavelet coefficients, chosen to produce least visible distortion as well as give highest robustness against compression. Robustness can be achieved by uniqueness of decomposition filter banks used. Another similar scheme sought to introduce more robustness by randomizing the block of embedding. In another approach, the wavelet coefficients of the LL block were treated as a low frequency image and its discrete cosine transforms were taken. Block to embed watermark was again randomly chosen and a certain digit of the coefficients was replaced by the watermark pixel values , considering a two tone image . In yet another approach, watermark was reduced to a low frequency signal and then modulation was achieved using the coverwork as carrier. Extraction requires demodulation of the carrier signals.

- Name of the Speaker: YASH BISWAS

- Number of slides: 47

- Time duration: 20 minutes

- Number of participants: 15

4.2.1   Watermarking of Digital Images

Topic Overview:
The ability to resolve ownership disputes and copyright infringement is difficult in the worldwide digital age. There is an increasing need to develop techniques that protect the owner of digital data. Digital Watermarking is a technique used to embed a known piece of digital data within another piece of digital data. The embedded piece of data acts as a fingerprint for the owner, allowing the protection of copyright, authentication of the data, and tracing of illegal copies. The goal of this work is to study and implement watermarking techniques, both robust and fragile, in spatial as well as transform domain, and compare their effectiveness, weakness and limitations. Out of the four techniques discussed here the first three are robust watermarking techniques. The first one uses a spatial watermarking technique, while the next two uses a frequency (discrete cosine transform) based technique. The last watermarking technique is a fragile watermarking technique in spatial domain.

- Name of the Speaker: DEVESH KATIYAR

- Number of slides: 53

- Time duration: 17 minutes

- Number of participants: 18

4.3   EI (1): Course Digital Watermarking of Still Images

Topic Overview:
Implementation of watermarking schemes in special domain and frequency domain. Watermarking using informed embedding and blind detection in spatial domain. Developed a GUI implementing all possible attacks on an image.

- Name of the Speaker: RISHABH MATHUR

- Number of slides: 51

- Time duration: 14 minutes

- Number of participants: 21

Feedback::
Web-based courses or video lectures distributed at IIT Kharagpur have got good response from the users because of the following reasons:

1. Any portion can be played back as many times as the student want.

2. Some students who has requirement for a small part of the course need not enroll to the full subject and it may not be always possible because of the conflict between subject slots.

3. Integration of slides with video of the Lecturer makes the topic more interesting and add some emotions to the slides.

5   httc e.V., Darmstadt

5.1   EI(5) - Course on Copyright Basics in International Research Projects

Name of the Course: Multimedia Technology

Didactical concept: The aim is to prepare baisc information about copyright in international research projects.

Topic Overview:

- General Provisions

- European Community regulations

- National law systems in Italy, India and Germany

Number of slides: 47.

Number of Lecturnity recordings: 4 recordings in total lenght of 120 minutes.

Number of course participants: httc is no university and holds no own courses. The material was at the disposition of all project partners.

Evaluation concept of the course: As project partners chosed.

Evaluation feedback: in gereral overall positive feedback of course structure and use of material.

Information about the use of material from other project partners: legal aspects highlighted in the courses on copyright, digital documents, virtual presence and data protection were used as lecture part at University Magdeburg.

5.2   EI(5) - Course on Data Protection in International Research Projects

Didactical concept: The aim is to prepare basicc information about data protection in international research projects.

Topic Overview:

- General provisions
- European Community regulations
- National law systems in Italy, India and Germany

Number of slides: 64.

Number of Lecturnity recordings: 4 recordings in total lenght of 120 minutes.

Number of course participants: httc is no university and holds no own courses. The material was at the disposition of all project partners.

Evaluation concept of the course: As project partners chosed

Evaluation feedback: in gereral overall positive feedback of course structure and use of material.

Information about the use of material from other project partners: legal aspects highlighted in the courses on copyright, digital documents, virtual presence and data protection were used as lecture part at University Magdeburg.

5.3   EI(5) - Course on Probative Force of Electronic Documents in International Court Procedures

Didactical concept: The aim is to prepare basicc information about probative force of electronic documents in international court procedures

Topic Overview:

- General provisions

- European Community regulations
- National law systems in Italy, India and Germany

Number of slides: 42.

Number of Lecturnity recordings: 3 recordings in total lenght of 90 minutes

Number of course participants: httc is no university and holds no own courses. The material was at the disposition of all project partners.

Evaluation concept of the course: As project partners chosed

Evaluation feedback: in gereral overall positive feedback of course structure and use of material.

Information about the use of material from other project partners: legal aspects highlighted in the courses on copyright, digital documents, virtual presence and data protection were used as lecture part at University Magdeburg.

5.4 EI(5) - Course on Virtual Presence in International University Examinations

Didactical concept: The aim is to prepare basicc information about virtual presence in international university examinations.

Topic Overview:

- Function of physical presence
- Legal Framework in universities
- Document features for oral examinations
- Document features for written examinations

Number of slides: 22.

Number of Lecturnity recordings: 1 recordings in total lenght of 30 minutes

Number of course participants: httc is no university and holds no own courses. The material was at the disposition of all project partners.

Evaluation concept of the course: As project partners chosed

Evaluation feedback: in gereral overall positive feedback of course structure and use of material.

Information about the use of material from other project partners: legal aspects highlighted in the courses on copyright, digital documents, virtual presence and data protection were used as lecture part at University Magdeburg.

On the mono-lingual and cross-lingual speaker identification for Indian and European languages

HEMANT A. PATIL[1], P. K. DUTTA[2] AND T. K. BASU[2]

[1] Department of Electronics and Instrumentation Engineering,
Dr. B. C. Roy Engineering College, Durgapur, West Bengal, India.

[2] Department of Electrical Engineering, IIT Kharagpur, West Bengal, India.

Email: hemant_patil1977@yahoo.com, hemant, pkd, tkb@ee.iitkgp.ernet.in

Contents

Abstract

Automatic Speaker Recognition (ASR) deals with authentication of a person based on his/her voice with the help of machines. ASR finds its applications in transactions authentication, forensic research, etc. In this paper, we present an ASR system for monolingual and cross-lingual mode for Indian (Marathi and Hindi) and European (German and English) languages. The experimental results are shown by using Linear Prediction Coefficients (LPC), Linear Prediction Cepstral Coefficients (LPCC) and Mel Frequency Cepstral Coefficients (MFCC) as feature sets and polynomial classifier of 2nd order approximation as speaker models. The work reported in this paper demonstrates that the cross-lingual ASR is more challenging than the monolingual case.

1 Introduction

Recognizing a person's voice with the help of machines has been an active area of research for several decades now, but it still remains active and it will continue to attract interest till a satisfactory and robust system evolves. In addition to this, speech remains the simplest method of input for personal biometrics, although its accuracy is lower than that of fingerprints or retinal scans. ASR is a data driven field, i.e., the performance of ASR is dependent on the database. The factors affecting the performance are recording conditions, gender type used in population, speaker characteristics, monolingual or cross-lingual corpora, etc. Success rates obtained in an ASR system are meaningless, if the recording or experimental conditions are not known.

Recently, Campbell et al. [3] developed cross-lingual and cross-channel corpora. In their work, for developing cross-lingual corpora, they have considered American English as the *default language* and any one of Arabic, Mandarin, Russian and Spanish as non-native language. India being a *multilingual* country, where there are 17 major languages and more than 200 partly developed dialects/native languages and where majority of the people has command over multiple languages, especially in the border areas of linguistics states, study of ASR performance for different Indian languages is worth pursuing. Moreover, at finer levels, criminals often move from one dialectal zone to another in a state and switchover to the native languages or dialect of that zone. So, in such situations, it is clear that ASR system needs to deal with ASR experiments in mono-lingual, cross-lingual and multilingual modes. In this paper, *text-independent* ASR system is presented in *monolingual and cross-lingual* modes for Indian and European languages. To the best of the authors' knowledge, this is the first study of its kind reported in the ASR literature.

2 Experimental Setup

A typical experimental setup consists of a close talking microphone, voice activated tape recorder and Pentium-III machine having speech processing software. The recording was done with the help of voice activated (VAS) tape recorders (Sanyo model no. M-1110C Aiwa model no. JS299) with microphone input and close talking microphones (viz. *Frontech and Intex*). The data is recorded on the Sony high fidelity voice and music recording cassettes (C-90HFB). A list consisting of five questions, isolated words, digits, combination-lock phrases, read sentences and a contextual speech of considerable duration was prepared in Marathi. The contextual speech consisted of description of nature or memorable events etc. of community or family life of the speaker. The topics were generally easy and simple for the speaker to think instantaneously and interact and the speech was usually conversational and quite varied. The interview was started with some questions to know about the personal information of the speaker such as his/her name, age, education, profession, etc. The data was recorded with 10 repetitions except for the contextual speech. Corpus is designed into single training segments of 30s, 60s, 90s and 120s durations and single testing segments of 1s, 3s, 5s, 7s, 10s, 12s and 15s in order to find the performance of the system for various training and testing durations [5].

3   Features Used

In this paper, LP-based features such as LPC and LPCC and filterbank-based features such as MFCC have been considered for ASR task. In the next sub-section, we will briefly review the computational details of LPCC and MFCC.

3.1   LPCC

The combined effect of glottal pulse, vocal tract and radiation at lips can be modeled by a simple filter function $h(n)$, for a speech signal as shown in Fig. 1. A quasi-periodic impulse train is assumed for the voiced part and a random noise as the input for the unvoiced part at the output speech. The gain factor G accounts for the intensity (assuming a linear system) [1], [5]. Combining the glottal pulse, vocal tract and radiation yields a single all-pole transfer function given by

$$H(z) = \frac{G}{1 - \sum\limits_{k=1}^{p} a_k z^{-k}}. \tag{1}$$

Given that all the poles $z = z_i$ are inside the unit circle and the gain is 1, the causal LP cepstral coefficients (LPCC) of $H(z)$ is given by [1], [5]: , for complex where are the poles of LP transfer function.

$$LPCC(n) = \frac{1}{n} \sum\limits_{i=1}^{p} |r_i|^n \cos(\theta_i n), \; n > 0, \text{ for complex } z_i = r_i \exp(j\theta_i), \tag{2}$$

where z_i's are the poles of LP tranfer function.

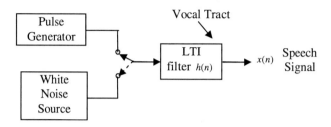

Fig. 1: Block diagram of a functional model of speech production (After Atal [1]).

3.2   MFCC

For a particular speech sound, the human perception process responds with better frequency resolution to lower frequency range and relatively low frequency resolution in high frequency range with the help of human ear. To mimic this process MFCC is developed. For computing MFCC, we warp the speech spectrum into Mel frequency scale. This Mel frequency warping is done by multiplying the magnitude speech spectrum for a preprocessed frame by magnitude of triangular filters in Mel filterbank. The frequency spacing of the filters used in Mel filterbank is kept as linear up to 1 kHz and logarithmic after 1 kHz. The frequency spacing is designed to simulate the *subjective spectrum* from *physical spectrum* to emphasize the *human perception process*. Davis and Mermelstein propose one such filterbank shown in Fig. 2 to simulate this in 1980 for speech recognition application [4]. This filterbank consists of filters having triangular bandpass frequency response with bandwidth and spacing determined by a constant Mel frequency interval (spacing=150 mels, bandwidth= 300 mels).

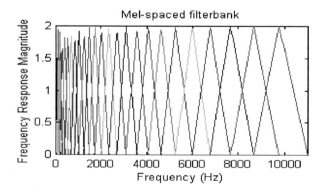

Fig. 2: Mel-spaced filterbank (After Davis and Mermelstein [4]).

To extract MFCC, the speech signal is passed through a frame blocking with 23.22 ms duration, each frame is pre-emphasized, hamming windowed, and the FFT is taken to get the spectrum. A magnitude spectrum (e.g., in human perception, it is more important to model the magnitude spectra of speech than their phase) is computed and frequency warped in order to transform the spectrum into the Mel frequency in which the filterbank is uniformly spaced. Twenty-four Mel-scale triangular filters are multiplied with the magnitude spectra of the frame and log energy is computed. It has been observed that 24 filters represent reasonably good approximation to cover whole speech bandwidth with perceptually meaningful scale, i.e., Mel scale. Finally, a Discrete Cosine Transform (DCT) of filterbank coefficients is taken to get the MFCC.

$$MFCC(k) = \sum_{l=1}^{L} \log[S(l)] \cos\left[\frac{k(l-0.5)}{L}\pi\right], \ k = 1, 2, \ldots, N_c, \tag{3}$$

where $\log[S(l)]$ is the log-filterbank energies and $MFCC(k)$ is the kth MFCC.

4   Experimental Results

In this paper, polynomial classier of 2nd order approximation is used as the basis for all the experiments [2]. Results are shown as average success rates (average computed over single testing segments of 1s, 3s, 5s, 7s, 10s, 12s, and 15s, i.e., average of 7 success rates) for different training (TR) durations. 12th orders LPC were extracted for a frame of 23.22 ms (512 samples) duration after pre-processing. LPCC was calculated from roots of LPC polynomial. The standard MFCC computations were performed as per method suggested in [4].

4.1   Results for German and English

In this section, results are reported on a small database of four speakers (with age ranging from 20-30) having German as their native language and English as a non-native language. Data is recorded in a laboratory environment (The data was supplied by the partners of the EU-India Culture Tech Project, University of Magdeburg, Germany, Dr. Claus Vielhauer and Dr. Jana Dittmann). Tables 1-4 show average success rates for monolingual and cross-lingual experiments with different feature sets (FS), *viz.*, LPC, LPCC and MFCC. Some of the observations from the results are as follows:

1. Success rates are 100% in all the cases of training and testing durations when training and testing are done with German. This may be due to the fact that the subjects considered were having German as their native language and the population size is very small.

2. Success rates degrade for some cases of training and testing durations when training and testing is done with English. This may be due to the fact that the subjects considered were having English as their *non-native* language.

3. The results demonstrate that the testing language significantly affects the performance of cross-lingual ASR as compared to the training language.

4. As the population size is very small, relative performances of different feature sets is very difficult to judge.

TABLE 1
AVERAGE SUCCESS RATES FOR TRL= GERMAN, TEL=GERMAN

TR FS	30s	60s	90s
LPC	100	100	100
LPCC	100	100	100
MFCC	100	100	100

TABLE 2
AVERAGE SUCCESS RATES FOR TRL= ENGLISH, TEL= ENGLISH

TR FS	30s	60s	90s
LPC	96.42	96.42	96.42
LPCC	96.42	100	100
MFCC	96.42	96.42	92.85

TABLE 3
AVERAGE SUCCESS RATES FOR TRL= GERMAN, TEL= ENGLISH

TR FS	30s	60s	90s
LPC	50.00	67.85	64.28
LPCC	96.42	92.85	92.85
MFCC	96.42	89.28	92.85

TABLE 4
AVERAGE SUCCESS RATES FOR TRL= ENGLISH, TEL=GERMAN

TR FS	30s	60s	90s
LPC	100	100	100
LPCC	100	100	100
MFCC	100	100	100

TRL=Training Language, TEL=Testing Language

4.2   Results for Marathi and Hindi

In this sub-section, results are discussed in tables 5-8 for monolingual and cross-lingual ASR tasks for Indian languages, viz., Marathi and Hindi for 11 female speakers. Some of the observations from the results are as follows:

1. MFCC performs better than LPC and LPCC in a majority of the cases of training speech durations. This may be due to the fact that when two women speak, our human perception process (so far as the human perception process is concerned, there is no difference in perceiving the voice of male and female. The difference in perception lies only in size and shape of vocal apparatus and their linguistic and stylistic use. The problem of recognizing female speakers with the help of machines is due to the signal processing issues, i.e., *spectral resolution* problem with female speech [5], [6], [7]. However, human perception process is related to MFCC so MFCC will perform better as compared to LP-based features) will be able to distinguish their voice better than the LPC-based features will do and hence will have greater discriminative power as compared to LPC and LPCC. It may also be mentioned that *LP-based features are dependent on the physiological characteristics of the vocal tract* and they represent the combined effects of glottal pulse, vocal tract impulse response (formant frequencies and their bandwidth) and radiation [5]. As discussed earlier, female speech suffers from the problem of spectral resolution and hence LP-based features will have poor discriminative power for different classes.

2. Success rates for Marathi are higher than that for Hindi for a majority of the cases in monolingual mode of ASR. This may be due to the fact that the subjects considered in this study have Marathi as native language and Hindi as non-native language. Speakers will have better pronunciation of the text material for Marathi as compared to that of Hindi (especially in case of small duration testing utterances).

3. The success rate decreases drastically in the cross-lingual mode of ASR. It is the testing language of the speaker which is more important than the training language (even if the training language is native or non-native), i.e., results are found to be better in the case when the testing language is Marathi and the machine is trained with Hindi than in the case when the testing language is Hindi and training language is Marathi. Thus, it is clear that the success rates are dependent on the closeness of the testing language to the *mother tongue* of the speaker than the training language (similar to that of section 4.1). Thus, in cross-lingual ASR, for a better success rate, the speaker should be tested with his or her native language.

TABLE 5
AVERAGE SUCCESS RATES FOR TRL= MARATHI, TEL=MARATHI (FEMALE SPID)

TR / FS	30s	60s	90s	120s
LPC	90.90	90.90	90.90	87.00
LPCC	88.30	90.90	87.00	89.60
MFCC	92.20	93.50	96.10	97.40

TABLE 6
AVERAGE SUCCESS RATES FOR TRL= HINDI, TEL=HINDI (FEMALE SPID)

TR / FS	30s	60s	90s	120s
LPC	79.21	72.72	71.42	71.42
LPCC	80.51	72.72	71.42	71.42
MFCC	80.51	80.51	80.51	80.51

TABLE 7
AVERAGE SUCCESS RATES FOR TRL= MARATHI, TEL= HINDI (FEMALE SPID)

TR / FS	30s	60s	90s	120s
LPC	16.88	19.47	16.88	14.28
LPCC	25.97	35.06	32.46	27.27
MFCC	36.36	32.46	31.16	29.86

TABLE 8
AVERAGE SUCCESS RATES FOR TRL= HINDI, TEL=MARATHI (FEMALE SPID)

TR / FS	30s	60s	90s	120s
LPC	46.74	44.15	44.15	45.45
LPCC	37.65	37.65	41.55	44.15
MFCC	45.45	45.45	44.15	42.85

SPID=Speaker Identification

5   Summary and Conclusions

ASR is the use of machines to identify a person's voice. In this paper, an investigation on sensitivity of training or testing language to ASR performance is presented for Indian and European languages.

The major contributions of the paper are as follows

1. Specialties of ASR for the cross-lingual mode in the sense that results degrade significantly (almost to 50%) as compared to monolingual mode.

2. For cross-lingual ASR, the success rates are dependent on the closeness of the testing language to the *mother tongue* of the speaker than the training language.

3. The success rates for all other ASR studies made earlier showed improvement when the classifier was selected with higher order. However, it requires more training time.[5].

The results reported in this paper can be further improved by some more refinements in the experimental conditions such as using a polynomial classifier of higher order approximation, using delta, delta-delta features, CMS features, etc.

6   Acknowledgements

The authors would like to thank the authorities of IIT Kharagpur and EU-India Culture Tech Project for their support to carry out this research work. They would like to all the subjects for their kind help and co-operation during data collection phase.

Bibliography

[1] Bishnu S. Atal. Effectiveness of Linear Prediction of the Speech Wave for Automatic Speaker Identification and Verification. *J. Acoust. Soc. Amer.*, volume 55, number 6, pp.1304-1312, June 1974.

[2] W. M. Campbell, K.T. Assaleh and C. C. Broun. Speaker recognition with polynomial classifiers. *IEEE Trans. Speech Audio Processing*, volume 10, number 4, pp. 205-212, May 2002.

[3] J. P. Campbell, H. Nakasone, C. Cieri, D. Miller, K. Walker, A. F. Martin and M. A. Przybocki. The MMSR Bilingual and Cross Channel Corpora for Speaker Recognition Research and Evaluation. *The Speaker and Language Recognition Workshop*, Odyssey'04, Toledo, Spain, pp. 29-32, May 31- June 3, 2004.

[4] S. B. Davis and P. Mermelstein. Comparison of parametric representations for monosyllabic word recognition in continuously spoken sentences. *IEEE Trans. Acoust., Speech, Signal Processing*, volume ASSP-28, number 4, pp. 357-366, Aug.1980.

[5] Hemant A. Patil, *Speaker recognition in Indian languages: A feature based approach*, Ph.D. Thesis, Department of Electrical Engineering, IIT Kharagpur, India, July 2005.

[6] Hemant A. Patil and T. K. Basu. Comparison and evaluation of LP based features for text-independent identification for female speakers. *Proc. National Conf. Control, Communication and Information Systems*, CCIS'04, Goa, India, pp.41-46, Jan.23-24, 2004.

[7] Aaron E. Rosenberg. Automatic speaker verification: A review. *Proc. IEEE*, volume 64, pp. 475-487, 1976.

Digital Repatriation of Heritage and Visualization Technologies. The Contribution of EPOCH

FRANCO NICCOLUCCI

EPOCH - Università di Firenze, Italy
Email: niccolucci@unifi.it

Contents

Abstract

Repatriation means returning cultural heritage to its place of origin and is based on legal reasons or justified by cultural or moral motivations. This often raises issues, especially when different countries are involved. Computer visualization technologies, as the one developed in the EU EPOCH project, may contribute to solve these issues, as shown by some past experiences. Also in those cases in which there is no controversy, as for the Indian cultural heritage located in UK, such technology may provide effective tools to turn dispersion of heritage into a factor of international cooperation and mutual understanding.

1   Introduction

The EPOCH[1] project is an ongoing EU-funded project on ICT applications to tangible cultural heritage [EPO] which started in 2004 for a duration of 4 years with the coordination of the University of Brighton, supervised by four executive directors (including the author of the present paper) and an Executive Committee of seven people, and with the involvement of more than 80 European partners. The overall goal of EPOCH is to overcome fragmentation of research in this domain and to foster interdisciplinarity and cross-fertilization between technology and humanities. EPOCH has a rich program of activities, including market survey and the definition of a research agenda, joint research activities, and dissemination and training. Socio-economic implications as well as business solutions are also included in EPOCH's investigation. Among other goals, EPOCH aims at producing a toolkit and a software common infrastructure to manage the different steps of the pipeline in producing valuable cultural communication. As it has been acknowledged that the production of communication may not be a linear process, but on the contrary it may avail of several parallel paths, the project now deals with a 'tool chain' that is a value chain that uses different software tools transforming raw data into communication to the public and in the meantime adding value to the content. Some of these tools are already available, others are missing; in most cases, there are inconsistencies at interfaces that prevent the outcomes of a previous step to be directly fed into the following one. Such gaps and inconsistencies are the target of EPOCH's research activity. Several tools are being produced internally, under the name of NEWTONs (NEW Tools Needed) addressing the needs and filling the gaps in the tool chain. It is planned to obtain, by the end of the project, a consistent toolkit, to be made available to the scientific community and to heritage professionals and practitioners. An important role in this effort is played by standards. Using standards guarantees a smoother interface at the beginning and end of the tool chain, and in the intermediate steps. It also guarantees immediate usability in all the external applications where standards are used. In other words, EPOCH is creating an intelligent cable to facilitate the flow of information;

---

[1]   EPOCH is funded by the European Commission under the Community's Sixth Framework Programme, contract no. 507382. However, this paper reflects only the author's views and the European Community is not liable for any use that may be made of the information contained herein.

when this will be ready using it will (hopefully) just require that the initial and terminal 'plugs' are standardized, and of course that there is information to flow along it.

2 The Issue of Repatriation

Repatriation can be defined as the return of cultural heritage to its place of origin. More precisely, it includes *restitution*, corresponding to the case in which the cultural property was illegally acquired or looted, and *return*, when the acquisition is not questioned on a legal basis, or a long time has occurred since acquisition, but there are moral issues concerning the present location of the property, for example when it was a acquired as a consequence of colonization or conquest. While there are no issues on restitution, which is compulsory under the UNIDROIT [UNI] Convention, return of cultural property sometimes raises a controversy of a legal, cultural and often also political nature. Most cases of repatriation concern native populations of America and Oceania and their cultural property or human remains. In such cases no international issue is involved. European cases consist more usually of heritage property taken away from other countries as a consequence of *conquest*, *colonization*, or *dubious acquisition*, occurred long ago when attention to heritage was lower and permits to export heritage were easy to obtain. The most famous such case concerns the Parthenon Marbles presently exhibited at the British Museum. A great deal of Indian artefacts was brought to UK during the British rule in the former British Indian Empire, embracing what nowadays corresponds to Pakistan, Bangladesh and India. This created a fashion and a style in England, and is now incorporated into English heritage. Many major British museums, including the British Museum and the Victoria and Albert Museum, have a rich collection of Indian antiquities. No large parts of buildings have been taken away, limiting the larger moved artefacts to isolated sculptures, as statues, columns or bas-relief. This situation creates a great opportunity to fully legitimize a complex period of intermingled cultural history in a collaborative way.

3 Digital Repatriation

The Parthenon Marbles [JCN+03] are one of the most successful cases in which digital repatriation has been attempted, possibly unawares. Created in 2003 by Paul Debevec and others of USC, with the collaboration of Roberto Scopigno's team of ISTI-CNR, and presented as a short movie at Siggraph 2004, it used state-of-art computer graphics research to present a visualization of the Parthenon and its sculptures. The sculptures were shown in their current location in the British Museum, as well as where they were originally placed on the Parthenon.The Parthenon Marbles were scanned using a custom-structured light 3D scanning system from high-quality replicas in the Skulpturhalle Basel, which hosts in the same place casts of the original sculptures now kept mainly at the British Museum but also in Paris, Copenhagen, Vienna and Rome, besides those remaining in Athens and exhibited there in the museum built for the purpose. Apart from showing impressive views of the reconstructed Parthenon, the work has virtually returned the sculptures where they once belonged, and has recreated the unity of the frieze putting together the parts now divided between Greece and UK, representing the subject, the Panathenaic procession, in the correct order. Not only it virtually brought home the Marbles but also collocated the sculptures where for preservation reasons they can never be put, on the temple. Thus a result usually obtained in virtual reconstructions, the recreation of past appearance, in this case doubled in repatriating a valuable piece of national heritage. Here, the product of valuable technology was enhanced and obtained a higher value because of the existing debate on the corresponding physical operation, and through the cultural interpretation of the outcome. As far as we know, the authors have never stressed these political and cultural implications, insisting instead on their remarkable technological achievements and their archaeological and artistic potential. To our knowledge, one of the first examples of a similar work dates back to 1996 [Got96] and concerning the interior of the Egyptian tomb of Horemheb, virtually reconstructed from images of wall paintings kept by several museums in different locations. Although not directly aimed at the repatriation of heritage, the paper proposed a way to virtual re-assemble the tomb integrity, currently dispersed in various European museums. Besides the two cases quoted above, quite a few other examples exist of digital assemblage of separate parts of the same heritage complex, which might turn into repatriation of cultural property if the parts are kept away from their original culture and location. The prevailing concept in such virtual reconstructions is the relocation of the parts, currently stored in a museum, in their original location to re-contextualize them, without understanding that such an operation has the political implication of repatriation. Therefore, the state-of-the-art in digital repatriation is that it is non-existing as such, although all the technology is in practice already available. In conclusion, the process of digital repatriation of dispersed cultural property consists of the following stages: i) digital acquisition of existing artefacts, objects or architectural details; ii) re-assembling of the original unity of the cultural property according to a local interpretation of the artefact; iii) optionally, digital restoration; iv) relocation of the digital artefact in the original place and cultural context. It may also include: v) presenting the virtual re-assemblage at the venues abroad where some of the materials are stored and exhibited. In the end, this would create, or reaffirm, the strong ties among the place of origin and the present locations, and turn what could be perceived as a spoliation into the evidence of a common, shared heritage.

4   The Contribution of the EPOCH Project

In EPOCH's first year of activity, several showcases were created, to demonstrate the potential of already available tools. Among others, those relevant for the scope of the present paper concern the production of virtual replicas of fragile artefacts to be also used as interfaces for multimedia communication/explanation, the production of 3D models of monuments and cities and the creation of virtual humans to populate them. EPOCH's showcases are detailed in [KYF+04]. Among the ongoing NEWTONs, those relevant to the scope of this paper are the following: CIMAD, implementing a framework for 'smart' cultural heritage environments that will support distributed and mobile on-site applications; IMODELASER, aimed at the integration of image-based and laserscan data for 3D modelling; CHARACTERISE, concerning the addition of avatars and virtual humans to 3D representations of cultural heritage sites; and 3DKIOSK, realizing an integrated turnkey solution, specially tailored for the needs and requirements of museums in terms of 3D representation of objects and contexts, for example a web service to automatically produce 3D models from images. All NEWTONs will develop an application scenario, that is a typical and exemplary application context demonstrating the practical use of the tool and how a specific heritage site may benefit from it.

5   Repatriation of Indian Heritage

EPOCH's technology can provide the basis for repatriating heritage, in particular the Indian one. Digital replicas of relevant exhibits may be created and displayed alongside with originals using EPOCH freely available technology. If the essence of a museum is not only preservation and exhibition of artefacts, but mainly communication and explanation [Ant04] for the 'study, education and enjoyment of the public' (see [ICO]), the remote and dispersed location of some of them - virtually present through their replicas - instead of being an inconvenience may create the bridge between different cultures and foster mutual understanding, and also facilitate the explanation of the exhibits that are physically present. For instance, different statues representing Lord Ganesha - physically located in such diverse locations, as India itself, Indonesia (where they belong to the local culture), and British museums (where they were brought as representative of an exotic culture) - may be better understood by comparison. Virtual replicas proposed by EPOCH may be an interface for explanation both to a local public, well aware of Ganesha's characteristics, and to a Western public, less familiar with the Lord's symbolism. In the meantime, such a virtual return is a problem-less repatriation: don't take away, but enrich. A big advantage of the technology resulting from EPOCH's research is cost-effectiveness. Without reducing quality and precision, the tools set up by the project result in significant savings of time and money. For example, 3D scanning technology and modelling is substantially improved; standardization gives consistent advantages also as far as the budget is concerned; complex reconstructions are facilitated and made available in an open-source software framework. In sum, EPOCH's technology may allow cost-effective exploitation of heritage as shown in the case study scenarios that the project is developing. They could effectively be developed also in a context like India, so rich of heritage and history. This would enable to turn the part of Indian heritage which is currently abroad into the ambassador of Indian culture and, going beyond the fascination of the exotic, witness to Westerners how much of their culture is indebted to it.

6   Conclusions

Apart from the above example, which is more a tribute to Ganesha's protection of new undertakings than an operational suggestion, we are not going to designate here specific items of Indian cultural property presently located elsewhere as susceptible of digital repatriation through the application of visualization technology. We believe that the technology EPOCH is assembling and creating for heritage applications may provide effective tools for such a task. What may be the best samples for the job, is a question that may be correctly answered only through a trans-national, and trans-cultural, collaboration, in which all those who believe that technology and culture may unite people are warmly welcomed to participate.

7 Acknowledgements

The work described in this article has been supported mainly by the EU-Project EPOCH . The Author also wants to thank the authorities of the EU-India Culture Tech project for the possibility to present and disseminate working results. The views and conclusions contained herein are those of the author and should not be interpreted as necessarily representing the official policies.

Bibliography

[Ant04]   Francesco Antinucci. *Comunicare nel Museo*. Laterza, Roma-Bari, 2004.

[EPO]   http://www.epoch-net.org, accessed 18/09/2006.

[Got96]   Antonio Gottarelli. Museografia e informatica: la ricostruzione virtuale della tomba menfita del generale Horemheb. *Archeologia e Calcolatori*, 16:1091–1100, 1996.

[ICO]   ICOM definition of museum. http://icom. museum/definition.html, accessed 18/09/2006.

[JCN+03] Jessi Stumpfel, Cristopher Tchou, Nathan Yun, Philippe Martinez, Timothy Hawkins, Andrew Jones, Brian Emerson, and P. Debevec. Digital reunification of the Parthenon and its sculptures. In David Arnold, Alan Chambers, and Franco Niccolucci, editors, *VAST 2003 4th International Symposium on Virtual Reality, Archaeology and Intelligent Cultural Heritage, Brighton 2003*, pages 41–50, Aire-La-Ville, CH, 2003. Eurographics.

[KYF+04] Kevin Cain, Yiorgos Chrysanthou, Franco Niccolucci, Daniel Pletinckx, and Neil Silberman, editors. *Interdisciplinarity or The Best of Both Worlds. The Grand Challenge for Cultural Heritage Informatics in the 21st Century. Selected papers from VAST2004*. Archaeolingua, Budapest, 2004. Also available from the EPOCH web site: http://www.epoch-net.org, accessed 18/09/2006.

[UNI]   UNIDROIT Convention on Stolen or Illegally Exported Cultural Objects, Rome 1995. http://www.unidroit.org/english/conventions/c-main.htm, accessed 18/09/2006.